The London Coffee Guide.

2018

20/6/18

we need to be in this book!

Edited by
Jeffrey Young

Author: Allegra Strategies
Reviewers: Richard Ehrlich & Kate Beard
Project Co-ordinator: Samantha Hughes
Researcher: India Jennings
Photography: Kate Beard, Horst A. Friedrichs
& provided by venues
Design: John Osborne
Website: Tim Spring
Publisher: Allegra Publications Ltd

D0234257

Visit our website:
www.londoncoffeeguide.com

@thelondoncoffeeguide

All information was accurate at time of going to press.

Published by Allegra Publications Ltd © 2018

Serendipity House, 106 Arlington Road, London, NW1 7HP, UK.

Foreword

by **Ruth Coppin and Darren Elliott,** Co-Founders, Timberyard

For those of us that grew up in the seventies, life was fun. It was a period of automation, convenience and instant gratification. We were just kids of course, so coffee came a distant second to fizzy drinks and we were easily distracted by space hoppers, roller discos, or bombing around on our Grifter bikes. But, nothing beat our mum's homemade coffee and walnut cake. Decorated with candied orange and chocolate sprinkles, this was probably the closest we ever came back then to identifying a flavour profile: caramel-like with nutty notes and a subtle citrus and chocolaty sweetness.

It was very much the Nescafé era for many families and, like today, quality and sophistication were way down the priority list when a family was on a budget. Artisan and craft products of old had been replaced with space age Smash and Angel Delight and, for some reason, we were all loving it.

Back then, premium quality coffee was largely absent in the workplace too. Vending machines were the norm: producing coffee that was sugary sweet and whitened with powdered milk, leaving the brew so red hot that it would come close to melting the flimsy plastic cups.

Yet, in Soho, espresso bars were a new obsession. Italian espresso coffee was captivating Londoners and being pushed out to the home counties with the energy and pulse of a musical beat. A new concept of coffee-to-go chains ensued; improving consistency, value and convenience, with its grande lattes and caramel cappuccinos. But it was our Antipodean friends who en masse led the next step; highlighting extraordinary speciality roasts, with carefully considered brew processes and a new focus on professionalism that enabled those of us with real passion to carve out legitimate careers.

The next wave slipped in discreetly: a more scientific approach to coffee, to roasting and 'brewology', that perhaps engaged more with the barista than the consumer. Yet now, the UK is poised as the most developed coffee shop market in Europe, and still continues to look forward.

Today, millennials make up a large proportion of customers and buy a coffee out of home regularly. They're a tough crowd. They're discerning and demand variety and choice. In parallel, as expectation of quality has become the norm, we as operators need to differentiate ourselves from the competition by offering an even higher level of customer experience that must be memorable.

Looking ahead, the future almost certainly involves consumer demand driven technology being part of our industry with personalisation and automation as key drivers. Also, speciality is moving into the workplace with the younger generation driving demand, but all demographics are now insisting on quality everywhere: at home, in a coffee shop, in a restaurant or at the office.

Consequently, we need to be proud of our profession: be proud of speciality and hospitality and focus closely on service and experience. There will be challenges for sure but the future is exciting and full of promise.

Contents

Introduction

Welcome to The London Coffee Guide 2018 - the definitive guide to London's independent coffee venues.

Year after year, we endeavour to bring you the crème de la crème of London's leading independent coffee shops, cafés and roasteries. We're here to spill the (coffee) beans on the latest and greatest places to get that all-important coffee boost. Whether you're searching for a morning flat white, a lunchtime long black, or an afternoon espresso, we've got plenty of top notch recommendations to keep you caffeinated.

With 31 new venues added to this 2018 edition, we now feature a total of 255 profiles in the guide. Look out for our 'New and Noteworthy' profiles dotted throughout the guide - these are venues we believe are exciting, must-visit new additions to London's flourishing speciality coffee scene.

The 5th Wave of coffee has become well and truly established in London, with independent specialists adopting a boutique-at-scale approach to coffee and opening multiple sites with their winning recipe for success, whilst still retaining their unique character and high quality.

Allegra is an established leader in consumer and business intelligence for the coffee industry in the UK and Europe. We have drawn upon this research as well as experts in the field to compile this eighth edition. We hope you enjoy it.

Photo: Horst A. Friedrichs

About the Guide

Ratings

Every venue featured in The London Coffee Guide 2018 has been visited and rated by our expert team. The ratings fall into two distinct categories: Coffee Rating and Overall Rating on a score of 1-5, with 5 being the highest possible score. Customer feedback received via The London Coffee Guide website and app also informs the venue shortlist and the final scores.

Coffee Rating

The Coffee Rating is about much more than just taste in the cup. An excellent coffee experience depends on a host of factors including: barista skills, coffee supplier, equipment, consistency, working processes and coffee presentation. The venue's coffee philosophy and commitment to excellence are also taken into consideration.

Overall Rating

In combination with the Coffee Rating, the Overall Rating reflects the total coffee shop experience for the customer. Factors taken into account include: service, café ambience, venue scale and impact, design and food quality. Feedback from the industry is also taken into consideration.

Key to symbols

Roaster

Alternative brew methods available

Coffee beans sold on site

Gluten-free products available

Venue has a loyalty card

Milk alternatives available

Toilets

Parent & baby friendly

Disabled access

WiFi available

Licensed

Coffee courses available

Outdoor seating

Brunch available at weekends

Cold Brew available

Pet friendly

Participating in UK Coffee Week™

Venues marked as are new to this edition of the Guide.

Venues marked as are recently opened venues we feel are worthy of special mention.

A Brief History of London Coffee

THE EARLY YEARS

800 AD The coffee plant (Coffea) attracts human interest and consumption as early as 800 AD in the Kaffe region of Ethiopia. According to legend, it was an Ethiopian goat herder named Kaldi who first discovered how animated his herd of goats became after chewing on the red berries.

MID 17TH CENTURY

Travellers to Middle Eastern areas such as the Ottoman Empire bring coffee to Europe and Britain.

1650 The first English coffee house is established in Oxford by a Jewish gentleman named Jacob at the Angel in the parish of St Peter.

Coffee houses become meeting places for political and literary debates between artists, intellectuals, merchants and bankers. Such venues are known as Penny Universities, in reference to the one penny entrance fee. They are closely associated with reading and provide pamphlets and newspapers, as well as copious amounts of coffee.

1652 London's first coffee house is established by Pasqua Rosée in St Michael's Alley, Cornhill, London EC3.

1668 Edward Lloyd's Coffee House in Lombard Street becomes a key meeting place for ship owners and marine insurance brokers. Situated on the site occupied by Lloyds bank today, this coffee house likely contributed to London becoming a global hub for insurance and financial services.

1674 The Women's Petition Against Coffee is set up in London in response to men spending less time at home due to the "excessive use of the drying and enfeebling liquor".

1675 There are now more than 3,000 coffee houses across England. King Charles II attempts to outlaw coffee houses as hotbeds of revolution, but following large public protests, his proclamation is revoked after 11 days.

1680 Jonathan's Coffee House is established by Jonathan Miles in Change Alley. It is a place where stockbrokers frequently meet and eventually becomes today's London Stock Exchange.

1706 Thomas Twining opens the first known tea room in London, which can still be found at 216 Strand.

18TH CENTURY

Coffee houses gradually decline in popularity and become more elite establishments, when they start charging more than one penny for entrance. Travelling taverns replace coffee houses as popular social spaces. Coffee also becomes a less important commodity as the East India Company and British trade in general focuses more on tea imports from India.

LAST CENTURY

1894 Lyons opens a chain of tea rooms followed by Lyons Corner Houses in London's West End in 1906.

1923 The Kenya Coffee Company Limited (Kenco) is established and soon begins selling coffee on Vere Street, Mayfair.

1950s Italian-run espresso houses featuring Formica-topped tables are a popular feature of this era, particularly in London's Soho.

1952 Moka Bar opens on Frith Street and is London's first espresso bar.

1971 Starbucks opens its first store at Pike Place Market in Seattle, USA.

First Costa Coffee shop opened by brothers Sergio and Bruno Costa at 9 Newport Street, London.

1978 An early pioneer of artisanal coffee, Monmouth Coffee Company opens in Monmouth Street, Covent Garden.

1986 Pret A Manger is established by college friends Julian Metcalf and Sinclair Beecham.

1992 Fairtrade Foundation is established in London by the Catholic Overseas Development Agency, Christian Aid, Oxfam, Traidcraft, the World Development Movement, and the National Federation of Women's Institutes.

1995 Whitbread Group acquires Costa Coffee with 41 stores and a roastery in Lambeth.

1997 Nescafé opens first Café Nescafé trial stores in London and UK, but closes all outlets several years later.

Gerry Ford acquires five Caffè Nero stores and begins building a chain, which grows to become the third-largest coffee shop brand in the UK.

1998 Starbucks launches in the UK, acquiring 65 Seattle Coffee Company stores for an estimated £52 million.

1999 Allegra Strategies releases the groundbreaking Project Café Report, which predicts a significant boom in coffee shops.

LAST DECADE

2000 Internet cafés grow in popularity during the dotcom era.

Marks & Spencer launches Café Revive concept.

2001 The caffè latte is added to the Consumer Price Index (CPI), the basket of goods the government uses to measure products purchased by a typical British household.

2005 Flat White coffee shop opens in Berwick Street, Soho, setting the stage for further Antipodean influences on coffee in the UK.

2006 The number of branded chain coffee shop outlets exceeds 1,000 in London alone.

2007 James Hoffmann is crowned World Barista Champion and founds Square Mile Coffee Roasters.

2008 The first-ever European Coffee Symposium is held at London's Park Lane Hotel.

2009 A host of new artisanal "third wave" coffee shops open in London.

The UK's Gwilym Davies is crowned World Barista Champion.

2010 Costa, Starbucks and several other mainstream coffee chains launch their versions of the flat white.

The World Barista Championships are held in London at Caffè Culture.

The first edition of The London Coffee Guide is published.

2011 Growth of artisanal coffee shops and micro coffee roasteries in London continues to accelerate with the arrival of Workshop (formerly St. Ali), and Prufrock Coffee.

First-ever London Coffee Festival held at the Old Truman Brewery on Brick Lane.

2012 Roastery/cafés increase in popularity with the opening of Caravan King's Cross, Ozone and TAP Wardour Street.

London Coffee Festival hosts UK Barista Championship finals.

Harris + Hoole opens first London store.

2013 Bulldog Edition opens at Ace Hotel London, in collaboration with Square Mile Coffee Roasters.

2014 Growth of speciality micro-chains, with leading independents such as Grind & Co and Workshop Coffee Co. opening multiple new sites.

2015 Coffee Masters launched at The London Coffee Festival.

Maxwell Colonna-Dashwood wins the UK Barista Championship for the third time.

Key openings; Allpress (Dalston), Kaffeine (Eastcastle Street), Origin Coffee (Charlotte Road).

2016 The London Coffee Festival is attended by over 30,000 visitors.

Key openings: Caravan Bankside, Clerkenwell Grind and Workshop Roastery (Vyner Street).

2017 Britain's Dale Harris (Has Bean Coffee) crowned World Barista Champion 2017.

London's West End is synonymous with the city's legendary theatre and music scene, as well as its restaurants, shopping and nightlife. Business people and actors rub shoulders with tourists and urbanites, and the area's café culture is just as diverse.

West End

* NEW
◊ TOP 35

26 Grains

1 Neal's Yard, WC2H 9DP

This tiny, attractive place goes very big on grain-based cooking (hence the name), which is also the subject of a best-selling cookbook published by its owner. Scandinavian in look and feel as well as cooking, it's a place where they want you to enjoy yourself rather than crack the MacBook and work. (There's no WiFi.) Milky drinks are the attraction here, with Assembly beans passing through a lovingly attended La Marzocco.

www.26grains.com
⊖ Covent Garden

MON-FRI.	8:00am - 5:00pm
SAT.	9:00am - 5:00pm
SUN.	10:00am - 4:00pm

First opened 2015
Roaster Assembly
Machine La Marzocco Linea PB, 2 groups
Grinder Victoria Arduino Mythos One

Espresso	£2.40
Cappuccino	£2.80
Latte	£2.80
Flat white	£2.80

MAP REF. ❶

COFFEE 4.00 / 5

OVERALL 4.00 / 5 ★★★★☆

The Attendant Fitzrovia

27a Foley Street, W1W 6DY

London's only coffee shop located in a former underground public lav still has plenty of shock value for first-time visitors. Veterans know it not for its setting - though that's impressive enough - but for the superb quality of its coffee. Attendant roasts its own beans, and the baristas love to show and explain how good those beans can be in the cup. Sandwiches and baked goods are fresh and well made. The only drawbacks are small size and lack of a view. But these are minor inconveniences in this public convenience. Attendant is waiting for you to discover it if you haven't already.

+44(0)20 7637 3794
www.the-attendant.com
⊖ Goodge Street

Sister locations Shoreditch / Clerkenwell

MON-FRI.	7:30am - 5:30pm
SAT-SUN.	9:00am - 5:30pm

First opened 2013
Roaster Attendant Roastery
Machine La Marzocco GB5, 2 groups
Grinder Victoria Arduino Mythos One, Mahlkönig EK 43

Espresso	£2.20
Cappuccino	£3.00
Latte	£3.00
Flat white	£2.90

MAP REF.

 COFFEE 4.25 / 5 OVERALL 4.25 / 5

Boki

20 Earlham Street, WC2H 9LG

Boki seems like something that shouldn't be possible: an all-day coffee shop and restaurant in expensive Covent Garden real estate that doesn't need to charge Covent Garden prices. And it thrives, as you'd expect. The key to success is a varied offering which shifts throughout the day: coffee and lunch in daytime, snacks and drinks later on, with an imaginative cocktail list using their house coffee infused liquors in the evening. The dinner menu is dominated by meat and cheese platters, simply presented, and their all-day menu features dishes influenced by their owners' backgrounds; an Asian/British fusion, with beautiful, delicate flavours and fresh ingredients.

The coffee is Allpress, all espresso-based, and as always with Allpress it performs best in its milky forms. The space is beautiful; coffee shop with plenty of tables and comfy seating in the front, and a gleaming horseshoe shaped cocktail bar beneath a halo of living plants and a stunning skylight at the back. Service is notably friendly, and the atmosphere may make you think you're in Paris or Berlin rather than London. A real West End gem.

MAP REF.

COFFEE 4.25 / 5	OVERALL 4.25 / 5

MON–FRI.	9:00am – 9:00pm
SAT.	10:00am – 10:00pm
SUN.	10:00am – 6:00pm

First opened 2017
Roaster Allpress Espresso
Machine La Marzocco Linea AV, 2 groups
Grinder Mazzer Robur

Espresso	£1.80
Cappuccino	£2.80
Latte	£2.80
Flat white	£2.80

+44(0)20 7836 8589
www.bokisevendials.com
⬤ Leicester Square / Covent Garden

The Borough Barista Marble Arch

60 Seymour Street, W1H 7JN

This attractive place, on a corner site in posh Marylebone, is all the more welcome because there isn't much competition in the area for low-key daytime dining with superior coffee. Food and coffee are served on the ground floor, where there are also a few tables. Downstairs there's more seating and a very chilled-out vibe at quiet times - perfect for both talking and working. Borough roasts its own beans and makes an excellent espresso blend, which is the basis for all drinks served here. Sample their very good lunch options, or just a slice of cake if that's more your speed.

+44(0)20 7563 7222
www.theboroughbarista.com
⊖ Marble Arch

Sister locations St James

MON–FRI.	7:30am – 4:30pm
SAT.	9:00am – 4:00pm
SUN.	Closed

First opened 2011
Roaster The Borough Barista
Machine La Marzocco Linea, 2 groups
Grinder Mazzer Super Jolly, Eureka

Espresso	£2.20
Cappuccino	£3.20
Latte	£3.20
Flat white	£3.20

MAP REF. **4**

COFFEE 4.25 / 5

OVERALL 4.25 / 5 ★★★★⯨

The Borough Barista St James

15 Charles II Street, SW1Y 4QU

Borough Barista's St James's branch, one of the few coffee joints in this blue-chip area, is surprisingly spacious: a fairly small ground-floor café and a bigger room downstairs. Around half their custom is takeaway for local office workers (no weekend opening). It's an attractive, low-priced lunch spot, and the company's own espresso blend makes a bright cup when pulled through the three-group Linea. Its central location makes Borough a welcome haven for coffee and a sandwich or cake after touring the nearby sights in Piccadilly or Trafalgar Square.

+44(0)20 3272 0222
www.theboroughbarista.com
⊖ Piccadilly Circus

MON-FRI.	7:45am – 5:30pm
SAT-SUN.	Closed

First opened 2013
Roaster The Borough Barista
Machine La Marzocco Linea, 3 groups
Grinder Mazzer Kony x2

Espresso	£2.20
Cappuccino	£3.20
Latte	£3.20
Flat white	£3.20

Sister locations Marble Arch

MAP REF. **5**

COFFEE 4.25 / 5		OVERALL 4.00 / 5	★★★★☆

Coffee Island

5 Upper St Martin's Lane, WC2H 9NY

Two things make Coffee Island such a welcome addition to the Leicester Square scene. One is the outstanding coffee, a wide range roasted by the company itself and featuring a number of lots from 'micro-farms' which they nurture through direct trade. The other is the food, which makes a real effort to excel in quality, freshness, and price. Latte art is great, but let yourself be tempted by the range of filters. Coffee Island is of Greek origin, with this being their first London store. We wouldn't be surprised if more branches follow.

+44(0)20 7836 3007
coffeeisland.co.uk
⊖ Leicester Square

MON-FRI.	7:30am – 9:00pm
SAT-SUN.	9:00am – 9:00pm

First opened 2016
Roaster Coffee Island
Machine Victoria Arduino Black Eagle, 3 groups
Grinder Mahlkönig EK 43 Limited Edition, Mahlkönig K30, Mahlkönig EKK43

Espresso	£2.00
Cappuccino	£2.90
Latte	£3.00
Flat white	£2.70

MAP REF. **6**

COFFEE 4.50 / 5		OVERALL 4.25 / 5	★★★★⯪

Covent Garden Grind

42 Maiden Lane, WC2E 7LJ

This is a medium-sized Grind, with a main dining area on the ground floor and a smaller, slightly quieter (important point here) basement room. Service is a pleasure, delivered efficiently and with a smile. The crowd is a mix of ages and types, with some lone workers, some holding meetings, and some just having a good time with well-made sandwiches and high-quality baked goods. Grind is a gem in the Covent Garden scene.

grind.co.uk
⊖ Covent Garden

Sister locations Multiple locations

MON.-THU.	7:30am - 11:00pm
FRI.	7:30am - 12:00am
SAT.	9:00am - 12:00am
SUN.	9:00am - 7:00pm

First opened 2016
Roaster Grind & Co.
Machine La Marzocco Linea PB, 3 groups
Grinder Victoria Arduino Mythos One x2, Mahlkönig Tanzania

Espresso	£2.30
Cappuccino	£3.00
Latte	£3.00
Flat white	£3.00

MAP REF.

 COFFEE 4.25 / 5   **OVERALL** 4.25 / 5

Curators Coffee Gallery

51 Margaret Street, W1W 8SG

The interior of this Fitzrovia venue dares to deviate from the bare brick and distressed furnishings seen in so many London independents. There is dark wood, a pristine white bar, and kettles made from blazing copper. Spectacular signature drinks such as iced Cascara make neat additions to an already appealing coffee selection. The Curators Coffee Gallery, as the name suggests, is a place to settle in and escape with coffee and art. Whether it's artistry in the cup, on the walls, or indeed on the cup itself, this is a unique coffee shop with a vitality which goes way beyond just the coffee.

+44(0)20 7580 2547
www.curatorscoffee.com
Oxford Circus

Sister locations Curators Coffee Studio / Curators Coffee Kitchen

MON-FRI.	7:30am - 6:00pm
SAT-SUN.	9:00am - 5:30pm

First opened 2014
Roaster Colonna Coffee
Machine La Marzocco Strada EP, 3 groups
Grinder Nuova Simonelli Mythos One, Mazzer Robur E, Anfim

Espresso	£2.40
Cappuccino	£3.00
Latte	£3.00
Flat white	£3.00

MAP REF. 8

COFFEE 4.50 / 5

OVERALL 4.50 / 5 ★★★★☆

11

Daisy Green

20 Seymour Street, W1H 7HX

Daisy Green is all about excellent coffee, friendly service, and Australian-style food with equal emphasis on good health and wicked self-indulgence. The upstairs corner room is light and airy, with two big windows. Downstairs has a 'garden' area that is simply one of London's most beautiful spaces for eating and drinking. And let's not gloss over the coffee quality: beans from The Roasting Party are skilfully pulled through the La Marzocco, so don't pass up a flat white while you're there.

+44(0)20 7723 3301
www.daisygreenfood.com
⊖ Marble Arch

Sister locations Multiple locations

MON–FRI.	7:00am – 6:00pm
SAT.	8:00am – 6:00pm
SUN.	9:00am – 6:00pm

First opened 2012
Roaster The Roasting Party
Machine La Marzocco FB80, 3 groups
Grinder Mazzer Robur

Espresso	£2.20 / £2.60
Cappuccino	£2.90 / £3.20
Latte	£2.90 / £3.20
Flat white	£2.90 / £3.20

MAP REF. 9

 COFFEE 4.25 / 5   **OVERALL** 4.50 / 5 ★★★★½

Élan Café

48 Park Lane, W1K 1PR

The first thing you'll notice upon approaching Élan is the queue out the door. But persist, and you'll enter a café unlike any you've experienced. Complete with a pink wall of flowers, Élan's aesthetic is truly special. The food and drink offering is equally notable, and coffee can be enjoyed late into the night. Union coffee is skilfully pulled through their La Marzocco GB5, and their designer patisserie from around the world compliments their clientele. If you're looking for something a little different, sample their exquisite caffeine-free Red Espresso rooibos. A real treasure, just moments from Hyde Park.

+44(0)20 7491 8880
www.elancafe.co.uk
⊖ Hyde Park Corner / Green Park

MON-SUN.   7:30am - 12:00am

First opened 2017
Roaster Union Coffee Roasters
Machine La Marzocco GB5
Grinder Victoria Arduino Mythos One x2

Espresso	£3.20
Cappuccino	£4.50
Latte	£4.80
Flat white	£4.30

Sister locations Knightsbridge

MAP REF. 10

COFFEE 4.25 / 5   🫘🫘🫘🫘🫘

OVERALL 4.50 / 5   ★★★★⯨

13

The Espresso Room Covent Garden

24 New Row, WC2N 4LA

This miniature coffee house is staffed by super-friendly coffee obsessives who discuss latte art in their downtime and prepare the best flat white on a street crammed with other outlets. Daily filter options are available at the bar, along with an enticing lemon drizzle cake, gourmet cookies, and a range of pastries and sandwiches. Fresh almond milk is prepared each day, and the pulp is used to make tasty almond biscuits.

+44(0)20 3583 6949
theespressoroom.london
◉ Leicester Square

Sister locations Bloomsbury / Holborn

MON-FRI.	7:30am – 7:30pm
SAT-SUN.	9:00am – 7:30pm

First opened 2011
Roaster Caravan Coffee Roasters and guests
Machine La Marzocco Linea, 2 groups
Grinder Mazzer Robur, Mazzer Super Jolly

Espresso	£2.20
Cappuccino	£2.80 / £3.60
Latte	£2.80 / £3.60
Flat white	£2.80 / £3.60

MAP REF. 11

COFFEE 4.25 / 5  **OVERALL** 4.00 / 5 ★★★★☆

Farmstand

42 Drury Lane, WC2B 5AJ

Farmstand is primarily a restaurant, featuring healthy salad boxes. The food's all gluten and dairy-free, and 100 per cent organic. On the coffee front they've gone with beans from Workshop, and they've also done something that's unusual and totally great: in addition to well-made espresso-based drinks from their La Marzocco, they sell filter coffee for just £1 a cup. Healthy for your bank balance. They sell dog food, just in case you're thinking of popping in with your pooch. And if you look at the bottom of your receipt, you're guaranteed a chuckle.

+44(0)20 7240 3866
www.farmstand.co.uk
◉ Covent Garden

MON-FRI.	7:30am – 9:00pm
SAT.	9:00am – 9:00pm
SUN.	10:00am – 5:00pm

First opened 2016
Roaster Workshop Coffee
Machine La Marzocco Linea, 2 groups
Grinder Victoria Arduino Mythos One

Espresso	£2.50
Cappuccino	£2.80
Latte	£2.80
Flat white	£2.80

MAP REF. 12

COFFEE 4.00 / 5   **OVERALL** 4.25 / 5 ★★★★½

Fernandez & Wells Somerset House

Somerset House, Strand, WC2R 1LA

This F&W has an enviable position inside the courtyard of one of central London's premier tourist attractions. The huge advantage of this venue is ample space within (rest your feet after gallery-going) and a bunch of tables in the glorious courtyard outside. Baked goods are the strong point in the food offer, and single origin filters from Has Bean may tempt you away from the espresso machine. A great place to sit and sip in peace, especially when there's an installation in the courtyard.

+44(0)20 7420 9408
www.fernandezandwells.com
⊖ Temple

Sister locations Denmark Street / Duke Street / Lexington Street / South Kensington

MON-TUE.	8:00am - 10:00pm
WED-FRI.	8:00am - 11:00pm
SAT.	10:00am - 9:00pm
SUN.	10:00am - 6:00pm

First opened 2011
Roaster Has Bean
Machine La Marzocco Linea PB, 3 groups
Grinder Nuova Simonelli Mythos One

Espresso	£2.60
Cappuccino	£2.95
Latte	£2.95
Flat white	£2.95

MAP REF. 13

COFFEE 4.25 / 5

OVERALL 4.50 / 5 ★★★★✭

The Gentlemen Baristas

The Building Centre, 26 Store Street, WC1E 7BT

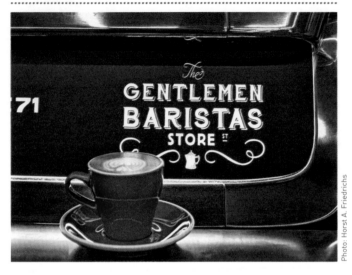

Photo: Horst A. Friedrichs

The Gentleman Baristas sets itself a tricky challenge: combining a dining area, coffee bar, and full kitchen in a small space in the crescent-shaped ground floor of The Building Centre. Despite the dinky size, they've managed to accommodate the crowds buying coffee to go, while providing comfortable seating. Coffee is mostly from their own roastery, and the espresso blend is outstanding when married to milk. The food menu has been developed by a highly skilled and quality-conscious chef who tries to make as much as possible in-house, including relishes, sauces, butter, and ricotta. Gentleman Baristas is right up there with the very best.

+44(0)7817 350 067
www.thegentlemenbaristas.com
Goodge Street

| MON-FRI. | 8:00am - 5:00pm |
| SAT-SUN. | Closed |

First opened 2016
Roaster The Gentlemen Baristas, Neighbourhood Coffee, Wogan Coffee Roasters
Machine Faema E71, 2 groups
Grinder Mazzer Major E, Mazzer Kony E, Mazzer Mini E

Espresso	£2.00
Cappuccino	£2.70
Latte	£2.70
Flat white	£2.70

Sister locations The Coffee House / The School House   **MAP REF.** 14

COFFEE 4.50 / 5

OVERALL 4.50 / 5 ★★★★½

Gitane

60 Great Titchfield Street, W1W 7QF

Gitane serves great coffee, all Ozone beans and all espresso-based. Drink it outside or at the tables in front, with a good view through the big windows. But that's not all that Gitane does. This lovely Fitzrovia spot is a showcase for food heavily influenced by Persian cooking (the owner is originally from Iran). It's a café menu in the day, with more 'serious' fare taking over at night and served at the tables at the back. And if all you want is coffee and a pastry, you've come to the right place.

+44(0)20 7631 5269
www.gitanelondon.co.uk
⊖ Oxford Circus

MON-SAT. 8:00am – 10:30pm
SUN. Closed

First opened 2012
Roaster Ozone Coffee Roasters
Machine La Marzocco Linea, 2 groups
Grinder Mazzer Robur E

Espresso	£2.40
Cappuccino	£2.90
Latte	£2.80
Flat white	£2.80

MAP REF. **15**

COFFEE 4.25 / 5

OVERALL 4.25 / 5

17

Jacob the Angel

16a Neal's Yard, WC2H 9DP

If you like perfectly brewed espresso from Square Mile's Red Brick blend, given a warm glow by a dose of perfectly textured milk, you're going to love Jacob the Angel. The coffee here is just great. But that's not the only thing you're going to love at this dinky room hidden in Neal's Yard. Jacob is the angelic brainchild of the people behind Palomar and Barbary (next door), renowned Israeli/Mediterranean restaurants. The food offering is outstanding, from stunning sandwiches to perfect pastries, nearly everything is home-made, even bagels. Your problem will be finding a table - it's no surprise that the place is incredibly popular.

jacobtheangel.co.uk
Covent Garden

MON-FRI.	8:00am - 5:00pm
SAT-SUN.	9:00am - 5:00pm

First opened 2017
Roaster Square Mile Coffee Roasters
Machine Victoria Arduino Black Eagle, 2 groups
Grinder Victoria Arduino Mythos One

Espresso	£2.50
Cappuccino	£2.50
Latte	£2.50
Flat white	£2.50

MAP REF. 16

 COFFEE 4.25 / 5   **OVERALL** 4.25 / 5 ★★★★½

Kaffeine Eastcastle Street

15 Eastcastle Street, W1T 3AY

TOP
35

West End

Photo: James Bryant

This second beautiful Kaffeine has a subtly different feel from the original: it's a tad bigger, and instead of bare brick has a sleek look featuring high ceilings, wood (both pale and dark), and a beautiful copper counter. Seating is on high stools or benches. What hasn't changed one bit is the superb quality of the coffee. Skilled baristas pull beautiful Square Mile beans through the Black Eagle espresso machine with assurance and consistency. The changing menu of in-house produced soups, salads, sandwiches and baked goods makes for great eating from breakfast through to the late afternoon.

+44(0)20 3730 5878
www.kaffeine.co.uk
⊖ Oxford Circus

Sister locations Great Titchfield Street

MON-FRI.	7:30am - 6:00pm
SAT.	8:30am - 6:00pm
SUN.	9:00am - 5:00pm

First opened 2015
Roaster Square Mile Coffee Roasters
Machine Victoria Arduino Black Eagle, 3 groups
Grinder Nuova Simonelli Mythos One Clima Pro

Espresso	£2.60
Cappuccino	£3.00
Latte	£3.00
Flat white	£2.90

MAP REF. **17**

COFFEE
4.75 / 5

OVERALL
4.75 / 5
★★★★⯪

19

Kaffeine Great Titchfield Street

66 Great Titchfield Street, W1W 7QJ

Kaffeine continues to follow the same path that's made it such a success all these years: excellent food, incredibly friendly service even when the room is a scrum, and close attention to detail in its espresso-based drinks. Salads and baked goods are the special stars in the food display, resupplied constantly from the kitchen downstairs. The best place to sit is on a bench at the back. Note that service can get stretched at maximum-peak times, so you might want to collect your coffee at the counter, so you get it as soon as it leaves the Synesso.

+44(0)20 7580 6755
www.kaffeine.co.uk
Ⓣ Oxford Circus

Sister locations Eastcastle Street

MON–FRI.	7:30am – 6:00pm
SAT.	8:30am – 6:00pm
SUN.	9:00am – 5:00pm

First opened 2009
Roaster Square Mile Coffee Roasters
Machine Synesso Cyncra, 3 groups
Grinder Mazzer, Mahlkönig EK 43

Espresso	£2.60
Cappuccino	£3.00
Latte	£3.00
Flat white	£2.90

MAP REF. **18**

COFFEE 4.75 / 5

OVERALL 5 / 5 ★★★★★

Kin Cafe

22 Foley Street, W1W 6DT

Everything from the food to the furniture furthers Kin's mission to source in an ethical and socially responsible way. Their sourdough bread, for example, is baked by Better Health Bakery, an East London social enterprise employing adults recovering from mental illness. Kin's soothing interior of clean lines and muted tones falls somewhere between a Scandinavian kitchen and Japanese tea room. It's an environment to calm the soul, providing a serene backdrop to the sumptuous menu of superfood salads, quiche, cakes, and baked goodies.

+44(0)20 7998 4720
www.kincafe.co.uk
⊖ Goodge Street / Oxford Circus

MON-FRI.	7:30am - 5:30pm
SAT.	10:00am - 5:00pm
SUN.	Closed

First opened 2014
Roaster Clifton Coffee Roasters
Machine La Marzocco Linea, 2 groups
Grinder Anfim Super Caimano, Mahlkönig EK 43

Espresso	£2.40
Cappuccino	£2.90
Latte	£2.90
Flat white	£2.80

MAP REF. **19**

COFFEE 4.25 / 5

OVERALL 4.25 / 5 ★★★★⯪

Lantana Fitzrovia

13 Charlotte Place, W1T 1SN

Lantana can do no wrong in the eyes of its faithful customers. They queue for the privilege of eating here, even outside peak mealtimes. This location is especially attractive, with just pedestrian traffic and bare-wood tables outside. The menu is that wonderful Australian combination of healthy and self-indulgent, and customers come for one or the other, or both. If it's just coffee you want, filter or espresso, you can order it to go from the separate space next door or drink it here. We recommend sitting in, with or without something from the bakery.

+44(0)20 7637 3347
www.lantanacafe.co.uk
⊖ Goodge Street / Tottenham Court Road

MON–FRI.	8:00am – 6:00pm
SAT–SUN.	9:00am – 5:00pm

First opened 2008
Roaster Alchemy Coffee and guests
Machine La Marzocco FB80, 3 groups
Grinder Mazzer Luigi

Espresso	£2.20
Cappuccino	£3.00
Latte	£3.00
Flat white	£2.90

Sister locations Shoreditch / London Bridge

MAP REF. **20**

 COFFEE 4.50 / 5  **OVERALL** 4.50 / 5 ★ ★ ★ ★ ✯

Monmouth Coffee Company Covent Garden

27 Monmouth Street, WC2H 9EU

This is where the Monmouth phenomenon began, back in 1978. The original Monmouth roastery occupied this site until 2007 when it moved to Bermondsey. The interior here is simple, focusing attention on the coffee. Wooden booths encourage strangers to share conversation and trade ideas, continuing the grand tradition of the capital's first coffee houses. Monmouth Coffee is nothing short of a London institution, and more often than not, queues snake out of the door, but it's definitely worth the wait.

+44(0)20 7232 3010
www.monmouthcoffee.co.uk
⊖ Covent Garden

MON–SAT.	8:00am – 6:30pm
SUN.	Closed

First opened 1978
Roaster Monmouth Coffee Company
Machine La Marzocco Linea, 3 groups
Grinder Mazzer Robur E

Espresso	£2.00
Cappuccino	£3.10
Latte	£3.10
Flat white	£3.10

Sister locations Borough

MAP REF. **21**

 COFFEE 4.50 / 5   **OVERALL** 4.50 / 5 ★ ★ ★ ★ ✯

Monocle Café

18 Chiltern Street, W1U 7QA

If you've read Monocle, the über-sophisticated international magazine that shows impeccable good taste in everything, you'll have an idea of what to expect here. While that may sound like a backhanded compliment, it isn't. The Monocle Café is indeed slick and in the best possible taste, but it's staffed by people who show genuine warmth. And who know how to make great coffee using Allpress beans. Food is international in outlook, with an emphasis on Asia and Scandinavia, and there is a super cool cocktail menu. A great, and affordable, place to eat and drink in this affluent area.

+44(0)20 7135 2040
cafe.monocle.com
◒ Baker Street

MON–WED.	7:00am – 7:00pm
THU–FRI.	7:00am – 8:00pm
SAT.	8:00am – 8:00pm
SUN.	8:00am – 7:00pm

First opened 2013
Roaster Allpress Espresso
Machine La Marzocco Linea PB, 2 groups
Grinder Victoria Arduino Mythos One

Espresso	£2.50
Cappuccino	£3.00
Latte	£3.00
Flat white	£3.00

MAP REF.

COFFEE 4.25 / 5

OVERALL 4.25 / 5 ★★★★☆

Notes Trafalgar Square

31 St Martin's Lane, WC2N 4ER

Notes always has good crowds - not surprising for a place that's minutes from Trafalgar Square. But what brings them is not just location but incredibly high quality. The food is terrific, and it transforms into a wine bar in the evening, popular with theatre-goers. Single origin filter is the most exciting option, but the espressos are equally enjoyable, all using beans from their own roaster.

+44(0)20 7240 0424
notes-uk.co.uk
⊖ Charing Cross / Leicester Square

Sister locations Canary Wharf / Gherkin / King's Cross / Moorgate

MON-WED.	7:30am - 9:00pm
THU-FRI.	7:30am - 10:00pm
SAT.	9:00am - 10:00pm
SUN.	10:00am - 6:00pm

First opened 2010
Roaster Notes Coffee Roasters
Machine La Marzocco FB80, 3 groups
Grinder Mahlkönig EK 43,
Nuova Simonelli Mythos

Espresso	£2.00
Cappuccino	£2.80
Latte	£2.80
Flat white	£2.80

MAP REF. 23

COFFEE 4.50 / 5	OVERALL 4.50 / 5 ★★★★⯪

The Providores and Tapa Room

109 Marylebone High Street, W1U 4RX

Providores is the fine-dining restaurant upstairs, the Tapa Room is the café downstairs. Nearly everyone comes here for chef Peter Gordon's ground-breaking take on fusion cooking inspired by his native country, New Zealand. But if you just want a coffee and maybe a plate of homemade biscuits, grab a seat. Funnily enough, the best restaurants sometimes take little care with their coffee. Not at all true here, where the antipodean ethos dictates exacting standards at the La Marzocco. And it's better still if you finish off your meal from the all-day or brunch menu with a beautifully pulled coffee.

+44(0)20 7935 6175
www.theprovidores.co.uk
⊖ Baker Street / Bond Street

Sister locations Kopapa

MON-FRI.	8:00am - 10:30pm
SAT.	9:00am - 11:00pm
SUN.	9:00am - 10:30pm

First opened 2001
Roaster Volcano Coffee Works
Machine La Marzocco GB5, 2 groups
Grinder Mazzer Super Jolly

Espresso	£2.35
Cappuccino	£3.25
Latte	£3.25
Flat white	£3.25

MAP REF. 24

COFFEE 4.25 / 5	OVERALL 4.25 / 5 ★★★★⯪

Sharps Coffee Bar

9 Windmill Street, W1T 2JF

At Sharps, a barber shop and coffee bar complement one another without a whisker of encroachment. Sharps is one of the few coffee shops to offer coffee from celebrated Berlin roastery, The Barn. The café feels very neatly pulled together as a whole; every detail from the trim tiling to clean-cut branding befits this dapper Fitzrovia location.

+44(0)20 7636 8688
www.sharpsbarbers.com
Goodge Street

MON-FRI.	8:00am - 5:00pm
SAT.	10:00am - 5:00pm
SUN.	Closed

First opened 2013
Roaster The Barn and guests
Machine Kees van der Westen Spirit, 3 groups
Grinder Mahlkönig K30, Mahlkönig EK 43

Espresso	£2.00
Cappuccino	£2.40
Latte	£2.60
Flat white	£2.40

MAP REF. **25**

  COFFEE 4.50 / 5

 OVERALL 4.50 / 5 ★★★★✩

Store Street Espresso

40 Store Street, WC1E 7DB

Any coffee place with a vast catchment area of university students is likely to do pretty well. Store Street does better than most because its quality is right through the skylight roof. Simple sandwiches and top-notch baked goods make for a good light lunch, and the laid-back staff never seem to object when customers dawdle over dessert or laptops. Their seriousness with coffee is evident in the three-group Black Eagle. It processes hundreds of drinks throughout the day, made with unfailing skill. Milk art can be awesome, too. Or choose filter coffee if you want something special.

www.storestespresso.co.uk

⊖ Goodge Street

Sister locations Tavistock Place / Paddington

MON-FRI.	7:30am – 7:00pm
SAT.	9:00am – 6:00pm
SUN.	10:00am – 5:00pm

First opened 2010
Roaster Square Mile Coffee Roasters
Machine Victoria Arduino Black Eagle, 3 groups
Grinder Victoria Arduino Mythos One, Mahlkönig EK 43

Espresso	£2.40
Cappuccino	£3.00
Latte	£3.00
Flat white	£3.00

MAP REF. **26**

COFFEE 4.50 / 5		OVERALL 4.50 / 5	★ ★ ★ ★ ⯪

TAP Coffee Rathbone Place

26 Rathbone Place, W1T 1JD

This diminutive outpost of TAP (now part of the Department of Coffee and Social Affairs group) is a pleasure to look at, with its dark wood floors and beautiful pictures. Sandwiches and baked goods are simple and outstanding, and the coffee, needless to say, is up to TAP's consistently high standard. Espresso is well made, but something from the AeroPress is a life-enhancing joy. Especially if you can sit on the bench outside to drink it.

+44(0)20 7637 4221
departmentofcoffee.com

⊖ Tottenham Court Road / Goodge Street

Sister locations Tottenham Court Road / Wardour Street / Russell Square

MON-FRI.	8:00am – 7:00pm
SAT.	10:00am – 6:00pm
SUN.	Closed

First opened 2010
Roaster The Roastery Department
Machine Nuova Simonelli Aurelia II, 3 groups
Grinder Mazzer Robur, Mazzer Kony, Mazzer Super Jolly

Espresso	£2.40
Cappuccino	£2.95
Latte	£2.95
Flat white	£2.95

MAP REF. **27**

COFFEE 4.50 / 5		OVERALL 4.50 / 5	★ ★ ★ ★ ⯪

TAP Coffee Tottenham Court Road

114 Tottenham Court Road, W1T 5AH

You won't find the name on the storefront, but just look for the company trademark bicycle and hip grey paintwork on their corner site with huge windows that let in loads of light. If you like people-watching, perch on a bench at the window or outside while enjoying one of their stellar cups, either espresso-based or in filter. Tottenham Court Road is not London's most atmospheric street. TAP makes it not just tolerable but pleasurable.

+44(0)20 7383 5000
departmentofcoffee.com
⊖ Warren Street

Sister locations Rathbone Place / Wardour Street / Russell Square

MON-FRI.	7:30am - 7:00pm
SAT.	10:00am - 6:00pm
SUN.	10:00am - 5:00pm

First opened 2011
Roaster The Roastery Department
Machine Nuova Simonelli Aurelia II, 2 groups
Grinder Mazzer Robur, Mazzer Kony, Mazzer Super Jolly

Espresso	£2.40
Cappuccino	£2.95
Latte	£2.95
Flat white	£2.95

MAP REF. **28**

Taylor St Baristas Mayfair

22 Brooks Mews, W1K 4DY

A cool coffee place right behind Claridge's? It's true. This is the most unexpected TSB location, and the clientele, though not short of a bob or two, recognise the simple virtues of a good filter or espresso; the place is always rammed with regulars. The look is more Muswell Hill than Mayfair, and the mews setting guarantees low(ish) traffic noise. Sandwiches, salads and baked goods provide the food offering, and the coffee, as always from this outfit, is as good as you'd expect. A real gem to be enjoyed by all.

+44(0)20 7629 3163
www.taylor-st.com
⊖ Bond Street

Sister locations Liverpool Street / Shoreditch / Canary Wharf / Monument / Bank / South Quay / St Paul's

MON-FRI.	7:30am – 5:30pm
SAT-SUN.	Closed

First opened 2011
Roaster Taylor St Baristas
Machine La Marzocco Linea, 3 groups
Grinder Mazzer Kony E, Mahlkönig EK 43, Nuova Simonelli Mythos

Espresso	£2.00
Cappuccino	£2.80 / £3.20
Latte	£2.80 / £3.20
Flat white	£2.80 / £3.70

MAP REF. **29**

COFFEE 4.75 / 5		OVERALL 4.50 / 5	★★★★✬

Timberyard

7 Upper St Martin's Lane, WC2H 9DL

If you walk around the area regularly, you will probably think there is no quiet time at this outpost of the successful Timberyard group. You won't be entirely wrong, but you may get lucky - try Monday, which seems often to be a slower day. And it's worth persisting, because this is a wonderful place in every way. Coffee standards are high, as they are throughout the group. Espresso-based drinks are well made, but filter coffee is an even brighter star. Don't forget the downstairs rooms (great for meetings) if upstairs is rammed.

www.tyuk.com

⊖ Leicester Square / Covent Garden

MON-FRI.	8:00am - 6:00pm
SAT-SUN.	9:00am - 6:00pm

First opened 2014
Roaster Climpson & Sons, The Barn, Round Hill Roastery
Machine La Marzocco Linea PB
Grinder Nuova Simonelli Mythos, Mahlkönig EK 43

Espresso	£2.40 / £2.60
Cappuccino	£3.00 / £3.20
Latte	£3.00 / £3.20
Flat white	£2.80 / £3.00

MAP REF. **30**

Workshop Coffee Fitzrovia

80a Mortimer Street, W1W 7FE

West End

Workshop Fitzrovia harks back to London's imperial zenith; its intricate tiling and gold details invoke Victorian grandeur. And then there's that bar: a sovereign slab of Madagascan granite, imbued with a magnetism which demands your gaze and touch. The coffee is precisely what you'd expect from Workshop: light-roasted and delicious. The baristas are efficient and deliberate, engaging customers with utmost politeness. There's a sense of mastery about the place; an irrefutable statement that in speciality coffee, London is enjoying a new heyday with Workshop at the vanguard.

+44(0)20 7253 5754
www.workshopcoffee.com
Oxford Circus

Sister locations Marylebone / Clerkenwell / Holborn / White Collar Factory

MON-FRI.	7:00am - 7:00pm
SAT-SUN.	9:00am - 6:00pm

First opened 2014
Roaster Workshop Coffee
Machine La Marzocco Linea PB, 3 groups
Grinder Nuova Simonelli Mythos One

Espresso	£2.60
Cappuccino	£3.10
Latte	£3.30
Flat white	£3.10

MAP REF.

COFFEE 4.75 / 5

OVERALL 4.75 / 5 ★★★★☆

Workshop Coffee Marylebone

1 Barrett Street, W1U 1AX

TOP 35

There is a dozen or more places to get coffee within a five-minute walk of this Workshop outlet. While some of them may have fancier seating and more decorative frills, the brew here beats everything in the area. It's heavily used as a source of takeaways (expect queues at peak times), but there is also some bench-type seating and it's a surprisingly peaceful haven from the Oxford/Wigmore Street crowds. If you're settling in for a chat or a laptop session, get your brew in an AeroPress.

www.workshopcoffee.com

⊖ Bond Street

Sister locations Clerkenwell / Holborn / Fitzrovia / White Collar Factory

MON-FRI. 7:00am - 7:00pm
SAT-SUN. 9:00am - 6:00pm

First opened 2015
Roaster Workshop Coffee
Machine Synesso Hydra, 3 groups
Grinder Victoria Arduino Mythos One

Espresso	£2.40
Cappuccino	£3.10
Latte	£3.30
Flat white	£3.10

MAP REF. 32

COFFEE 4.75 / 5		OVERALL 4.50 / 5	★★★★⯪

Famous for its outrageous nightlife, Soho is also well-known for its cutting-edge bars, clubs and restaurants. This spirit of experimentation and adventure extends to coffee and many of London's most exciting artisanal cafés can be found here.

Soho

39 Steps Coffee Haus

8 D'Arblay Street, W1F 8DP

Hailing originally from Germany, 39 Steps Coffee Haus has hit Soho with an impressive offering of both coffee and food. Stepping inside, you immediately feel the difference from most cafés of a similar calibre in London - no modern minimalism to be found here. It has the feel of a bustling European street café, yet the syphon on the counter and the nitro cold brew bring your attention back to the fact that they are serious about their coffee.

Another testament to their seriousness about the bean is their unique three group Reneka machine, a white whale in the London coffee scene, and no less than four grinders. A milky espresso is a welcome treat, but don't pass up the opportunity to

sample one of their delicious pour overs. Be sure to sample their tempting cakes, all baked in house.

The welcome couldn't be more friendly, and the barista's skills are impressive. Prepare to see much more of this little outfit over the coming months, with plans to not only serve their own beans, but also to open two new sites within the next year, you'll want to keep an eye on this little gem.

MAP REF. **33**

COFFEE
4.25 / 5

OVERALL
4.25 / 5

Soho

MON-SAT.	7:00am - 7:00pm
SUN.	8:00am - 7:00pm

First opened 2018
Roaster 39 Steps Coffee and guests
Machine Reneka Life, 3 groups
Grinder Compak F10 Master Conic OD x3,
Santos 63

Espresso	£2.20
Cappuccino	£2.80
Latte	£3.10
Flat white	£2.90

+44(0)20 7287 6682
39stepscoffee.com
⊖ Piccadilly Circus / Oxford Circus

Bar Termini

7 Old Compton Street, W1D 5JE

Bar Termini is half coffee bar and half cocktail bar, with the two sides run by figures of distinction: Marco Arrigo of Illy on the coffee side, Tony Conigliaro - of 69 Colebrooke Row, Zetter Town House and other top bars - on the cocktail side. It offers little in the way of food, so all the focus is on 'the liquids' - and what liquids they are. Intriguingly, they don't believe in delaying delivery of your coffee by doing latte art: if you want to create your own, they'll give you a barista's pitcher.

+44(0)7860 945 018
www.bar-termini.com
⊖ Leicester Square

| MON-THU. | 11:30am - 1:00pm |
| FRI-SUN. | 10:00am - 1:00am |

First opened 2015
Roaster Illy
Machine Faema Legend E61, 2 groups
Grinder Faema

Espresso	£1.00 / £2.50
Cappuccino	£3.50
Latte	£3.50
Flat white	£3.50

MAP REF. 34

| COFFEE 4.00 / 5 | OVERALL 4.00 / 5 ★★★★☆ |

TOP 35 Department of Coffee and Social Affairs
Carnaby Street 3 Lowndes Court, W1F 7HD

Occupying a light, modern space just off Carnaby Street, this branch of Department is home to some of London's most talented baristas. The café offers an impressive choice of coffee beans: two espresso roasts complemented by two different single origins on filter. There's more to this stylish coffee bar than meets the eye: Department encourages a hands-on approach to coffee making, operating a coffee school in the dedicated downstairs space.

www.departmentofcoffee.com
⊖ Oxford Circus

Sister locations Multiple locations

MON-FRI.	8:00am - 7:00pm
SAT.	9:30am - 7:00pm
SUN.	10.00am - 7:00pm

First opened 2011
Roaster The Roastery Department
Machine La Marzocco Linea PB, 3 groups
Grinder Mazzer Robur E x2, Mazzer Super Jolly

Espresso	£2.50
Cappuccino	£3.00
Latte	£3.00
Flat white	£3.00

MAP REF. 35

| COFFEE 4.50 / 5 | OVERALL 4.50 / 5 ★★★★⯪ |

Department of Coffee and Social Affairs
Piccadilly 15 Sherwood Street, W1F 7ED

This compact venue is a modern and sophisticated take on the traditional Italian espresso bar. Department is ideal for picking up an expertly-made brew before dashing to your next Soho appointment. Alongside Department's house-roasted espresso blend, coffee aficionados will delight in the rotating range of single origin filter coffees.

www.departmentofcoffee.com
⊖ Piccadilly Circus

Sister locations Multiple locations

MON–FRI.	7:30am – 5:00pm
SAT.	10:30am – 5:00pm
SUN.	Closed

First opened 2013
Roaster The Roastery Department
Machine La Marzocco FB80, 2 groups
Grinder Mazzer Robur x2,
Mazzer Super Jolly

Espresso	£2.00
Cappuccino	£3.00
Latte	£3.00
Flat white	£3.00

MAP REF. **36**

 COFFEE 4.25 / 5   **OVERALL** 4.25 / 5 ★★★★

Fernandez & Wells Denmark Street

1-3 Denmark Street, WC2H 8LP

Fernandez & Wells is a food and drink emporium satisfying the most fervid foodies. Do you have a hankering for ham? Try the Iberian cured meats from Brindisa. Are you partial to pressed juice? Freshly squeezed blood orange is also available. Coffee comes from Has Bean, and you're sure to get a great cup whether you opt for a fragrant flat white or a well brewed filter.

+44(0)20 3302 9799
www.fernandezandwells.com
⊖ Tottenham Court Road

Sister locations Duke Street / Lexington Street / Somerset House / South Kensington

MON-TUE.	8:00am - 9:00pm
WED-FRI.	8:00am - 11:00pm
SAT.	9:00am - 10:00pm
SUN.	10:00am - 6:00pm

First opened 2014
Roaster Has Bean
Machine La Marzocco Linea PB, 3 groups
Grinder Nuova Simonelli Mythos One

Espresso	£2.60
Cappuccino	£2.95
Latte	£2.95
Flat white	£2.95

MAP REF. **37**

| COFFEE 4.25 / 5 | | OVERALL 4.25 / 5 | ★★★★⯪ |

Flat White

17 Berwick Street, W1F 0PT

Established in 2005, Flat White was perhaps the first café to bring Antipodean-style coffee to the UK. For a time it became a London coffee institution, celebrated as a pioneer of third wave coffee in the capital. The venue has changed management several times since those heady days, but fortunately there's a continued focus on quality. The interior has been refreshed and customers can expect a range of beans from Dark Arts, pulled through an impressive 4-group Synesso, affectionately dubbed "The Great White".

+44(0)20 7734 0370
www.flatwhitesoho.co.uk
⊖ Oxford Circus / Tottenham Court Road

Sister locations Milkbar

MON-FRI.	8:00am - 6:00pm
SAT.	9:00am - 6:00pm
SUN.	9:30am - 6:00pm

First opened 2005
Roaster Dark Arts Coffee
Machine Synesso Hydra, 4 groups
Grinder Nuova Simonelli Mythos, Mazzer

Espresso	£2.40
Cappuccino	£3.00
Latte	£3.00
Flat white	£2.80

MAP REF. **38**

| COFFEE 4.50 / 5 | | OVERALL 4.50 / 5 | ★★★★⯪ |

Milkbar

3 Bateman Street, W1D 4AG

When you've been around as long as Milkbar, and undergone some changes of ownership, you're sure to have some ups and downs. At the moment, the ups are running the show in Bateman Street. The dark room looks little different, but both food and coffee have regained the heights that originally made this such a star of London's coffee scene. Milky drinks rather than straight up espresso are the top choice from the well-tended La Marzocco, and Kalita drip is the best option if you have time on your hands and love a single origin cup. Baked goods are stars, as you'd expect from an Oz-owned place. Service is laid back but efficient. If you haven't been for a while, or if you've never been, go now.

+44(0)20 7287 4796
www.milkbarsoho.co.uk
◉ Tottenham Court Road /
Leicester Square

MON-FRI. 8:00am - 5:30pm
SAT-SUN. 9:30am - 6:00pm

First opened 2008
Roaster Dark Arts Coffee
Machine La Marzocco FB80, 3 groups
Grinder Mazzer

Espresso £2.60
Cappuccino £3.20
Latte £3.20
Flat white £3.00

Sister locations Flat White

MAP REF. **39**

 COFFEE 4.50 / 5   **OVERALL** 4.25 / 5 ★★★★✭

39

Rapha London Soho

85 Brewer Street, W1F 9ZN

The perfectionism Rapha applies to its cycling gear is readily apparent in its approach to coffee; the espresso here is extraordinarily good. Try a shot made with Allpress beans, pulled through a La Marzocco PB. Bike locks are available for those arriving on two wheels, and the vintage Italian cycling memorabilia adds to the café's sense of energy and momentum. Coffee is no afterthought here; Rapha has established itself as a coffee destination in its own right.

+44(0)20 7494 9831
www.rapha.cc
⊖ Piccadilly Circus

Sister locations Spitalfields

MON–SAT.	8:00am – 6:30pm
SUN.	12:00pm – 5:30pm

First opened 2012
Roaster Allpress Espresso and guests
Machine La Marzocco Linea PB, 2 groups
Grinder Mazzer Kony E x2, Mahlkönig Guatemala

Espresso	£2.30
Cappuccino	£3.00
Latte	£3.20
Flat white	£3.00

MAP REF. **40**

COFFEE 4.50 / 5		OVERALL 4.50 / 5	★ ★ ★ ★ ⯪

Sacred Ganton Street

13 Ganton Street, W1F 9BL

Food has been an increasingly important part of the offer at Sacred for some time now, and the trend continues at full blast. They've always had a wide range of sandwiches and enticing baked stuff - check out a sausage roll so huge you may doubt it's just one portion. But they also have cheese and charcuterie platters which you can accompany with cocktails, beer or wine, so you can get a proper meal if you need it. Or just sit with coffee, ideally the espresso blend with a dose of milk in whatever form you prefer. There's plenty of Antipodean-inspired coffee in London, but Sacred retains its large congregation of devout worshippers.

+44(0)20 7700 1628
www.sacredcafe.com
⊖ Oxford Circus

MON-FRI.	7:00am - 7:30pm
SAT.	8:00am - 7:30pm
SUN.	9:00am - 5:00pm

First opened 2005
Roaster Sacred
Machine La Marzocco Linea
Grinder Mahlkönig K30

Espresso	£2.20
Cappuccino	£3.00
Latte	£3.00
Flat white	£3.00

Sister locations The Strand / Highbury Studios / Westfield   MAP REF. **41**

Soho Grind

19 Beak Street, W1F 9RP

The Grind & Co. empire is on a mission to make coffee sexy, and what better neighbourhood to do it in than Soho? The second store from entrepreneur David Abrahamovitch and Australian DJ Kaz James is an enticing coffee and cocktail den complete with sanguine lighting and bass soundtrack. Satisfy your coffee cravings with a seductive flat white, then descend the steps - beneath the neon sign promising 'French lessons given downstairs' - to the basement speakeasy for an espresso martini.

+44(0)20 7287 7073
www.sohogrind.com
⊖ Piccadilly Circus

Sister locations Multiple locations

MON-THU.	7:30am - 11:00pm
FRI.	7:30am - 12:00am
SAT.	9:00am - 12:00am
SUN.	9:00am - 7:00pm

First opened 2014
Roaster Grind & Co.
Machine La Marzocco Linea PB, 3 groups
Grinder Victoria Arduino Mythos One x2, Mahlkönig Tanzania

Espresso	£2.30
Cappuccino	£3.00
Latte	£3.00
Flat white	£3.00

MAP REF. 42

COFFEE 4.50 / 5   OVERALL 4.50 / 5

TAP Coffee Wardour Street

193 Wardour Street, W1F 8ZF

This branch of TAP provides one of the speediest escapes from the Oxford Street shopping crowds. Lots of people know about it, so you can be sure of some pretty serious crowds here too - though nothing like Oxford Street, of course. There's a small food offering, but the main draws are the always excellent coffee (try the single origin filters) and the handsome room, long and slim and lit from above by big skylights. Unlike some places that attract local creatives and their laptops, TAP also has a good contingent of talkers - so the buzz is almost always lively. A top choice in coffee-crowded Soho.

+44(0)20 7734 4605
departmentofcoffee.com
⊖ Tottenham Court Road

Sister locations Rathbone Place / Tottenham Court Road / Russell Square

MON–FRI.	8:00am – 7:00pm
SAT.	9:30am – 7:00pm
SUN.	9:45am – 6:00pm

First opened 2012
Roaster The Roastery Department
Machine Nuova Simonelli Aurelia II, 2 groups
Grinder Mazzer Robur, Mazzer Kony, Mazzer Super Jolly

Espresso	£2.40
Cappuccino	£2.95
Latte	£2.95
Flat white	£2.95

MAP REF. **43**

 COFFEE 4.75 / 5 **OVERALL** 4.50 / 5 ★★★★⯪

43

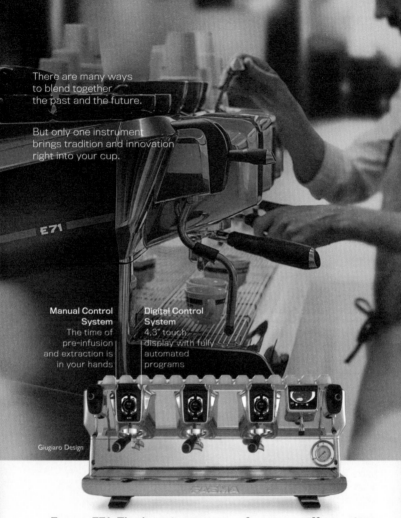

There are many ways
to blend together
the past and the future.

But only one instrument
brings tradition and innovation
right into your cup.

E71

**Manual Control
System**
The time of
pre-infusion
and extraction is
in your hands

**Digital Control
System**
4,3" touch
display with fully
automated
programs

Giugiaro Design

Faema E71. The best interpreter of master coffee artists.

The perfect blend between tech and tradition has found its shapes.
The natural evolution of a classic icon such as E61, is finally here.
E71, studied and designed for all those who seek perfection
and superior quality, with every sip and every cup of coffee.

EXPRESS YOUR ART

@FaemaOfficial   @faema_official

e71.faema.com

Dotted with beautiful squares and grand architecture, Bloomsbury offers refined, contemplative surroundings to enjoy coffee. Home to thinkers for centuries, the neighbourhood is anchored by numerous academic institutions and the imposing British Museum, as well as boasting a wealth of literary connections. Busy Holborn to the south is frequented by lawyers and journalists, conducting business in and around the many cafés.

Holborn & Bloomsbury

The Black Penny

34 Great Queen Street, WC2B 5AA

This popular Covent Garden café uses its own The Roastery Department blend. There is evident skill behind the machine, resulting in a beautifully pulled espresso. Where quality also shines brightly is in the food, which rises several notches above the West End café norm. Delicious baked goods, sandwiches and salads are all outstanding. You can get a takeaway, but the back room is a splendidly comfortable place to spend part of your morning, lunchtime or even a full leisurely afternoon.

+44(0)20 7242 2580
www.theblackpenny.co.uk
⊖ Covent Garden / Holborn

MON–FRI.	8:00am – 6:00pm
SAT.	9:00am – 6:00pm
SUN.	9:00am – 5:00pm

First opened 2015
Roaster The Roastery Department
Machine La Marzocco Linea PB, 3 groups
Grinder Anfim SCODY II

Espresso	£2.30
Cappuccino	£2.80
Latte	£2.80
Flat white	£2.80

MAP REF. **44**

| COFFEE 4.25 / 5 | OVERALL 4.50 / 5 ★★★★⯪ |

The Espresso Room Bloomsbury

31-35 Great Ormond Street, WC1N 3HZ

The original Espresso Room is approaching its tenth year in this tiny space. It has a huge local following, with Great Ormond Street Hospital across the street and lots of academics and lawyers nearby. But they're not resting on their laurels: the pursuit of quality remains intense. Any milky drink is a thing of beauty, brewed with scientific precision that the GOSH medics would recognise. The food offering is tiny but good. And the benches outside make a perfect perch to sit and sip when the weather is good.

+44(0)7760 714 883
www.theespressoroom.com
⊖ Russell Square

Sister locations Covent Garden / Holborn

MON–FRI.	7:30am – 5:00pm
SAT.	9:00am – 3:30pm
SUN.	Closed

First opened 2009
Roaster Caravan Coffee Roasters and guests
Machine Synesso Hydra, 2 groups
Grinder Mazzer Robur E, Mahlkönig EK 43

Espresso	£1.80 / £2.20
Cappuccino	£2.80 / £3.40
Latte	£2.80 / £3.40
Flat white	£2.80 / £3.40

MAP REF. **45**

| COFFEE 4.75 / 5 | OVERALL 4.25 / 5 ★★★★⯪ |

The Espresso Room Holborn

23 Southampton Row, WC1B 5HA

Raising the banner for craft coffee in Holborn, The Espresso Room's experienced baristas serve excellent coffee with a dose of American-style enthusiasm. Beautifully mismatched furniture and an old school gym bench add character to the sunny interior. Customers with time to linger can opt for single estate filter coffee served at the dedicated brew bar.

+44(0)20 7998 1017
www.freestatecoffee.co.uk
⊖ Holborn

Sister locations Bloomsbury / Covent Garden

MON-FRI.	7:00am – 7:00pm
SAT-SUN.	8:30am – 6:00pm

First opened 2013
Roaster Caravan Coffee Roasters
Machine La Marzocco Strada EP, 3 groups
Grinder Mazzer Robur E x2, Mahlkönig EK 43

Espresso	£2.20
Cappuccino	£2.80 / £3.50
Latte	£2.80 / £3.50
Flat white	£2.80 / £3.30

MAP REF. **46**

COFFEE 4.50 / 5   ●●●●●

OVERALL 4.25 / 5   ★★★★✩

Half Cup

100-102 Judd Street, WC1H 9NT

You know how you sometimes walk into an unfamiliar coffee place and think, 'I wish I lived around the corner'? Half Cup is that sort of place. It looks great, you get a big smile and hello when you set foot inside the door, and Nude beans from the Linea turn into excellent coffee whether milky or black. Your fellow customers might be device-bound workers, office-lunchers, or discerning tourists during the week, but at weekends it's a thriving local scene. The food is priced very fairly for this part of town, and the carrot cake has a devoted following.

+44(0)20 8617 7835
www.halfcup.co.uk
⊖ King's Cross

| MON-FRI. | 8:00am - 7:00pm |
| SAT-SUN. | 9:00am - 5:00pm |

First opened 2014
Roaster Nude Coffee Roasters
Machine La Marzocco Linea, 2 groups
Grinder Compak K10,
Nuova Simonelli Mythos One

Espresso	£2.20
Cappuccino	£2.70
Latte	£2.70
Flat white	£2.70

MAP REF. **47**

| COFFEE 4.25 / 5 | | OVERALL 4.25 / 5 |  |

Hopper Coffee

4 Roger Street, WC1N 2JX

Hopper is a tiny place (it was originally a sandwich takeaway) and has just a few seats if you want to eat and drink on the premises. But it's memorable nonetheless, simply because the coffee is exceptionally good and the food exceptionally inexpensive. (Sandwiches here are roughly half the price of some comparable coffee shops.) The beans come from Coffee Compass, and their espresso blend is round and sweet enough to drink without sugar. Locals love the place: at times the queue snakes right around the corner. It's easy to see why.

+44(0)7590 075 101

⊖ Holborn

MON-FRI.	7:00am - 5:00pm
SAT-SUN.	Closed

First opened 2016
Roaster Coffee Compass
Machine La Marzocco Linea AV, 2 groups
Grinder Mazzer Major

Espresso	£1.80
Cappuccino	£2.40 / £2.70 / £3.00
Latte	£2.40 / £2.70 / £3.00
Flat white	£2.40 / £2.70 / £3.00

MAP REF. **48**

COFFEE 4.25 / 5	🫘🫘🫘🫘🫘	OVERALL 4.25 / 5	★★★★✫

Hubbard & Bell

199-206 High Holborn, WC1V 7BD

Hubbard & Bell is a café, bar and grill occupying a swathe of the open plan foyer of the Hoxton Hotel. This slick, midcentury-inspired space hums with activity as hotel guests mingle with fashionably dressed media workers. The talented barista team have a background at some of London's top cafés, ensuring that the standard of coffee preparation is consistently high. Hubbard & Bell demonstrates that with the right approach, top-notch coffee can be served in a modern, fast-paced hotel environment.

+44(0)20 7661 3030
www.hubbardandbell.com
⊖ Holborn

Sister locations Barber & Parlour

MON-FRI.	7:00am – 2:00am
SAT.	8:00am – 2:00am
SUN.	8:00am – 12:00am

First opened 2014
Roaster Origin Coffee Roasters and guests
Machine La Marzocco Strada, 3 groups
Grinder Nuova Simonelli Mythos x2, Mahlkönig EK 43

Espresso	£2.50
Cappuccino	£2.80
Latte	£2.80
Flat white	£2.80

MAP REF. **49**

COFFEE 4.50 / 5	OVERALL 4.50 / 5 ★★★★★

Knockbox Coffee

29 Lamb's Conduit Street, WC1N 3NG

With its array of outfitters, Lamb's Conduit Street is a destination for the dapper man about town. The road is also home to another well-pulled-together outfit in the shape of Knockbox Coffee. Turkish owner, Mete Dogrul, has a meticulous eye for detail, creating the furniture and fittings himself with plywood and copper. Occupying a sunny corner, the café is perfectly positioned for people-watching. Relax with a Workshop coffee whilst tucking into a hearty sandwich or a glorious pastry.

+44(0)20 3489 7325
⊖ Russell Square / Holborn

MON-FRI.	7:00am – 6:00pm
SAT.	8:00am – 5:00pm
SUN.	9:00am – 5:00pm

First opened 2014
Roaster Workshop Coffee
Machine Synesso Cyncra, 2 groups
Grinder Mazzer Major

Espresso	£2.30
Cappuccino	£2.70
Latte	£2.70
Flat white	£2.70

MAP REF. **50**

COFFEE 4.25 / 5	OVERALL 4.25 / 5 ★★★★★

Redemption Roasters

84b Lamb's Conduit Street, WC1N 3LR

This Redemption location is a thing of beauty. Residing in a corner building with huge windows on two sides, this venue is awash with natural light, even on a cloudy day. The interior is light and simple, with both low and high seating. But the focus here is on the coffee, and it shows. The espresso-based drinks are stunning, with milk art that will blow you away, but the real heroes are the filter brews. And it's not just the great coffee that makes Redemption such a stand-up company - they work with young offenders to train them in roasting and barista skills and go on to help secure them jobs in the coffee industry when they re-enter the outside world. A truly outstanding outfit.

+44(0)20 7404 1927
 Russell Square

MON-FRI. 7:30am - 5:30pm
SAT-SUN. 9:00am - 4:00pm

First opened 2017
Roaster Redemption Roasters
Machine Slayer Steam, 2 groups
Grinder Mahlkönig EK 43, Mahlkönig K30 Vario

Espresso	£2.20
Cappuccino	£2.80
Latte	£2.90
Flat white	£2.90

Sister locations Barbican

MAP REF. **51**

COFFEE 4.50 / 5

OVERALL 4.25 / 5 ★★★★⯨

TAP Coffee Russell Square

72 Russell Square, WC1B 5BA

Unless you work around Russell Square, it may well be a place you pass through on your way to somewhere else. Though one of London's most famous Georgian squares, it's one of those 'in between' places, not brilliant for public transport and without any major attractions in the immediate vicinity. What's more, the east side has lost its old architecture to nondescript post-war boxes. Tourist hotels make up a lot of the foot traffic, and local colour is in short supply.

But TAP's vast new outlet here will quickly make you change your tune about the attractions of the square. It's a great big place on the east side, with views of the old parts: trees in the square and Georgian splendour in the terraces to south and north. The space itself is highly attractive, spacious and high-ceilinged and light-filled, and there's no shortage of well-spaced seating. You're unlikely to be disturbed if you set yourself up at one of the tables with laptop and phone for a good long work session. There's a small selection of food to sustain you, and the Aurelia is in good hands here, as at all TAP venues. If you're lingering, however, a single origin brew from the V60 should be on your shopping list. The final plus: there isn't much competition providing top-quality coffee in the area. Russell Square, a coffee drinking destination - will wonders never cease?

MAP REF. **52**

COFFEE 4.50 / 5	OVERALL 4.50 / 5

MON–FRI.	7:30am – 5:00pm
SAT.	8:30am – 5:00pm
SUN.	9:00am – 5:00pm

First opened 2017
Roaster The Roastery Department
Machine Nuova Simonelli Aurelia, 3 groups
Grinder Mazzer Robur, Mazzer Kony

Espresso	£2.30
Cappuccino	£2.70
Latte	£2.70
Flat white	£2.70

departmentofcoffee.com
🚇 Russell Square

Sister locations Tottenham Court Road / Wardour Street / Rathbone Place

Holborn & Bloomsbury

Workshop Coffee Holborn

60a Holborn Viaduct, EC1A 2FD

TOP
35

Workshop Holborn is a coffee bar for perfectionists. Its design can be summed up in just one word: uncompromising. The interior details look like they were agonised over during many long nights of planning. The meticulously dosed coffee flows from immaculate portafilters into satisfyingly weighty porcelain cups. Workshop's exacting philosophy might not be to everybody's taste, but there's no question it has redefined what we've come to expect from a coffee bar.

+44(0)20 7324 7797
www.workshopcoffee.com
 Farringdon / Chancery Lane

MON-FRI.	7:00am – 6:30pm
SAT-SUN.	Closed

First opened 2014
Roaster Workshop Coffee
Machine La Marzocco Linea PB, 3 groups
Grinder Victoria Arduino Mythos One

Espresso	£2.60
Cappuccino	£3.10
Latte	£3.30
Flat white	£3.10

Sister locations Marylebone / Fitzrovia / Clerkenwell

MAP REF. **53**

COFFEE
4.75 / 5

OVERALL
4.75 / 5

★★★★⯪

Formerly hubs of manufacturing and enterprise, the districts of Farringdon and Clerkenwell now house smart offices, loft apartments, night clubs and restaurants. Some of the most exciting coffee venues in town can also be found here, making this the new heart of London's burgeoning coffee culture.

Farringdon & Clerkenwell

Caravan Exmouth Market

11-13 Exmouth Market, EC1R 4QD

The original, and many still would say the best. Caravan's roasting and brewing skills need no special mention: they've become an integral part of London's coffee scene. The special charms of this place lie in its location at the western end of Exmouth Market, and in its ample outdoor seating. On a nice day, even a not-so-nice day, there are few more pleasurable places to sit in London. When ordering, don't restrict yourself to espresso-ey stuff: a changing roster of filter brews offers plenty of excitement.

+44(0)20 7833 8115
www.caravanonexmouth.co.uk
⊖ Angel / Farringdon

Sister locations King's Cross / Bankside / City

MON–FRI.	8:00am – 10:30pm
SAT.	10:00am – 10:30pm
SUN.	10:00am – 4:00pm

First opened 2010
Roaster Caravan Coffee Roasters
Machine Faema Teorema, 3 groups
Grinder Mazzer Kold E, Mazzer Robur E, Mahlkönig EK 43

Espresso	£2.20
Cappuccino	£2.80
Latte	£2.80
Flat white	£2.80

MAP REF. **54**

COFFEE
4.75 / 5

OVERALL
4.50 / 5 ★★★★⯪

Catalyst Café & Coffee Roasters

48 Gray's Inn Road, WC1X 8LT

Unless you work or live around there, or have an appointment at the Eastman Dental Hospital, Gray's Inn Road is unlikely to feature on your list of must-go London hotspots. It's not the loveliest of London streets, and apart from the southernmost and northernmost ends, there isn't much retail activity to look at. And it is an official coffee desert.

Or so you might have assumed. Into the desert has leapt Catalyst, which is an official coffee oasis - and definitely not a mirage. Opening here was either a huge risk in such a non-destination area or a stroke of genius, since there was nothing else around. A loyal local gathering would suggest the latter explanation is the correct one.

You see the place well in advance, its big windows and gleaming bright interior like a beacon in the uninspiring Gray's Inn surroundings. And it's a pleasure to spend time here, whether at the bar or one of the well-spaced tables. Downstairs are the tiny kitchen, where very serious Mediterranean-accented food is prepared from top ingredients, and the Diedrich roaster that provides beans for service, wholesale and for mail order. Barista skills are high both in pulling and in milk art. As daytime yields to the evening, the place looks even lovelier - and caffeine gives way to alcohol as the drink of choice with a tempting and reasonably priced cocktail list. A real oasis in every sense of the word.

MAP REF.

COFFEE
4.50 / 5

OVERALL
4.50 / 5 ★★★★✦

MON-WED.	7:00am – 7:00pm	
THU-FRI.	7:00am – 10:00pm	
SAT-SUN.	Closed	

+44(0)20 7242 8777
www.catalyst.cafe
Chancery Lane / Farringdon

First opened 2016
Roaster Catalyst Café & Coffee Roasters
Machine Victoria Arduino Black Eagle,
2 groups
Grinder Nuova Simonelli Mythos One,
Mahlkönig EK 43

Espresso	£2.20
Cappuccino	£2.70
Latte	£3.00
Flat white	£2.70

Farringdon & Clerkenwell

Clerkenwell Grind

2-4 Old Street, EC1V 9AA

This is the biggest and most ambitious Grind yet, a 100-cover restaurant/café/bar with long hours Thursday to Saturday. The menu covers everything from breakfast to dinner, with particularly well-priced starters and mains, and cocktails are a big feature on the drinks list. Most of the ground-floor space is for dining, with beautiful light fixtures and comfortable long banquettes along the walls, but there's a smaller café at the front if you just want coffee. The three-group Linea shares the honours with single-origin filter, and the professionalism of Grind's customer service is never less than assured.

grind.co.uk
⊖ Barbican

Sister locations Multiple locations

MON-THU.	8:00am - 11:00pm
FRI-SAT.	8:00am - 2:00am
SUN.	9:00am - 7:00pm

First opened 2016
Roaster Grind & Co.
Machine La Marzocco Linea PB, 3 groups
Grinder Nuova Simonelli Mythos One x2, Mahlkönig Tanzania

Espresso	£2.30
Cappuccino	£3.00
Latte	£3.00
Flat white	£3.00

MAP REF. **56**

COFFEE
4.50 / 5

OVERALL
4.50 / 5 ★★★★⯪

Department of Coffee and Social Affairs
Leather Lane 14-16 Leather Lane, EC1N 7SU

Long one of Leather Lane's most popular coffee spots, DCSA goes from strength to strength. It looks exactly the same as it did when it opened in 2010, with some of London's coolest brickwork, and there's little change in the food and drink formula: well filled sandwiches (more attractively priced than we remember them from recent years), beautiful baked goods, and coffee that's brewed with consistent care. The small room at the back has a big table that makes a comfortable perch for meetings, solo working, or just a good old-fashioned chinwag. Despite the wealth of local competition, you'll almost always find a sizeable crowd here, especially at mealtimes.

+44(0)20 7419 6906
www.departmentofcoffee.co.uk
Chancery Lane / Farringdon

MON-FRI. 7:00am - 5:00pm
SAT-SUN. Closed

First opened 2010
Roaster The Roastery Department
Machine La Marzocco Linea PB, 3 groups
Grinder Mazzer Robur x2, Mazzer Super Jolly

Espresso	£2.50
Cappuccino	£3.00
Latte	£3.00
Flat white	£3.00

Sister locations Multiple locations
MAP REF. 57

COFFEE 4.50 / 5
OVERALL 4.50 / 5 ★★★★✦

Exmouth Market Grind

8-10 Exmouth Market, EC1R 4QA

Grind's beautiful corner spot in Exmouth Market is a real winner. With large windows on two sides, and light yet rustic interior, the numerous tables in the long room have a spacious and charming aesthetic. Make sure to bag yourself a seat at the high bar if you like to watch the skilled baristas demonstrate milk art. As with all Grind locations, coffee drinks are only part of the draw. The tempting food menu will keep you lounging around this beautiful venue from morning 'til night.

The coffee should absolutely not be overlooked. Using their own beans, choose from a delicious range of brews. Whether you're in the mood for a delicate pour-over or a beautifully decorated flat white, the highly trained baristas know just how to get the most out of the Grind.

Looking for something with a bit more of a kick? The imaginative Grind cocktail menu, with a variety of coffee-infused spirits, is a sure-fire way to get your evening off to a great start (although, there's no bad time for a Grind espresso martini in our opinion). Whether you're in the area or not, this Grind is a beautiful place to stop off for a quick cuppa or a full feast, especially on the outdoor seating when the sun is shining.

MAP REF. **58**

| COFFEE 4.50 / 5 | | OVERALL 4.50 / 5 | |

MON-WED.	8:00am - 11:00pm
THU-FRI.	8:00am - 12:00am
SAT.	8:00am - 11:00pm
SUN.	9:00am - 7:00pm

+44(0)20 3019 7709
grind.co.uk
 Angel / Farringdon

Sister locations Multiple locations

First opened 2017
Roaster Grind & Co.
Machine La Marzocco Linea PB, 2 groups
Grinder Nuova Simonelli Mythos One

Espresso	£2.30
Cappuccino	£3.00 / £3.30
Latte	£3.00 / £3.30
Flat white	£3.00 / £3.30

 Farringdon & Clerkenwell

Fix

161 Whitecross Street, EC1Y 8JL

Discreetly occupying a former pub adjacent to the Whitecross St Market, Fix is a spacious and stylish place to drop in for a coffee and bite to eat. Fix serves a Climpson & Sons blend custom-roasted to their exact specification. Big leather couches, well-chosen vintage furniture, and quirky light fittings make this a comfortable and dynamic space in which to hang out. Creatives and visitors to the Whitecross Street market keep Fix buzzing on weekdays.

+44(0)20 7998 3878
www.fix-coffee.co.uk
⊖ Old Street / Barbican

Sister locations Fix 126

MON–FRI.	7:00am - 7:00pm
SAT.	8:00am - 7:00pm
SUN.	9:00am - 7:00pm

First opened 2009
Roaster Climpson & Sons and guests
Machine La Marzocco Linea, 3 groups
Grinder Mazzer Robur E, Nuova Simonelli Mythos

Espresso	£1.80 / £2.20
Cappuccino	£2.75
Latte	£2.75
Flat white	£2.75

MAP REF. 59

COFFEE 4.25 / 5

OVERALL 4.25 / 5 ★★★★⯪

Granger & Co Clerkenwell

Clerkenwell Green, 50 Sekforde Street, EC1R 0HA

Bill Granger's dictionary of restaurant design does not contain the word 'unattractive'. Even by his standards, however, Granger Clerkenwell is a stunner. Huge and sprawling over two floors of a window-lined corner spot, it makes an incredibly soothing place for chilling outside mealtimes. (They welcome third-space cadets when the place isn't busy.) Espresso-based drinks are well made, but the real star here is cold drip, served on ice. Sip it slowly with a piece of cake on the side. If you dawdle long enough, it will be cocktail hour and time to sample their evening menu.

+44(0)20 7251 9032
grangerandco.com
⊖ Farringdon

MON–FRI.	7:00am – 11:00pm
SAT.	9:00am – 11.00pm
SUN.	10:00am – 6:00pm

First opened 2014
Roaster Allpress Espresso
Machine La Marzocco Linea AV, 3 groups
Grinder Mazzer Robur, Mazzer Super Jolly

Espresso	£2.80
Cappuccino	£2.80
Latte	£2.80
Flat white	£2.80

Sister locations Notting Hill / King's Cross

MAP REF.

COFFEE 4.50 / 5

OVERALL 4.50 / 5 ★★★★⯪

67

Ground Control

61 Amwell Street, EC1R 1UR

Ground Control is a one-off: London's only coffee shop roasting and serving 100 per cent Ethiopian beans. Put through a Kees van der Westen Mirage (or a filter), these beans can produce some of the most exciting and distinctive coffees on earth. The location itself is a curiosity, in the little-known interlude between Farringdon and Angel. It's a lovely area, quiet and relatively unspoiled, and Ground Control is just another good reason to visit.

+44(0)20 7502 1201
www.theethiopiancoffeecompany.co.uk
⊖ Angel

MON.	7:30am - 4:00pm
TUE-FRI.	7:30am - 5:00pm
SAT.	8:00am - 5:00pm
SUN.	9:00am - 4:00pm

First opened 2012
Roaster The Ethiopian Coffee Company
Machine Kees van der Westen Mirage, 2 groups
Grinder Anfim Titanium

Espresso	£2.50
Cappuccino	£2.90
Latte	£2.90
Flat white	£2.80

MAP REF. **61**

COFFEE 4.00 / 5

OVERALL 4.00 / 5   ★ ★ ★ ★ ☆

Look Mum No Hands!

49 Old Street, EC1V 9HX

Photo: Horst A. Friedrichs

Look Mum No Hands! is one of the city's best destinations for those who love bikes and coffee in equal measure. This lively café and workshop is decorated with bicycles, bike parts, and vintage cycling memorabilia. A range of British craft beer is available on tap, and during the Tour de France, this place is a full-on party zone. The café frequently hosts a range of bike-related events, including cyclist speed dating nights. If you love bikes, coffee, or both, No Hands! is an essential pit-stop.

+44(0)20 7253 1025
www.lookmumnohands.com
⊖ Old Street / Barbican

Sister locations Lmnh Kitchen

MON–FRI.	7:30am – 10:00pm
SAT.	8:30am – 10:00pm
SUN.	9:00am – 10:00pm

First opened 2010
Roaster Square Mile Coffee Roasters
Machine Kees van der Westen Mirage, 2 groups
Grinder Anfim Super Caimano, Victoria Arduino Mythos

Espresso	£2.20
Cappuccino	£2.90
Latte	£2.90
Flat white	£2.70

MAP REF. **62**

COFFEE
4.50 / 5

OVERALL
4.50 / 5

Prufrock Coffee

23-25 Leather Lane, EC1N 7TE

TOP 35

Prufrock has achieved legendary status in London, and international recognition for its progressive methods and tireless pursuit of coffee excellence. Founded by Gwilym Davies and Jeremy Challender, Prufrock is a premier destination to see unusual brew methods and sample rare coffees. Prufrock features a broad range of 85+ coffees, including guest roasts from The Barn, Five Elephant and Koppi just to name a few, so if you are looking for something new they can certainly help. The space also incorporates an SCAE accredited coffee training school catering to novices and barista champions alike. With a fantastic space and welcoming staff, Prufrock is one of the best.

+44(0)20 7242 0467
www.prufrockcoffee.com
⊖ Farringdon / Chancery Lane

MON–FRI. 7:30am - 6:00pm
SAT–SUN. 10:00am - 5:00pm

First opened 2011
Roaster Square Mile Coffee Roasters and multiple guests
Machine Victoria Arduino Black Eagle Gravimetric, 3 groups
Grinder Mahlkönig EK 43, Victoria Arduino Mythos One, Victoria Arduino Mythos Two

Espresso	£2.20
Cappuccino	£3.00
Latte	£3.00
Flat white	£2.80

MAP REF. **63**

COFFEE
5 / 5

OVERALL
4.75 / 5

ROCKET ESPRESSO AT HOME

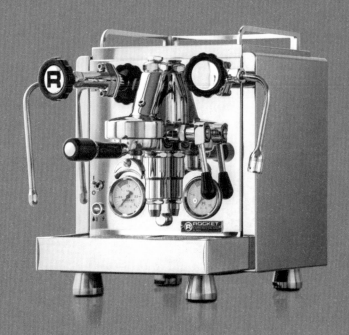

ROCKET®
ESPRESSO MILANO

THIRD WAVE
COFFEE SOURCE

PRIMAVERA
COFFEE IMPORTERS
WWW.PRIMAVERA.COFFEE

specialty coffee producers

from guatemala

London's centre of finance and commerce may not boast the sheer number of cafés as Soho or the West End, but several recent high-profile openings have rapidly transformed its coffee fortunes. The City is surprisingly quiet at weekends (and many coffee bars open Monday to Friday only), so the area is best experienced during the bustling work week.

The City

The City

Moorgate

Liverpool Street

WHITECROSS ST

SCRUTTON STREET

CURTAIN ROAD

WORSHIP STREET

PRIMROSE ST

CITY ROAD

WILSON STREET

ELDON STREET

FINSBURY CIRCUS

LIVERPOOL STREET

BISHOPSGATE

74

75
84

83

68

82

89

WALL

LONDON WALL

MOORGATE

OLD BROAD ST

HOUNDSDITCH

ST. BOTOLPH ST

Aldgate

88

81

66

POULTRY

Bank **86**

LEADENHALL STREET

MINORIES

79

CANNON ST

69

72

73

FENCHURCH ST

78

Cannon Street

80

FENCHURCH STREET

Fenchurch Street

THAMES ST

Monument

LONDON BRIDGE

200   400m

Alchemy Café

8 Ludgate Broadway, EC4V 6DU

Alchemy does a huge takeaway trade, as you would expect in this office-heavy location. Order and run, if that's what you want. But if you can, make time to perch on a stool and enjoy their exquisite beans as their roaster intended them: piping-hot and brewed to perfection. If you're a coffee geek, the people behind the bar can talk tech with you all day long. The food offering is small but high-quality, like the place itself. And don't ignore the filter brews, which perfectly showcase Alchemy's roasting skills.

+44(0)20 7329 9904
www.alchemycoffee.co.uk
⊖ Blackfriars / ⇌ City Thameslink Rail

MON-FRI.	9:00am - 6:00pm
SAT-SUN.	Closed

First opened 2013
Roaster Alchemy Coffee
Machine La Marzocco GB5, 2 groups
Grinder Mazzer Robur E x2, Mahlkönig EK 43

Espresso	£2.40
Cappuccino	£3.05
Latte	£3.05
Flat white	£2.85

MAP REF. 64

 COFFEE 4.75 / 5

 OVERALL 4.50 / 5

Artigiano Espresso and Wine Bar

1 Paternoster Square, EC4M 7DX

Café by day and wine bar by night, Artigiano should be top of your pitstop-list while on a visit to St Paul's. The design inside is stunning; with wooden floors, bare brick and grey steel all presented beautifully. There's plenty of seating on two floors, with lots of outdoor space as well. In this location you could get away with average coffee, but Artigiano cuts no corners. Origin beans come from a gleaming La Marzocco Linea carefully brewed and piping hot, and milk art is skilful. The cathedral may be the official place of worship, but there's plenty to worship here, too.

+44(0)20 7248 0407
www.artigiano.uk.com
⊖ St Paul's

MON-WED.	7:00am - 10:00pm
THU-FRI.	7:00am - 11:00pm
SAT.	10:30am - 6:00pm
SUN.	Closed

First opened 2013
Roaster Origin Coffee Roasters
Machine La Marzocco Linea PB, 2 groups
Grinder Nuova Simonelli Mythos One

Espresso	£2.30
Cappuccino	£2.95
Latte	£2.95
Flat white	£2.75

MAP REF. **65**

COFFEE
4.25 / 5

OVERALL
4.50 / 5 ★★★★☆

Association Coffee Creechurch Lane

10-12 Creechurch Lane, EC3A 5AY

Association brings gourmet coffee and quality food from small suppliers to the heart of the City. A meticulously prepared range of pastries, cakes and sandwiches are served in sleek but accessible surroundings. The interior follows a familiar industrial template while adding City-influenced twists including a tiled communal table studded with banker's lamps, offering a great spot for meetings or casual lunches. Association's brew bar should not be missed, manned by professional baristas who are serious about their craft.

+44(0)20 7283 1155
www.associationcoffee.com
⊖ Aldgate

MON-FRI.	7:30am – 5:00pm
SAT-SUN.	Closed

First opened 2012
Roaster Square Mile Coffee Roasters
Machine Victoria Arduino Black Eagle
Gravimetric, 3 groups
Grinder Mahlkönig K30

Espresso	£2.30
Cappuccino	£2.90
Latte	£2.90
Flat white	£2.90

Sister locations Ludgate Hill

MAP REF. 66

COFFEE 4.75 / 5

OVERALL 4.75 / 5

Association Coffee Ludgate Hill

56 Ludgate Hill, EC4M 7AW

This second branch of Association occupies a lovely space (dominated by pale wood in various guises) in a prime location, surrounded as it is by thirsty office workers. Popular within weeks of opening, the venue boasts not only two three-group Black Eagles but two Marco SP9s single-serve filter brewers to speed up service when things get busy. Espresso is as well made here as at the original in Creechurch Lane, with newspapers - plus a small food offering - serving the needs of those who want to linger.

+44(0)20 7283 1155
www.associationcoffee.com
City Thameslink / St Paul's / Blackfriars

Sister locations Creechurch Lane

MON-FRI.	7:30am - 5:00pm
SAT-SUN.	Closed

First opened 2012
Roaster Square Mile Coffee Roasters and guests
Machine Victoria Arduino Black Eagle Gravimetric, 3 groups x2
Grinder Mahlkönig Peak

Espresso	£2.30
Cappuccino	£2.90
Latte	£2.90
Flat white	£2.90

MAP REF.

COFFEE 4.50 / 5

OVERALL 4.50 / 5 ★★★★✬

Bean & Wheat

13 Artillery Passage, E1 7LP

The little warren of pedestrian walkways just south of Spitalfields Market is a lovely survivor of old London, and a great place to recover after a shopping tour. Top spot for this: Bean & Wheat. This really is a lovely place in every possible way, whether for a light lunch, sandwiches or platters of meat or cheese. Much of the food comes from the nearby Frog, also owned by chef Adam Handling. The Union espresso blend yields its usual velvety results even without milk, and there are nice wood tables in the back where you can sit with your laptop and get some serious work (or surfing) done. And if you arrive later in the day, warm up for the evening with drinks and a nibble.

+44(0)20 3802 2190
www.beanandwheat.co.uk
⊖ Liverpool Street

| MON-FRI. | 7:00am - 8:00pm |
| SAT-SUN. | Closed |

First opened 2017
Roaster Union Coffee Roasters
Machine La Marzocco Linea AV, 2 groups
Grinder Sanremo

Espresso	£2.40
Cappuccino	£2.60
Latte	£2.60
Flat white	£2.60

MAP REF. 68

COFFEE 4.25 / 5

 OVERALL 4.25 / 5 ★★★★★

81

The City

Caravan City

22 Bloomberg Arcade, EC4N 8AR

Coffee places in the City tend to be big on business-friendly but small on cosy or intimate. And for obvious reasons: this is where people deal in money, not in meaningful interpersonal interaction. You expect the bustle of a trading floor, not the hush of a candlelit bistro.

So London's business centre is probably the last place you would expect to find a branch of Caravan, with a really seductive atmosphere, but that's exactly what you get here. The secret lies in the remarkably intelligent design of its brand-new space, both the way it's divided into separate seating areas and especially the lighting. By day this is an attractive, contemporary-looking café/restaurant. When the sun dips,

and the lights go on, those separate seating areas - especially the ones at the back, which are what you should ask for if you're booking a table - become private spaces for dining and drinking.

Caravan has pretty much perfected its business model of faithfully excellent food, good lists of alcoholic drinks, and beautifully brewed beans. In this City location, it has also achieved something remarkable in going against the neighbourhood stereotype. Sex and The City - who knew?

MAP REF. **69**

COFFEE 4.50 / 5	OVERALL 4.50 / 5 ★★★★⯪

MON-FRI.	7:00am - 10:30pm	
SAT.	10:00am - 10:30pm	
SUN.	10:00am - 4:00pm	

First opened 2017
Roaster Caravan Coffee Roasters
Machine Faema E71, 3 groups
Grinder Mazzer Luigi

Sister locations Exmouth Market / King's Cross / Bankside

Espresso	£2.20
Cappuccino	£2.80
Latte	£2.80
Flat white	£2.80

+44(0)20 3957 5555
www.caravanrestaurants.co.uk
⊖ Bank

Carter Lane Coffee House

50a Carter Lane, EC4V 5EA

If you've not yet done so, you urgently need to walk down Carter Lane even if you don't drink coffee. One of the narrowest streets in London, it will make you think you're in another century. Of course, coffee lovers will get the full benefit of the experience. This minute place can barely accommodate half a dozen drinkers, and it offers a compact food menu, but everything is first-rate. Especially their treatment of Climpson's Baron espresso blend in a Synesso Hydra. Friendly service tops off the picture. Small but perfectly formed, just like the street outside.

+44(0)20 7248 9493
www.carterlane-coffee.co.uk
St Paul's / City Thameslink Rail

MON-THU.	7:30am – 4:30pm
FRI.	7:30am – 4:00pm
SAT-SUN.	Closed

First opened 2012
Roaster Climpson & Sons
Machine Synesso Hydra, 2 groups
Grinder Mahlkönig Vario, Mazzer Robur x2, Mazzer Super Jolly Mini

Espresso	£1.80 / £2.00
Cappuccino	£2.70 / £2.95
Latte	£2.70 / £2.95
Flat white	£2.60

MAP REF. 70

COFFEE 4.25 / 5

OVERALL 4.25 / 5 ★★★★

Chancery Press

81 Chancery Lane, WC2A 1DD

The first thing to be said about this lawyer-land branch of Press is that you won't find it where you'd expect to find it, unless you're familiar with the weird street-numbering in Chancery Lane. It's at the southern end, not the Holborn end. And it's worth finding. As well as the ever-impressive coffee, this is a really pretty, quiet space, with high windows and a few places to perch in the pedestrian walkway running off Chancery Lane. Whether you choose a milky espresso, or opt for a slow drip, the Allpress Beans perform beautifully.

www.presscoffee.london
⊖ Chancery Lane

MON-FRI.	7:00am - 6:00pm
SAT-SUN.	Closed

First opened 2016
Roaster Press Coffee Roasters
Machine La Marzocco Linea PB, 2 groups
Grinder Mahlkönig Tanzania,
Victoria Arduino Mythos One

Espresso	£2.10
Cappuccino	£2.70
Latte	£2.70
Flat white	£2.70

Sister locations Fleet Street / St Bride

MAP REF. **71**

COFFEE
4.25 / 5

OVERALL
4.00 / 5
★★★★☆

The Coffee Works Project Leadenhall

Leadenhall Market, Whittington Avenue, EC3V 1PP

Diminutive size isn't always a handicap when it comes to coffee bars. But when the tiddler in question occupies prime real estate in the City with a massive customer base, there's a need to keep throughput of punters at a certain level. Within those limitations, however, Coffee Works Project Leadenhall is a dream come true. The gourmet toasted sandwiches from former chef and owner Peter are superb, as is the coffee, of course: beans from their own roaster, brewed on a Slayer V2.

+44(0)20 7621 0040
www.coffeeworksproject.com
⊖ Bank

Sister locations Angel / Blackfriars Road / Battersea / Hackney

MON-FRI.	7:30am - 5:00pm
SAT-SUN.	Closed

First opened 2015
Roaster The Coffee Works Project
Machine Slayer V2, 3 groups
Grinder Nuova Simonelli Mythos x2, Mahlkönig EK 43

Espresso	£2.20
Cappuccino	£2.80
Latte	£2.80
Flat white	£2.80

MAP REF.

COFFEE 4.50 / 5

OVERALL 4.25 / 5

Curators Coffee Studio

9a Cullum Street, EC3M 7JJ

For fans who have been popping in ever since it opened in 2012, this original branch of Curators - not much bigger than a matchbox - is still a firm favourite. Most people regard it as a takeaway place, but if you can find a place to stand (or sit outside) it's also an ideal respite from the City crowds. The roasters on offer will vary constantly, so this is a good place to make new discoveries. And get one of their mouth-watering bakery items while you're at it.

+44(0)20 7283 4642
www.curatorscoffee.com
 Monument / Bank

Sister locations Curators Coffee Gallery / Curators Coffee Kitchen

| MON-FRI. | 7:30am - 5:30pm |
| SAT-SUN. | Closed |

First opened 2012
Roaster Colonna Coffee and guests
Machine La Marzocco Strada, 3 groups
Grinder Mazzer Robur E, Nuova Simonelli Mythos One, Anfim

Espresso	£2.40
Cappuccino	£3.00
Latte	£3.50
Flat white	£3.00

MAP REF. **73**

| COFFEE 4.50 / 5 | | OVERALL 4.50 / 5 | ★★★★★ |

Department of Coffee and Social Affairs
Norton Folgate 201 Bishopgate, EC2M 3UG

Norton Folgate was a tiny self-governing area of East London that spanned just a few blocks up until 1855 and still gives its name to a short stretch of the A10. This narrow, sun-filled venue features a takeaway zone at one end and an eat-in area at the other. Custom-made lights inspired by the molecular structure of caffeine combine with a minimal black-and-white decor, high ceilings and huge windows to create a serene, crystalline space.

www.departmentofcoffee.com
 Liverpool Street / Shoreditch High Street

Sister locations Multiple locations

| MON-FRI. | 7:00am - 5:00pm |
| SAT-SUN. | Closed |

First opened 2012
Roaster The Roastery Department
Machine La Marzocco FB80, 3 groups
Grinder Mazzer Robur x2, Mazzer Super Jolly

Espresso	£2.50
Cappuccino	£3.00
Latte	£3.00
Flat white	£3.00

MAP REF. **74**

| COFFEE 4.50 / 5 | | OVERALL 4.25 / 5 | ★★★★★ |

Department of Coffee and Social Affairs
Spitalfields Market
Spitalfields Arts Market, 6 Lamb Street, E1 6EA

Old Spitalfields Market has more coffee hangouts than ever, but there are still strong reasons to come here. You can watch the market crowds roll by from an outdoor seat or chill in the basement. Baked items provide a light lunch or afternoon sugar rush. But the main reason is the great coffee. It's all single-origin, with two espressos (one specifically for milky drinks) and one filter. The baristas combine the precision of scientists with the passion of lay preachers. Despite the competition, long queues prove that locals have got the message.

www.departmentofcoffee.com
⊖ Liverpool Street /
Shoreditch High Street

Sister locations Multiple locations

MON-FRI.	8:00am - 5:00pm
SAT-SUN.	10:00am - 5:30pm

First opened 2015
Roaster The Roastery Department
Machine La Marzocco FB80, 3 groups
Grinder Mazzer Super Jolly,
Mazzer Robur x2

Espresso	£2.50
Cappuccino	£3.00
Latte	£3.00
Flat white	£3.00

MAP REF. **75**

COFFEE 4.50 / 5		OVERALL 4.25 / 5	

Dose Espresso

70 Long Lane, EC1A 9EJ

You should consider Dose as your coffee spot of choice when you're looking for something hot and bracing while you're exploring the Barbican or Farringdon area. With the Barbican centre just minutes away, pop in for a pre-show pick-me-up. It's small and it can get busy at mealtimes, but it's worth waiting to enjoy above-average hot dishes, sandwiches and baked goods. Square Mile is the principal roaster, but rotating guest beans are a major attraction. This place is simply one of the best, year after year.

+44(0)20 7600 0382
www.dose-espresso.com
🔴 Barbican

MON-FRI. 7:00am - 5:00pm
SAT-SUN. Closed

First opened 2009
Roaster Square Mile Coffee Roasters and guests
Machine Synesso Hydra, 3 groups
Grinder Ceado E92, Mahlkönig EK 43, Anfim Super Caimano

Espresso	£2.00
Cappuccino	£2.90
Latte	£2.90
Flat white	£2.90

MAP REF. **76**

COFFEE 4.50 / 5	OVERALL 4.50 / 5

 ★★★★⯨

Fleet Street Press

3 Fleet Street, EC4Y 1AU

Fleet Street Press occupies a listed building complete with stunning stained glass window, and serves a mixed crowd of lawyers and students. Owners Davide Pastorino and Andy Wells oversee a friendly team pulling shots of their own Press coffee on a gleaming La Marzocco. Expect top notch supplies and a healthy dose of witticisms dispensed to passers-by on what is surely London's most amusing pavement A-board sign.

+44(0)20 7583 7757
www.presscoffee.london
🔴 Temple

Sister locations Chancery Lane / Ludgate Circus / Fleet Street

MON-FRI. 6:30am - 7:00pm
SAT-SUN. 9:00am - 6:00pm

First opened 2011
Roaster Press Coffee Roasters
Machine La Marzocco Linea PB, 3 groups
Grinder Victoria Arduino Mythos One, Mahlkönig EK 43

Espresso	£2.10
Cappuccino	£2.70
Latte	£2.70
Flat white	£2.70

MAP REF. **77**

COFFEE 4.25 / 5	OVERALL 4.00 / 5

★★★★☆

Flock

105a Minories, EC3N 1LA

Flock lies just a few minutes' walk from the Tower of London, but it's not on the beaten tourist track - you have to know it's there if you want to nip in after visiting the Tower. And it is definitely worth paying a visit, because this is a seriously high-quality place. It's fun to be in, thanks to a nicely eccentric approach to interior decoration. The owners opened the place with a major emphasis on good food, which has if anything grown over the months. But they wanted the coffee to have a starring role, and that too has become even stronger. Square Mile's espresso blend gets royal treatment in the three-group Black Eagle, and milk art is outstanding. We hope customers flock to Flock at every opportunity.

flockbeyond.com
⊖ Tower Hill

MON-WED.	7:00am - 6:00pm
THU-SAT.	7:00am - 8:00pm
SUN.	Closed

First opened 2017
Roaster Square Mile Coffee Roasters
Machine Victoria Arduino Black Eagle Dublin, 3 groups
Grinder Nuova Simonelli Mythos One, Mahlkönig Tanzania

Espresso	£2.40
Cappuccino	£2.90
Latte	£2.90
Flat white	£2.90

MAP REF.

 COFFEE 4.50 / 5

 OVERALL 4.25 / 5 ★★★★☆

Host

St Mary Aldermary Church, Watling Street, EC4M 9BW

Host may be the most tranquil place in the City of London that serves top-notch coffee - and perhaps the most heavenly, since it's inside a Gothic-revival church designed by Sir Christopher Wren. The City office workers who buy coffee here seem to love a quiet interlude in their working day. Coffee comes (appropriately) from Mission and is well made in double shots at reasonable prices. Food is minimal but you can bring in your own food if you buy a drink. And buying a 'caffe sospeso' (suspended coffee) will provide a hot drink for one of the local homeless people who come in regularly. Hallelujah!

+44(0)20 7248 9902
www.moot.uk.net/host
Mansion House

| MON-FRI. | 7:15am - 4:45pm |
| SAT-SUN. | Closed |

First opened 2012
Roaster Mission Coffee Works
Machine La Marzocco Linea, 2 groups
Grinder Anfim

Espresso	£2.00
Cappuccino	£2.40
Latte	£2.60
Flat white	£2.40

MAP REF. **79**

COFFEE
4.25 / 5

OVERALL
4.25 / 5 ★★★★☆

The New Black

9-10 Philpot Lane, EC3M 8AA

This London outpost of the original in Singapore is awash with lively, vivid colour. And it's not only the look of the place that is unique, so too is the coffee offering. There's not one house roaster but a raft of them, from all over the world. All are explained stylistically on the wall menu, with excellent advice from the staff if you need pointers. The brewed coffees are the stars here, especially when consumed in the elegant back room (or cute little courtyard in good weather). And in case you're wondering about the name, here's a clue: all the staff wear orange uniforms.

+44(0)20 3051 4696
www.thenewblack.coffee
Monument

| MON-FRI. | 6:00am - 6:00pm |
| SAT-SUN. | Closed |

First opened 2016
Roaster Multiple roasters
Machine Modbar, 2 groups
Grinder Mahlkönig EK 43

Espresso	£2.50
Cappuccino	£2.90
Latte	£2.90
Flat white	£2.90

MAP REF.

  COFFEE 4.50 / 5   OVERALL 4.50 / 5

Notes The Gherkin

The Gherkin, 30 St Mary Axe, EC3A 8EP

Notes has a knack for turning small, quirky spaces into distinctive dining and drinking destinations. This one at the base of the Gherkin is, like their King's Cross venue, on two levels. It's a very small space, but when you're sitting upstairs, size doesn't matter at all. Notes is a seriously good roaster, and drinks are of top quality whether from the La Marzocco or in filter. In the evening it turns into a wine bar with food. But not at weekends, when it's closed. This being the City and all.

+44(0)20 7283 2773
notes-uk.co.uk

⊖ Aldgate

Sister locations King's Cross / Moorgate / Trafalgar Square

MON-TUE.	7:30am - 7:00pm
WED-FRI.	7:30am - 10:00pm
SAT-SUN.	Closed

First opened 2016
Roaster Notes Coffee Roasters
Machine La Marzocco Linea PB, 2 groups
Grinder Nuova Simonelli Mythos One, Mahlkönig EK 43

Espresso	£2.00
Cappuccino	£2.80
Latte	£2.80
Flat white	£2.80

MAP REF. 81

 COFFEE 4.25 / 5

 OVERALL 4.00 / 5 ★★★★☆

Nude Espresso Bell Lane

8 Bell Lane, E1 7LA

Nude Bell Lane is notably smaller than their original Hanbury Street location, with seating for just 20 people (at notably lovely tables) and no weekend opening. It's less neighbourhood hangout than a haven for local office workers. None of that detracts from the charms of this Nude. The coffee is made with the customary Nude Espresso care and the gleaming Strada packs a nicely fruity kick. Sandwiches, salads and baked goods (all homemade) are attractively presented, and, the service couldn't be friendlier.

www.nudeespresso.com

⊖ Aldgate East

Sister locations The Roastery (Hanbury Street) / Hanbury Street / Spitalfields Market

MON-FRI.	7:30am - 4:00pm
SAT-SUN.	Closed

First opened 2015
Roaster Nude Coffee Roasters
Machine La Marzocco Strada EE, 2 Groups
Grinder Nuovo Simonelli Mythos One x2, Compak K30

Espresso	£2.40
Cappuccino	£3.00
Latte	£3.00
Flat white	£3.00

MAP REF. **82**

COFFEE 4.50 / 5   **OVERALL** 4.25 / 5

Nude Espresso Spitalfields Market

Spitalfields Market, 4 Market Street, E1 6EW

The City

Nude's most recent opening, in a big, high-ceilinged space on the south side of Old Spitalfields, competes against a number of other nearby coffee places - including another Nude just north of the market. But you should still expect to find it packed, even outside mealtimes. The Nude formula always works well, with a good brunch/lunch menu and excellent baked goods. And, of course, their fine beans brewed by skilled baristas. Don't neglect their pour overs. And do grab a seat outside if weather permits, either before or after a stroll through the market.

www.nudeespresso.com

⊖ Aldgate East

Sister locations The Roastery (Hanbury Street) / Hanbury Street / Bell Lane

MON–FRI.	7:30am – 5:30pm
SAT–SUN.	10:00am – 5:00pm

First opened 2016
Roaster Nude Coffee Roasters
Machine La Marzocco FB80, 3 groups
Grinder Nuova Simonelli Mythos One, Mahlkönig K30

Espresso	£2.20
Cappuccino	£2.80
Latte	£2.80
Flat white	£2.80

MAP REF.

  COFFEE 4.25 / 5   OVERALL 4.25 / 5 ★★★★⯪

Rapha Cycle Club Spitalfields Market

Old Spitalfields Market, 61-63 Brushfield Street, E1 6AA

You don't need to be a cycle-maniac to enjoy spending time with Rapha. They bring the same dedication to coffee and cooking as they do to two-wheeled matters, hiring outstanding baristas and sourcing top-quality beans served from the La Marzocco machine or in filters. There's not much in the way of seating inside, though there's extra outdoors for good weather. The location makes this a good place to start (or end) an exploration of the market or of nearby Brick Lane. Despite the abundant competition, Rapha Cycle Club is a true winner.

+44(0)20 7426 2000
www.rapha.cc/gb/en/clubhouses/
londonspitalfields
🚇 Liverpool Street

MON-FRI.	8:00am - 7:00pm
SAT.	9:00am - 7:00pm
SUN.	11:00am - 6:00pm

UK COFFEE WEEK

First opened 2015
Roaster Allpress Espresso, Catalyst Café & Coffee Roasters
Machine La Marzocco Strada, 2 groups
Grinder Mazzer Kony E

Espresso	£2.30
Cappuccino	£3.00
Latte	£3.20
Flat white	£3.00

Sister locations Soho   MAP REF. 84

COFFEE 4.25 / 5

OVERALL 4.25 / 5

Rosslyn Coffee

78 Queen Victoria Street, EC4N 4SJ

Any café that springs from a team of former Caravan members is almost certain to live up to its fine pedigree. Thankfully, Rosslyn coffee delivers on these promises. The café, flooded with natural light and beautifully-designed, is sure to join London's cohort of 'Instagram darling' cafés. With a rotating lineup of incredible roasteries - anchored by Bath's Colonna Coffee on espresso and Bristol's Round Hill on filter - the focus here is entirely on creating the perfect cup of coffee. Be sure to check out the gorgeous bespoke ceramic cups by Melisa Dora while you sip your filter.

www.rosslyncoffee.com
⊖ Mansion House

MON-FRI.	6:30am - 5:00pm
SAT-SUN.	Closed

First opened 2018
Roaster Modern Standard, Colonna Coffee, Round Hill Roastery and guests
Machine Synesso MVP Hydra, 3 groups
Grinder Mahlkönig, Fiorenzato

Espresso	£2.70
Cappuccino	£3.00
Latte	£3.00
Flat white	£3.00

MAP REF.

Royal Exchange Grind

34 Royal Exchange, EC3V 3LP

No two Grinds are alike, but there's something special about this little branch in the Royal Exchange. You'll find crowds of caffeinistas coming for takeaways throughout the day, but the place is a very pleasant place to sit, too. And at 5pm on a Friday, you might well find a group of City gents sitting down for espresso Martinis rather than a plain old espresso. The food offering is Grind's usual delicious assortment of sandwiches and baked goods, and the staff are notably fun and friendly.

+44(0)20 3019 1807
grind.co.uk
⊖ Bank

Sister locations Multiple locations

| MON-FRI. | 6:30am – 7:00pm |
| SAT-SUN. | Closed |

First opened 2016
Roaster Grind & Co.
Machine La Marzocco Linea PB, 3 groups x2
Grinder Victoria Arduino Mythos One x2, Mahlkönig Tanzania

Espresso	£2.30
Cappuccino	£3.00
Latte	£3.00
Flat white	£3.00

MAP REF. **86**

 COFFEE 4.25 / 5    OVERALL 4.25 / 5 ★★★★☆

Saint Bride Press

11 Saint Bride Street, EC4A 4AS

This newest Press location occupies a tiny space just off Ludgate Circus. Nearby office-bees rush in for al-desko brews, but there's seating for around a dozen people. For such a small space, St Bride creates a lively vibe. A dinky kitchen turns out breakfast, sandwiches, soups and stews. Baked goods beckon from the counter. Behind the bar, top-notch baristas produce shots from the gleaming Faema, enjoyed with or without milk. Using beans from their own roastery, the filter brews are always a top choice if you take your coffee black.

www.presscoffee.london
⊖ Blackfriars

Sister locations Chancery Lane / Fleet Street

| MON-FRI. | 6:30am – 6:30pm |
| SAT-SUN. | Closed |

First opened 2016
Roaster Press Coffee Roasters
Machine Faema E71
Grinder Nuova Simonelli Mythos One, Mazzer Mini

Espresso	£1.90
Cappuccino	£2.50
Latte	£2.50
Flat white	£2.60

MAP REF. **87**

 COFFEE 4.25 / 5   OVERALL 4.00 / 5 ★★★★☆

Taylor St Baristas Bank

125 Old Broad Street, EC2N 1AR

The bustle rarely lets up at this big branch of TSB. Even outside mealtimes, there are always customers here - sometimes City workers discussing a deal, but also visitors enjoying a well-deserved break in their sightseeing. The draw is obvious. Apart from location, this place has good looks, ample seating, a constantly refreshed food offering, and the usual Taylor St coffee expertise, happily expressed in both espresso and a changing roster of single origin filters. Though there's no shortage of places to drink coffee in the area, this still stands out even after almost a decade in business.

+44(0)20 7256 8665
www.taylor-st.com
⊖ Bank / Liverpool Street

Sister locations Multiple locations

MON-FRI.	7:00am - 5:00pm
SAT-SUN.	Closed

First opened 2010
Roaster Taylor St Baristas
Machine Nuova Simonelli Aurelia II T3, 3 groups, Victoria Arduino White Eagle, 3 groups
Grinder Nuova Simonelli Mythos One x3, Anfim

Espresso	£2.00
Cappuccino	£2.80 / £3.20
Latte	£2.80 / £3.20
Flat white	£2.80 / £3.70

MAP REF. 88

COFFEE 4.50 / 5

OVERALL 4.50 / 5 ★ ★ ★ ★ ⯪

Taylor St Baristas Liverpool Street

1a New Street, EC2M 4TP

The atmosphere at the smallest Taylor St venue is thick with intoxicating coffee aromas layered with heavy bass from the oversized sound system. The morning rush swells the narrow space, steam rolls and grinders spin up as the team of baristas perform in perfect synchronisation, deftly working the queue to a quickening tempo. This accelerated coffee bar is a slingshot for the City's office workers, propelling them towards offices, meetings, and spreadsheets. It's a far cry from the larger Taylor St cafés - this store marches to an altogether different beat.

+44(0)20 7929 2207
www.taylor-st.com
⊖ Liverpool Street

Sister locations Multiple locations

MON-FRI.	7:00am - 5:00pm
SAT-SUN.	Closed

First opened 2008
Roaster Taylor St Baristas
Machine Victoria Arduino Black Eagle, 3 groups, Victoria Arduino White Eagle, 2 groups
Grinder Victoria Arduino Mythos One x2, Anfim, Mazzer Robur, Mahlkönig Tanzania

Espresso	£2.20
Cappuccino	£3.00
Latte	£3.00
Flat white	£3.00

MAP REF. 89

COFFEE 4.50 / 5

OVERALL 4.00 / 5 ★ ★ ★ ★ ☆

The City

The **Watch House** Fetter Lane

92 Fetter Lane, EC4A 1EP

Watch out for the Watch House. This small group knows how to roll out new start-ups that are perfectly well suited to their surroundings. And in the case of Watch House number three, the surroundings are a bit of a challenge: a long, narrow room with space for just a few tables and a long counter facing the big windows opposite the bar. Nor is the location the most obvious place to look for good coffee: it's not quite Fleet Street, not quite Inns of Court.

But Watch House is well worth hunting down. And in fact, it's not very far from Holborn even if it does seem to be rather isolated. It's also a very good-looking place (check out the stunning light fittings),

especially attractive in the evening and far more intriguing than you'd expect from the rather anonymous office block that towers over it. There's a cool cocktail list, good wines, and some interesting food based on carefully sourced British ingredients - consider it for dinner if you're in need of a meal. But coming for coffee is just as smart a move. It's well made from Ozone beans, and they show their seriousness by serving V60 and AeroPress in addition to espresso-based drinks. Baked goods are a cut above, and service is friendly. Don't be surprised to see more branches opening up.

MAP REF. **90**

COFFEE
4.25 / 5

OVERALL
4.25 / 5

★ ★ ★ ★ ⯨

MON-FRI.	7:30am - 10:00pm
SAT-SUN.	Closed

First opened 2017
Roaster Ozone Coffee Roasters
Machine La Marzocco PB, 2 groups
Grinder Nuova Simonelli Mythos One

Espresso	£2.20
Cappuccino	£2.80 / £3.30
Latte	£2.80 / £3.30
Flat white	£3.00

+44(0)20 7242 6993
www.thewatchhouse.com
⊖ Chancery Lane / Farringdon

STRM

BARISTA ATTITUDE

The fashionable boroughs of North London contain a huge variety of venues, from the colourful cafés of Camden – the rock 'n' roll hub of yesteryear – to chic neighbourhood delis in Islington. Moneyed Hampstead retains an English village style charm, just a short tube ride away from central London. Home to both busy professionals and counter-culture figures, the area's coffee culture reflects North London's diversity and fascinating history.

North

Beam

40-41 Topsfield Parade, N8 8PT

Sidar Akyuz, the Crouch End native who owns Beam, says that locals 'move to Shoreditch when they're 18 and move back here when they start a family.' Akyuz has catered for the local population brilliantly in this big, opulently gorgeous restaurant-café. If you're not eating, let yourself be guided to one of the 'comfy chairs', low and long enough to sleep in. Sweet things on the counter make a perfect partner for Allpress espresso, brewed expertly in a three-group La Marzocco. This is a true local gem.

+44(0)20 8348 3748
www.cafebeam.co.uk
⊖ Finsbury Park

MON-SUN. 8:00am - 6:30pm

First opened 2013
Roaster Allpress Espresso
Machine La Marzocco Linea, 3 groups
Grinder Mazzer Robur, Mazzer Super Jolly

Espresso	£2.20
Cappuccino	£2.80
Latte	£2.80
Flat white	£2.80

MAP REF. **91**

COFFEE 4.00 / 5		OVERALL 4.00 / 5	

Bear and Wolf

153 Fortress Road, NW5 2HR

Owner Matthew Neel planned B&W as a gathering place for parents with young children, right down to the playroom ('Cubroom') in the back. Seating in the minimally decorated dining area comprises a large window table, a counter opposite the serving area, and long, closely spaced reclaimed wood tables in the back. The setup encourages conversation with your neighbours, and there is a winning community feel here. Well-made coffee from Ozone beans makes a fine conclusion to a light meal of notably good food.

+44(0)20 3601 1900
www.bearandwolfcafe.com
⊖ Tufnell Park

MON-FRI. 7:30am - 5:30pm
SAT-SUN. 8:30am - 5:30pm

First opened 2014
Roaster Ozone Coffee Roasters
Machine La Marzocco Linea, 2 groups
Grinder Mazzer

Espresso	£2.00
Cappuccino	£2.75
Latte	£2.75
Flat white	£2.50

MAP REF. **92**

COFFEE 4.25 / 5		OVERALL 4.25 / 5	

Black Truffle

41 England's Lane, NW3 4YD

Black Truffle is one of the three excellent coffee spots in England's Lane, Belsize Park. It has a well-stocked deli selling a good range of high-quality products, much of it organic. In short, the emphasis here is on food - the owner has a cheffing background. But coffee is taken very seriously: all espresso-based Climpson's and pulled from a three-group La Marzocco. The long dining space is divided, front from back, by the serving area. It's all very light-filled and has a modern but cosy look. Come here after a walk on Primrose Hill for well extracted coffee and an indulgent cake, or an imaginative healthy salad.

+44(0)20 7483 1623
www.blacktruffledeli.com
 Belsize Park

MON-SAT.	7:30am - 7:00pm
SUN.	8:30am - 7:00pm

First opened 2013
Roaster Climpson & Sons
Machine La Marzocco Linea AV, 3 groups
Grinder Anfim Milano V240

Espresso	£2.30
Cappuccino	£2.90
Latte	£2.90
Flat white	£2.90

MAP REF. **93**

Bonjour Brioche

2a England's Lane, NW3 4TG

Bonjour Brioche is very popular with locals for its Monmouth coffee (expertly brewed daily to hit all the right sweet notes) and especially its excellent food. They make everything fresh, and even bake their own bagels (and brioche of course). If you go for just one thing, go for something sweet: a slice of unfathomably moist, red velvet cake suggests they have one of the best bakers in London. With notably friendly staff, Bonjour Brioche is another local hero for the lucky inhabitants of Belsize Park.

+44(0)20 7846 0202
www.bonjourbrioche.co.uk
⊖ Chalk Farm

| MON–FRI. | 7:30am – 5:00pm |
| SAT–SUN. | 8:00am – 5:00pm |

First opened 2013
Roaster Monmouth Coffee
Machine La Marzocco FB, 2 groups
Grinder Mazzer Robur

Espresso	£2.20
Cappuccino	£2.70
Latte	£2.70
Flat white	£2.70

MAP REF. 94

COFFEE 4.25 / 5

OVERALL 4.25 / 5 ★★★★✩

Campbell & Syme

9 Fortis Green, N2 9JR

East Finchley may not be fashionable territory for a roastery café, but don't let this make you underestimate Campbell & Syme. The business was established by Joe Syme, an experienced hand in the catering sector, and Jon Cowell, a musician and long-time coffee aficionado. The team offer a variety of blends and single origins, and they have established direct relationships with individual producers, underlining their commitment to responsibly sourcing top-quality coffee.

+44(0)7977 514 054
www.campbellandsyme.co.uk
⊖ East Finchley

MON-FRI.	7:30am - 5:00pm
SAT-SUN.	8:30am - 5:00pm

First opened 2013
Roaster Campbell & Syme
Machine Sanremo Opera, 3 groups
Grinder Nuova Simonelli Mythos One, Mahlkönig EK 43

Espresso	£2.20
Cappuccino	£2.80
Latte	£2.80
Flat white	£2.70

MAP REF. 95

Caravan King's Cross

1 Granary Square, N1C 4AA

TOP 35

This was the second Caravan to open, and it couldn't have been more different from the first: vast and ultra-modern-looking, with an expansive view onto Granary Square. Caravan's roasting skills are best appreciated in single origin filter form, though espresso-based milky drinks are carefully crafted. And as always, Caravan is as much about the whole dining experience as the appreciation of their beans. This venue is particularly good during the day with the lovely courtyard view, but it's a deservedly popular dinner spot as well. Camp out in Caravan for a delicious brew any time of day.

+44(0)20 7101 7661
www.caravankingscross.co.uk
⊖ King's Cross St Pancras

Sister locations Exmouth Market / Bankside / City

MON-FRI.	8:00am - 11:30pm
SAT.	10:00am - 11:30pm
SUN.	10:00am - 4:00pm

First opened 2012
Roaster Caravan Coffee Roasters
Machine Faema E71, 3 groups
Grinder Mazzer Robur E x3, Mahlkönig EK 43

Espresso	£2.00
Cappuccino	£2.60
Latte	£2.60
Flat white	£2.60

MAP REF. **96**

COFFEE 5 / 5 🫘🫘🫘🫘🫘   OVERALL 5 / 5 ★★★★★

Coffee Circus

136 Crouch Hill, N8 9DX

With its circus theme and vintage tearoom feel, Coffee Circus is a friendly, whimsical place to discover. The café's hidden location seemingly cultivates the eccentricity and playfulness hidden within: it wouldn't surprise us if it concealed a cupboard with a portal to a fantasy-land. In addition to the well-poured coffee, expect a fanciful food menu including eggs and buttered soldiers. Coffee Circus transforms into an occasional evening performance space. The curious visitor is more likely to stumble upon jazz nights than performing elephants, but one can always hope.

+44(0)20 8340 8221
www.coffeecircus.co.uk
⊖ Crouch Hill

| MON–FRI. | 8:00am – 6:00pm |
| SAT–SUN. | 9:00am – 6:00pm |

First opened 2010
Roaster Mission Coffee Works, Campbell & Syme
Machine La Marzocco Linea PB, 2 groups
Grinder Mazzer Robur E, Ditting, Nuova Simonelli Mythos Clima Pro, Sage Pro

Espresso	£2.00
Cappuccino	£2.60
Latte	£2.60
Flat white	£2.60

MAP REF.

COFFEE 4.25 / 5

OVERALL 4.25 / 5 ★★★★½

111

The Coffee Jar

83 Parkway, NW1 7PP

If you're a newcomer, you may be greeted with the words 'Is this your first time here?' or something along those lines. Coffee Jar has been trading in this minute spot since 2013, and most people are regulars. It's easy to see why. Monmouth beans are brewed with exceptional care, food is good and well-priced (try a chocolate chip cookie), and the welcome is naturally warm. There's little seating, so be prepared to wait if you want to get comfortable. An independent gem in a part of north London that's seeing lots of chains move in.

www.thecoffeejar.co.uk
⊖ Camden Town

MON-FRI.	7:30am - 5:30pm
SAT-SUN.	9:00am - 5:30pm

First opened 2013
Roaster Monmouth Coffee Company
Machine La Marzocco Linea, 2 groups
Grinder Mazzer Robur E

Espresso	£2.00
Cappuccino	£2.60
Latte	£2.70
Flat white	£2.60

MAP REF. **98**

COFFEE **4.00 / 5** 🫘🫘🫘🫘🫘   OVERALL **4.00 / 5** ★★★★☆

The Coffee Works Project Angel

96-98 Islington High Street, N1 8EG

Even in coffee-crowded Upper Street, the CWP ranks high on the A-list. The place looks great, and it's always so busy (even outside primetime) that you're guaranteed a good buzz. No such guarantees apply to a seat, sadly, especially at weekends when the market is in full flow. Arrive early for the best chance of getting some of their excellent grub: suppliers are all gold-plated, and the skill levels in the kitchen are fantastically high. The same applies behind the bar, whether from the big Slayer or in filter. This group is one of London's finest; this venue is probably their best.

+44(0)20 7424 5020
www.coffeeworksproject.com
⊖ Angel

Sister locations Leadenhall
/ Blackfriars Road / Battersea / Hackney

MON-FRI.	7:30am - 6:00pm
SAT.	9:00am - 6:00pm
SUN.	10:00am - 5:00pm

First opened 2012
Roaster The Coffee Works Project
Machine Slayer V3, 3 groups
Grinder Nuova Simonelli Mythos x2, Mahlkönig EK 43

Espresso	£2.20
Cappuccino	£2.80
Latte	£2.80
Flat white	£2.80

MAP REF. **99**

COFFEE 4.50 / 5	OVERALL 4.75 / 5 ★★★★⯪

113

Cricks Corner

80 Dartmouth Park Hill, N19 5HU

Some coffee places may not have the wow-factor yet still make a big impression. Crick's Corner is one of them. Set in two tiny rooms on a corner site, it offers a small selection of sandwiches and baked goods - all of very high quality. The barista skills do full justice to Dark Arts beans. The front room is where people seem to socialise, while at the back there's a little lending library and sheets of paper for the kiddies to draw on. This quiet neighbourhood, far from the nearest tube, is lucky to have Cricks in its midst.

+44(0)20 7686 2967
crickscorner.co.uk
⊖ Archway

MON-FRI.	8:00am - 4:00pm
SAT-SUN.	9:00am - 3:00pm

First opened 2015
Roaster Dark Arts Coffee
Machine La Marzocca Linea PB, 2 groups
Grinder Nuova Simonelli Mythos One, Mahlkönig EK 43

Espresso	£2.00
Cappuccino	£2.60
Latte	£2.60
Flat white	£2.50

MAP REF. 100

COFFEE		OVERALL	
4.00 / 5	🫘🫘🫘🫘🫘	3.75 / 5	★★★⯨☆

Dark Habit

72a Salusbury Road, NW6 6NU

Dark Habit is a bright light in Queen's Park's coffee scene. The best specialist in the area, it pursues excellence in every cup with a quiet fanaticism - and in fitting surroundings, understated but lovely. The wide spacing of tables is a rarity and a pleasure. They need lots of floor space so people (sometimes with buggies and prams in tow) can queue in comfort. You can see why the Q-Parkers queue happily when you taste the coffees, all espresso-based, with Workshop beans pulled through a La Marzocco FB80. Take it away if you must, but you'll get the most from DH if you perch for a while, perhaps with something from their small selection of baked goods.

darkhabitcoffee.co.uk

⊖ Queen's Park / Brondesbury Park

MON-SUN. 8:00am - 4:00pm

First opened 2018
Roaster Workshop Coffee and guests
Machine La Marzocco FB80, 2 groups
Grinder Victoria Arduino Mythos One

Espresso	£2.20
Cappuccino	£2.50 / £2.90
Latte	£2.50 / £2.90
Flat white	£2.50 / £2.90

MAP REF. **101**

 COFFEE 4.25 / 5

 OVERALL 4.25 / 5

The Fields Beneath

52a Prince of Wales Road, NW5 3LN

Named after Gillian Tindall's 1977 historical study of Kentish Town, this small speciality coffee outpost has rallied a loyal local following. Owned by long-time coffee aficionado Gavin Fernback, the converted railway arch at Kentish Town West station is a small but attractive coffee bar. The space is bathed in floods of light, and their own beans perform well in the La Marzocco Linea. They recently became fully vegan, so prepare for some delicious meat and dairy-free treats.

+44(0)20 7424 8838
⊖ Kentish Town West

MON–FRI.	7:00am – 4:00pm
SAT.	8:00am – 5:00pm
SUN.	9:00am – 5:00pm

First opened 2012
Roaster Fields Beneath Coffee
Machine La Marzocco Linea, 2 groups
Grinder Nuova Simonelli Mythos Clima Pro

Espresso	£2.00
Cappuccino	£2.70
Latte	£2.80
Flat white	£2.70

MAP REF. 102

COFFEE 4.25 / 5

OVERALL 4.25 / 5 ★★★★⯨

Fink's Salt and Sweet

70 Mountgrove Road, N5 2LT

Fink's is a shop, deli, café and restaurant. Above all else, however, it's an exemplary neighbourhood hangout. Mealtimes can be mental, especially at weekends, but out of peak hours it's great for mums with babies, laptop users or friends meeting for coffee and a chat. The big front room is best for socialising, and the nook at the back for working. Beans from Caravan call out for milk, perhaps with something gluten-free (there's a good selection) on the side. Locals have been keeping Fink's busy since the day it opened; they know a good thing when they see it.

+44(0)20 7684 7189
finks.co.uk
 Arsenal

MON-WED.	9:00am - 7:00pm
THU.	9:00am - 10:30pm
FRI-SAT.	9:00am - 11:00pm
SUN.	10:00am - 5:00pm

First opened 2014
Roaster Caravan Coffee Roasters
Machine La Marzocco Linea, 2 groups
Grinder Mazzer Major

Espresso	£2.00
Cappuccino	£2.60
Latte	£2.60
Flat white	£2.60

MAP REF. **103**

 COFFEE 4.00 / 5

 OVERALL 4.25 / 5 ★★★★

117

Ginger & White Belsize Park

2 England's Lane, NW3 4TG

Ginger & White is always a pleasure, as long as you can get a seat – and a seat downstairs or outside by preference, as the upstairs mezzanine can feel a bit cramped. If you're in on the ground floor, however, you're in for a treat. A big central communal table is almost always crowded with large parties or sharing twosomes eating excellent salads or wickedly fabulous baked indulgences. Coffee is all espresso-based and comes from Square Mile. It's served by people who took Advanced Smiling classes wherever they went to school. You'll be hard pushed to leave without a smile of your own.

+44(0)20 7722 9944
www.gingerandwhite.com
⊖ Chalk Farm / Belsize Park

Sister locations Hampstead

MON-FRI.	7:30am – 5:30pm
SAT-SUN.	8:30am – 5:30pm

First opened 2012
Roaster Square Mile Coffee Roasters
Machine La Marzocco FB80, 3 groups
Grinder Victoria Arduino Mythos One, Mazzer Luigi

Espresso	£2.90
Cappuccino	£3.25
Latte	£3.25
Flat white	£3.25

MAP REF.

COFFEE 4.25 / 5   **OVERALL** 4.25 / 5 ★★★★⯪

Ginger & White Hampstead

4a-5a Perrin's Court, NW3 1QS

Hampstead contains countless historic streets and alleys of mind-blowing beauty, and Perrin's Court is one of the loveliest. And it sometimes seems that every tourist walking up the street has a legal obligation to eat at Ginger & White - that's how busy it can get. And the space is not a large one, even with its handful of outside tables. It's worth coming outside mealtimes and trying to get seated either in the window or one of the sofas. Order something sweet to go with your Square Mile latte or cappuccino, and rest your feet before heading off for more sightseeing.

+44(0)20 7431 9098
www.gingerandwhite.com
⊖ Hampstead

Sister locations Belsize Park

| MON-FRI. | 7:30am - 5:30pm |
| SAT-SUN. | 8:30am - 5:30pm |

First opened 2009
Roaster Square Mile Coffee Roasters
Machine La Marzocco FB80, 3 groups
Grinder Victoria Arduino Mythos One, Mazzer Luigi

Espresso	£2.50
Cappuccino	£3.25
Latte	£3.25
Flat white	£3.25

MAP REF. **105**

North

COFFEE 4.25 / 5 | OVERALL 4.25 / 5 ★★★★✯

Granger & Co King's Cross

Stanley Building, 7 Pancras Square, N1C 4AG

The area around King's Cross is hardly short of places to eat and drink, but Granger is deservedly popular. This is a lovely space, like all Granger restaurants, with huge windows that give an ample view of the throngs passing by. Most people come for a meal from their Australia-derived all-day menus. Others come and sit at the bar for a coffee and a scrumptious cake or pastry. Espresso-based drinks are well made, and plenty of people come in for something milky to take to the office, but the real star is the cold drip.

+44(0)20 3058 2567
grangerandco.com
⊖ King's Cross

Sister locations Clerkenwell / Notting Hill

MON-FRI.	7:00am - 11:00pm
SAT.	9:00am - 11:00pm
SUN.	10:00am - 6:00pm

First opened 2014
Roaster Allpress Espresso
Machine La Marzocco Linea AV, 3 groups
Grinder Mazzer Robur, Mazzer Super Jolly

Espresso	£2.80
Cappuccino	£2.80
Latte	£2.80
Flat white	£2.80

MAP REF. **106**

COFFEE 4.25 / 5 | OVERALL 4.25 / 5 ★★★★✯

Guy Gold Coffee Bar & Treatment Rooms

85 Jamestown Road, NW1 7DB

We're used to seeing coffee shops pop up in so many unlikely places that they barely seem unlikely any more. Bicycle shop? Old hat. Boutique? Same old same old. But even jaundiced observes of London's bean scene might think they you couldn't make this one up. Unless we're very much mistaken, Guy Gold is the first retail premises where you can order both a perfect macchiato and a session of osteopathic treatment.

The back story: Guy Gold is an osteopath who wrote his degree thesis on the consumption of coffee by osteopathic practitioners. He is clearly a man in love with two very different disciplines. So what was the next logical step? To open up a venue that provides both of these useful services. We have not visited the consulting rooms, but the café is tiny and light-filled - just a few tables in the very tip of an old building, with windows on two sides, it's a pleasure to sit in. The beans are from Climpson, and the barista knows everything there is to know about how to treat them. One of the best macchiatos we've had all year.

If Guy Gold knows his kind of treatment as well as the barista here, we'd place ourselves in his hands any time. Make no bones about it: this is pure gold in a Camden backwater.

MAP REF. **107**

COFFEE 4.25 / 5	OVERALL 4.00 / 5
	★★★★☆

MON-THU.	7:30am - 5:00pm
FRI.	7:30am - 4:00pm
SAT.	9:00am - 4:00pm
SUN.	Closed

First opened 2017
Roaster Climpson & Sons
Machine La Marzocco Linea PB, 2 groups
Grinder Nuova Simonelli Mythos One,
Mahlkönig Vario

Espresso	£2.20
Cappuccino	£2.80
Latte	£3.00
Flat white	£2.80

guygolds.com
⊖ Camden Town

Harris + Hoole

9 The Broadway, N8 8DU

This branch of Harris + Hoole, a perfect fit with Crouch End, attracts a varied crowd. The long, attractive space has generous seating on either chairs or sofas, and there's table space for workers with laptops. Coffee is expertly made on the three-group Simonelli, though there's also a choice of filter methods for single-origin beans. The word 'friendly' doesn't begin to describe the welcome here - so it's hardly surprising that the place is full of regulars.

+44(0)20 8347 6269
www.harrisandhoole.co.uk
≥ Crouch Hill Rail

Sister locations Tooley Street / Kensington / Imperial Wharf / Fulham Reach

MON-FRI.	7:00am - 6:00pm
SAT.	8:30am - 6:00pm
SUN.	9:00am - 5:00pm

First opened 2013
Roaster Harris + Hoole
Machine Nuova Simonelli Aurelia, 3 groups
Grinder Nuova Simonelli Mythos One

Espresso	£2.15
Cappuccino	£2.55 / £2.95 / £3.35
Latte	£2.55 / £2.95 / £3.35
Flat white	£2.55 / £2.95 / £3.35

MAP REF. 108

COFFEE 4.25 / 5   **OVERALL** 4.25 / 5 ★★★★½

Leyas

20 Camden High Street, NW1 0JH

Leyas would be a star wherever it happened to set up shop. Once you've ordered from the raised-ground-floor counter, you can grab a seat on the bright ground floor or walk down a few steps to the larger lower level. Whether you opt for a milky espresso or a delicate pour-over, the Leyas baristas treat the Saint Espresso beans with care and attention. Southern Camden Town needs more places of this superb quality.

www.leyas.co.uk
⊖ Mornington Crescent

Sister locations Saint Espresso Angel / Saint Espresso Baker St / Saint Espresso & Kitchen Kentish Town

| MON-FRI. | 7:30am - 5:30pm |
| SAT-SUN. | 9:00am - 5:30pm |

First opened 2011
Roaster Saint Espresso
Machine La Marzocco GB5, 2 groups
Grinder Nuova Simonelli Mythos One, Mahlkönig EK 43

Espresso	£2.30
Cappuccino	£2.80
Latte	£2.80
Flat white	£2.70

MAP REF. 109

122

COFFEE 4.25 / 5   **OVERALL** 4.25 / 5 ★★★★½

Local Blend

587 Green Lanes, N8 0RG

This place is just great. Everything about it is great. The food, the look, the welcome, and the coffee. There are other places that could be described that way, but this branch of Blend is exceptional because of its extra activities for local residents, exhibition space for local artists, and the imaginative restaurant popups that appear on a regular basis. Coffee is expertly made in their Linea PB using Climpsons beans, and there are crafty cocktails if you're interested in something stronger than caffeine. This is the very model of a local coffee hangout. Lucky Harringay.

+44(0)20 8341 2939
www.localblend.co.uk
⊖ Turnpike Lane / Harringay Green Lanes

Sister locations Notting Hill

MON–FRI.	8:30am – 5:00pm
SAT.	9:30am – 5:00pm
SUN.	10:00am – 5:00pm

First opened 2013
Roaster Climpson & Sons
Machine La Marzocco Linea PB, 3 groups
Grinder Mazzer Major E, Mazzer Mini E

Espresso	£2.00
Cappuccino	£2.65
Latte	£2.65
Flat white	£2.65

MAP REF. **110**

COFFEE 4.25 / 5

OVERALL 4.25 / 5 ★★★★⯨

Loft Coffee Company

4 Canfield Gardens, NW6 3BS

Loft is one of London's smallest sources for fine coffee, with seating for just a handful of people. That's not so important, because a lot of their custom comes from commuters. And it matters even less because the quality here is sky-high. Sung-Jae Lee, originally from South Korea, is a coffee fanatic from way back. The fanaticism shows in their perfectly brewed, velvety-sweet espresso blend. Loft is one of the relatively few places in London where milk and sugar aren't needed to round out the cup. Lofty indeed.

+44(0)20 7372 2008
⊖ Finchley Road

MON-FRI.	7:00am - 5:00pm
SAT.	8:00am - 4:00pm
SUN.	9:30am - 3:00pm

First opened 2012
Roaster Square Mile Coffee Roasters
Machine La Marzocco Linea PB, 3 groups
Grinder Mazzer Kold

Espresso	£2.30
Cappuccino	£2.70
Latte	£2.70
Flat white	£2.70

MAP REF.

COFFEE 4.25 / 5   OVERALL 4.25 / 5 ★ ★ ★ ★ ⯪

Maison d'Etre Coffee House

154 Canonbury Road, N1 2UP

If you had to name north London's unlikeliest spot for a coffee shop, you might go for Highbury roundabout. But improbably, Maison d'Etre is one of the area's best - and there's plenty of competition. It's fun to look at, every decorative detail carefully chosen. And it has the happiest buzz imaginable, so friendly that customers and workers seem to be one big happy group. Sandwiches are well above average quality. Most baked goods are homemade, a perfect accompaniment to a milky brew made from Square Mile's ubiquitous Red Brick blend. Maison d'Etre might well be Highbury roundabout's raison d'etre.

+44(0)20 7226 4711
www.maisondetrecafe.co.uk
⊖ Highbury & Islington

MON-FRI.	7:30am - 6:00pm
SAT-SUN.	10:00am - 5:00pm

First opened 2011
Roaster Square Mile Coffee Roasters
Machine La Marzocco Linea, 2 groups
Grinder Nuova Simonelli Mythos

Espresso	£2.10
Cappuccino	£2.80
Latte	£2.80
Flat white	£2.80

MAP REF.

Melrose and Morgan

42 Gloucester Avenue, NW1 8JD

This grocer and deli in leafy Primrose Hill is a cornucopia of beautifully prepared, locally sourced food. Homemade preserves fill the shelves, alongside a daily selection of seasonal salads, sandwiches, soups, and breads. Enjoy your coffee in the relaxing seating area while contemplating the irresistible range of cakes, tarts, and tray bakes. Melrose and Morgan is one of London's very best purveyors of artisan produce, recognised with two 'Great Taste' awards.

+44(0)20 7722 0011
www.melroseandmorgan.com
⊖ Chalk Farm / Camden Town

Sister locations Hampstead

MON-FRI.	8:00am - 7:00pm
SAT.	8:00am - 6:00pm
SUN.	9:00am - 5:00pm

First opened 2004
Roaster Mission Coffee Works
Machine La Marzocco Linea, 2 groups
Grinder Anfim

Espresso	£1.95
Cappuccino	£2.60
Latte	£2.60
Flat white	£2.60

MAP REF. 113

 COFFEE 4.00 / 5   **OVERALL** 4.00 / 5 ★★★★☆

Notes King's Cross

Unit 2, One Pancras Square, N1C 4AG

Notes has struck just the right chord with this branch. The office complexes around King's Cross are not exactly over-filled with cosy hangouts, but Notes manages it surprisingly well on two floors - a ground floor and mezzanine with total capacity of around 35. Notes' in-house roasting has gone from strength to strength, and a changing roster of single-origin espressos includes some unusual lots handled with skill. The food offer is smaller in range than at other branches, but there's enough to keep the place busy when it turns into a wine bar at 5pm.

+44(0)20 3479 1576
www.notes-co.uk
⊖ King's Cross St Pancras

Sister locations Multiple locations

MON-WED.	7:30am - 9:00pm
THU-FRI.	7:30am - 10:00pm
SAT.	10:00am - 5:30pm
SUN.	10:30am - 5:30pm

First opened 2015
Roaster Notes Coffee Roasters and guests
Machine La Marzocco Linea PB, 2 groups x2
Grinder Nuova Simonelli Mythos x2

Espresso	£2.20 / £2.50
Cappuccino	£3.00
Latte	£3.00
Flat white	£3.00

MAP REF.

COFFEE
4.25 / 5

OVERALL
4.25 / 5 ★★★★⯪

127

Origin Coffee Roasters British Library

British Library, 96 Euston Road, NW1 2DB

The British Library made a great decision when it gave the franchise for its café to Origin. There are two separate Origin spaces here, and they couldn't be more different. The first to open is on the right-hand side of the airy foyer of the main library building. The other space is a snug sliver of a room with a big window and stools overlooking Euston Road. Origin trains its baristas very well, and the single-origin batch brews are as much of a draw as espresso-based brews. This is a small place of mega quality. Full marks to the Library for inviting Origin to this great learning institution.

+44(0)20 7729 6252
www.origincoffee.co.uk
⊖ King's Cross

Sister locations Hammersmith / Shoreditch

MON–FRI.	7:00am – 6:00pm
SAT.	9:30am – 5:00pm
SUN.	11:00am – 5:00pm

First opened 2016
Roaster Origin Coffee Roasters
Machine Spirit Triplette, 3 groups
Grinder Mahlkönig EK 43,
Nuova Simonelli Mythos One

Espresso	£2.20
Cappuccino	£2.80
Latte	£2.80
Flat white	£2.60

MAP REF. **115**

COFFEE
4.50 / 5

OVERALL
4.25 / 5
★★★★☆

Ripe Kitchen

136 Regents Park Road, NW1 8XL

This friendly Primrose Hill local does everything right. It's a lovely place to sit and serves food from breakfast onwards – which makes it a shame just to order takeaway, as many customers do. In addition to the Antipodean-inspired brunch offer, Ripe offers a soup of the day and a stew of the day, at prices that are extremely reasonable for such an upscale location. Ripe Kitchen's rendition of Square Mile espresso brings out all its rounded fruity notes. And this little gem even has its own blends of tea.

+44(0)7572 480 102
www.ripekitchen.co.uk
 Chalk Farm

Sister locations Six Degrees

MON-FRI.	7:30am – 5:00pm
SAT.	8:00am – 5:30pm
SUN.	8:30am – 5:30pm

First opened 2014
Roaster Square Mile Coffee Roasters
Machine La Marzocco GB5, 2 groups
Grinder Macap MXD Xtreme, Mazzer Super Jolly

Espresso	£2.30
Cappuccino	£2.80
Latte	£2.80
Flat white	£2.70

MAP REF. **116**

COFFEE 4.25 / 5		OVERALL 4.25 / 5	★★★★✩

Saint Espresso Angel

Angel House, 26 Pentonville Road, N1 9HJ

Saint Espresso says a lot about the status of coffee in London today. Aptly named due to its location in Angel House, Saint's interior is clean and understated. The elegant branding and subtle lighting creates a refined ambiance. The service is attentive and the baristas direct the attention of the curious customer towards tasting notes for the various beans on offer. If it wasn't for the espresso machine and retail display of coffee home brewing gear, this could just as easily be an upscale wine bar. Saint extols the virtues of the cult of espresso, and Londoners are converting in droves.

www.saintespresso.com

⊖ Angel

Sister locations Baker Street / Kentish Town / Leyas

MON-FRI.	7:30am – 6:00pm
SAT-SUN.	9:00am – 6:00pm

First opened 2014
Roaster Saint Espresso
Machine La Marzocco Strada, 2 groups
Grinder Mahlkönig EK 43, Nuova Simonelli Mythos One

Espresso	£2.20
Cappuccino	£2.80
Latte	£2.80
Flat white	£2.70

MAP REF. 117

 COFFEE 4.50 / 5 OVERALL 4.50 / 5 ★★★★⯪

Saint Espresso & Kitchen Kentish Town

296 Kentish Town Road, NW5 2TG

Kentish Town has come up massively in the food and drink world, but top-notch coffee isn't always as easy to find. All the more reason to welcome Saint Espresso to the scene. While most people order something espresso-based, the single origin offerings from V60 and AeroPress should definitely get your attention too. Expanding the food offering to give more choice at brunch and lunch shows how serious Saint is about making this a local destination - and we couldn't be happier.

www.saintespresso.com
⊖ Kentish Town

Sister locations Angel / Baker Street / Leyas

| MON-FRI. | 7:30am - 5:30pm |
| SAT-SUN. | 9:00am - 5:30pm |

First opened 2017
Roaster Saint Espresso
Machine La Marzocco Linea PB, 2 groups
Grinder Mahlkönig EK 43,
Nuova Simonelli Mythos One

Espresso	£2.30
Cappuccino	£2.80
Latte	£2.80
Flat white	£2.70

MAP REF. 118

COFFEE 4.50 / 5

OVERALL 4.25 / 5 ★★★★⯪

131

Sawyer & Gray

290 St Paul's Road, N1 2LH

'We wanted it to be a nice place for everyone.' That's how the owners describe their goal here, and they certainly live up to that. The interior could be described as 'quirky brilliance'. Origin beans get the full respect and the food covers lots of bases, from breakfast and brunch basics to more adventurous cooking in the evening. Sawyer & Gray is the type of place you would love as your local.

+44(0)20 3417 5950
www.sawyerandgray.co.uk
🚇 Highbury & Islington

MON.	7:30am – 3:00pm
TUE.	Closed
WED-FRI.	7:30am – 3:00pm
SAT.	8:30am – 4:00pm
SUN.	9:30am – 4:00pm

First opened 2015
Roaster Origin Coffee Roasters
Machine La Marzocco GB5, 2 groups
Grinder Mazzer Major, Mazzer Super Jolly

Espresso	£2.20
Cappuccino	£2.80
Latte	£2.80
Flat white	£2.70

MAP REF. **119**

COFFEE 4.00 / 5

OVERALL 4.25 / 5 ★★★★☆

Sunday

169 Hemingford Road, N1 1DA

Sunday is the place you daydream about on a sullen Monday morning. Snuggled on a residential street in Barnsbury, this tiny neighbourhood café aims to make every day feel like a weekend. It's a glowing composition of cappuccinos, broadsheets, broad smiles, pancakes, and imaginative egg dishes. The Caravan coffee is made with care and the brunch is one of the best in London. Sunday truly is a victory over the week gone by, but be prepared to queue.

+44(0)20 7607 3868

 Caledonian Road & Barnsbury / Highbury & Islington

MON.	Closed
TUE.-FRI.	8:30am - 6:00pm
SAT.-SUN.	9:00am - 6.00pm

First opened 2013
Roaster Caravan Coffee Roasters
Machine La Marzocco Linea, 2 groups
Grinder Mazzer Super Jolly

Espresso	£2.30
Cappuccino	£2.90 / £3.30
Latte	£2.90 / £3.30
Flat white	£2.90 / £3.30

MAP REF. 120

 COFFEE 4.25 / 5

 OVERALL 4.25 / 5 ★★★★

Tintico

2-4 Station Road, N3 2SP

Tintico is just a two-minute walk from Finchley Central tube, so it's a perfect place to pitch up for the pre-commute pick-me-up. But those who stay a while are those get the full benefit of this lovely, lively local. It's on a corner site with big windows that let in lots of light even on a dull day. Service is warm and efficient, sandwiches are tasty. As are the well-made brews pulled through their three-group La Marzocco. And if you're a fan of the blues, you'll love what's on the sound system.

+44(0)20 3674 1717
tinti.co
 Finchley Central

MON-FRI.	7:00am - 5:30pm
SAT-SUN.	9:00am - 5:30pm

First opened 2014
Roaster Campbell & Syme
Machine La Marzocco GB5, 3 groups
Grinder Mazzer Robur

Espresso	£1.80
Cappuccino	£2.40
Latte	£2.60
Flat white	£2.40

MAP REF. 121

 **COFFEE** 4.25 / 5

 **OVERALL** 4.00 / 5 ★★★★☆

133

Vagabond N7

105 Holloway Road, N7 8LT

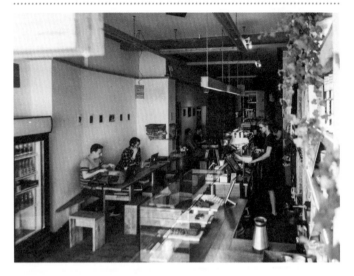

Vagabond N7 has a deliberately unfinished interior look with pockmarked walls and weathered wooden floorboards creating a delightfully grungy vibe, and the enormous back room is home to an impressive Giesen roaster. There's also an inviting, if somewhat ramshackle, rear garden. The coffee is made with exceptional care, and single origins are available brewed by AeroPress or V60. Vagabond is an energetic, young coffee business with a roasting operation that offers some excellent coffees.

www.vagabond.coffee

⊖ Highbury & Islington

| MON-FRI. | 7:30am – 5:00pm |
| SAT-SUN. | 9:00am – 6:00pm |

First opened 2013
Roaster Vagabond Coffee Roasters
Machine Conti Monte Carlo, 3 groups
Grinder Compak R120, Compak E8, Ceado

Espresso	£2.00
Cappuccino	£2.80
Latte	£2.80
Flat white	£2.80

MAP REF.

COFFEE 4.50 / 5

OVERALL 4.50 / 5 ★★★★½

Velasquez and Van Wezel

78 Park Road, N8 8JQ

There's a kind of stripped-back simplicity about Velasquez and Van Wezel. It's a smallish space dominated by a huge window, with little seating and just a few sandwiches and baked goodies to eat. The one thing that's huge is coffee quality, from a custom-built Kees van der Westen or filters. The owners grew up in the coffee business and they handle Square Mile's beans with consummate skill. But they also know how to make even a simple space into a warm and welcoming hangout, both for locals and for those coming in to enjoy the area's attractions.

+44(0)7715 881 949
www.velasquezandvanwezel.co.uk
 Archway

MON-FRI.	7:30am - 5:00pm
SAT.	8:00am - 5:00pm
SUN.	8:30am - 5:00pm

First opened 2016
Roaster Square Mile Coffee Roasters
Machine Kees van der Westen Spirit
Duette, 2 groups
Grinder Victoria Arduino, Nuova Simonelli
Mythos One, Mahlkönig EK 43

Espresso	£2.00
Cappuccino	£2.70
Latte	£2.50
Flat white	£2.50

MAP REF.

COFFEE 4.25 / 5

OVERALL 4.00 / 5 ★★★★☆

135

Wired Co.

194 Broadhurst Gardens, NW6 3AY

Wired brings a bit of hipster cool - and that's a compliment in this case - to a patch of sedate West Hampstead where cool is not exactly in ample supply. And its continuing success proves that the locals appreciate it, coming here even when there's competition from the chains just a few minutes away. Climpson coffee is brewed expertly and decorated with love. Food is simple but attractive and the welcome is always warm. There's a larger room downstairs if the small ground floor is full, and a few tables outside when the weather's good. We can't imagine how this place could be any better.

⊖ West Hampstead

Sister locations Cable Co.

MON–FRI.	7:30am – 5:00pm
SAT–SUN.	9:00am – 5:00pm

First opened 2013
Roaster Climpson & Sons and guest roasters
Machine La Marzocco Linea, 2 groups
Grinder Nuova Simonelli Mythos One, Mazzer Major E, Mazzer Mini, Anfim

Espresso	£2.10
Cappuccino	£2.70
Latte	£2.70
Flat white	£2.60

MAP REF.

COFFEE 4.25 / 5

OVERALL 4.25 / 5  ★★★★⯪

Developed with baristas for baristas

UNSWEETENED

BLUE DIAMOND
ALMONDS

Almond Breeze®

Rich & Creamy

BARISTA BLEND
Created for Use by Professionals
Dairy and Soya Free

Baristas know their coffee better than anyone. That's why they he
us make our new, low calorie Almond Breeze® Barista Blend.
deliciously creamy and frothy, making it perfect for the world's fi
coffee. And because it's an almond drink, it's dairy free and soya

● Perfect for latte art   ● No added sugar   ● Cholesterol free, low fat alternative to

For more information & stockists visit **bluediamondalmonds**

Brick Lane and Shoreditch provide London's creative pulse and are areas of tremendous diversity that have undergone rapid change in recent years. Many of the city's best new roasteries are based in East London and a range of artisan coffee venues provide fuel for the artists, students and urbanites who flock here for the weekend markets.

Inner East

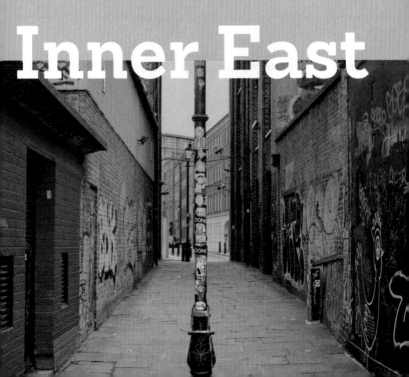

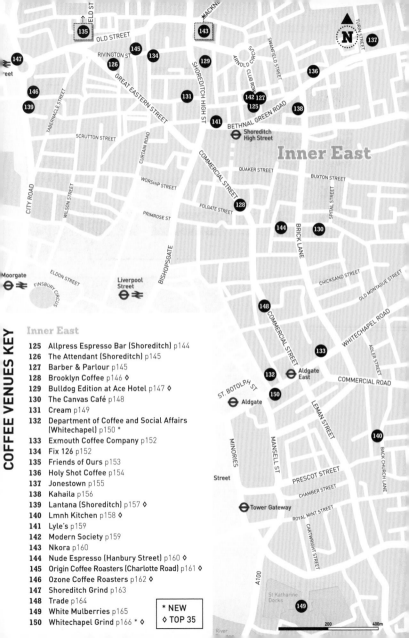

* NEW
◊ TOP 35

Inner East

Allpress Espresso Bar Shoreditch

58 Redchurch Street, E2 7DP

The famous Allpress Redchurch Street café helped catapult a once neglected side road into one of East London's hippest retail streets. The Kiwi roaster's influence extends well beyond the local area though, with wholesale coffee customers spanning the length and breadth of the country. Following the opening of the company's new Dalston Roastery Café, this original site was refurbished with a smaller, yet still perfectly-formed footprint, ideally positioned for a post-shopping espresso and a spot of people-watching.

+44(0)20 7749 1780
uk.allpressespresso.com
⊖ Shoreditch High Street

Sister locations Dalston

MON-FRI. 7:30am - 5:00pm
SAT-SUN. 9:00am - 5:00pm

First opened 2010
Roaster Allpress Espresso
Machine La Marzocco Linea PB, 3 groups
Grinder Nuova Simonelli Mythos One

Espresso	£2.30
Cappuccino	£2.90
Latte	£2.90
Flat white	£2.90

MAP REF. **125**

COFFEE 4.50 / 5

OVERALL 4.25 / 5

The Attendant Shoreditch

74 Great Eastern Street, EC2A 3JL

The original Attendant in Foley Street might seem a hard act to follow, between its excellent quality and its inimitable location. This one is quite a big place, light and airy, and beautifully decorated with lots of greenery. With the expanded space comes an expansive food offering, baked goods in the morning leading on to brunch or lunch of soup, sandwiches, salads and the like. Attendant's roastery produces beans that make for a rounded, fruity cup, and for a very pleasant Shoreditch sojourn.

+44(0)20 7729 0052
www.the-attendant.com
⊖ Old Street

Sister locations Fitzrovia / Clerkenwell

| MON-FRI. | 8:00am - 6:00pm |
| SAT-SUN. | 9:00am - 6:00pm |

First opened 2015
Roaster The Attendant Roastery
Machine La Marzocco GB5, 2 groups
Grinder Victoria Arduino Mythos One, Mahlkönig EK 43

Espresso	£2.20
Cappuccino	£3.00
Latte	£3.00
Flat white	£2.90

MAP REF. 126

| COFFEE 4.25 / 5 |  | OVERALL 4.00 / 5 | ★★★★☆ |

Barber & Parlour

64-66 Redchurch Street, E2 7DP

Barber and Parlour is a hybrid space on achingly hip Redchurch Street, catering for the East Londoner's every whim. The visitor will encounter a cinema, hair salon, nail bar, and gentleman's barber before reaching the kitchen on the upper floor. Skilled baristas diligently oversee the coffee preparation and with excellent Origin beans in the hopper, coffee aficionados have their caffeine fix sorted. Only one choice remains: will you be following your espresso with a moustache trim or a manicure?

+44(0)20 3376 1777
www.barberandparlour.com
⊖ Shoreditch High Street

Sister locations Hubbard & Bell

| MON-SUN. | 9:00am - 9:30pm |

First opened 2014
Roaster Origin Coffee Roasters and guests
Machine La Marzocco Linea PB, 3 groups
Grinder Nuova Simonelli Mythos, Mazzer Super Jolly

Espresso	£2.50
Cappuccino	£3.00
Latte	£3.00
Flat white	£3.00

MAP REF. 127

| COFFEE 4.25 / 5 | | OVERALL 4.25 / 5 | ★★★★⯪ |

145

Brooklyn Coffee

139 Commercial Street, E1 6BJ

The slick interior design of Brooklyn Coffee divides opinion. It's all clean lines, sharp corners and plate glass. The effect is multiplied by the monolithic concrete bar. Well-extracted coffee from their own beans is made with precision by co-owner Bryan, who originally hails from New York City himself. Complement your flat white with a bar of artisan chocolate crafted by Williamsburg's achingly hip Mast Brothers. The store's interior may be austere, but the North American-style hospitality at Brooklyn Coffee is attentive and friendly.

+44(0)7845 394 695
www.brooklyncoffee.co.uk
Shoreditch High Street / Liverpool Street

| MON-FRI. | 7:00am – 5:00pm |
| SAT-SUN. | 9:00am – 5:00pm |

First opened 2014
Roaster Brooklyn Coffee
Machine La Marzocco Linea PB, 2 groups
Grinder Mazzer Robur, Mazzer Kony

Espresso	£2.40
Cappuccino	£2.80
Latte	£3.00
Flat white	£2.80

MAP REF. 128

COFFEE 4.50 / 5

OVERALL 4.50 / 5 ★★★★⯪

Bulldog Edition at Ace Hotel

100 Shoreditch High Street, E1 6JQ

The Ace Hotel is an official HQ for Shoreditch hipsterdom. Step into its sizeable lobby any time of day and you're in a sea of bearded, sock-less humanity, with a soundtrack provided by the click-clicks of keyboards and mouse pads. Eye contact isn't prohibited, but it's rare. This is a shame - the oustanding coffee offering here should fuel a bit more conversation. The coffee bar is on one side of the lobby, with its own entrance and a few seats outside. If the weather doesn't allow that, get a macchiato or cortado from the experts manning the Strada, carry it into the lobby, and grab a seat (if you can).

+44(0)20 7613 9800
www.acehotel.com/london
⊖ Shoreditch High Street / Old Street

MON-SUN. 6:30am - 6:00pm

First opened 2013
Roaster Square Mile Coffee Roasters
Machine La Marzocco Strada, 3 groups
Grinder La Marzocco Vulcano, Mahlkönig EK 43

Espresso	£2.00 / £2.20
Cappuccino	£2.60
Latte	£3.00
Flat white	£2.60

MAP REF. **129**

The Canvas Café

42 Hanbury Street, E1 5JL

There are lots of places to have a coffee around Brick Lane, but Canvas is a standout. This pleasantly shabby-looking place is part of a network of 'Happy Cafés,' aimed at promoting contentment through spiritual, artistic, and intellectual improvement. Don't worry: Canvas is a place for fun, even if you don't want a compassion course or storytelling session. Weekday food is eggs, salads, baked things and sandwiches. Brunch reigns at weekends. Friendly, well trained staff pull tiptop espresso-based coffees using Square Mile beans. Check out the writing on the walls, and add to it.

+44(0)20 7018 1020
www.thecanvascafe.org/cafe
⊖ Liverpool Street / Shoreditch High Street

MON-WED.	11:00am - 8:00pm
THU.	11:00am - 10:00pm
FRI.	11:00am - 12:00am
SAT-SUN.	10:00am - 8:00pm

First opened 2014
Roaster Square Mile Coffee Roasters
Machine La Marzocco Linea, 2 groups
Grinder Mazzer, Mazzer Kony

Espresso	£2.50
Cappuccino	£2.80
Latte	£2.80
Flat white	£2.70

MAP REF. 130

COFFEE
4.00 / 5

OVERALL
4.25 / 5 ★★★★⯪

Cream

31 New Inn Yard, EC2A 3EY

Now well established on the East London scene, Cream continue to bring their innovative cooking to their large converted warehouse space. The Dark Arts coffee is very well prepared, but the food deserves a special mention. With a daily changing menu featuring what's market fresh, you can be sure to find something to tempt you. When it comes to brunch, Cream definitely rises to the top.

+44(0)7931 289 260
www.cream-shoreditch.com
⊖ Shoreditch High Street

MON-FRI. 8:00am - 4:00pm
SAT-SUN. 10:00am - 5:00pm

First opened 2015
Roaster Dark Arts Coffee
Machine Kees van der Westen Mirage, 2 groups
Grinder Compak K-10 x2, Compak K-3

Espresso	£2.00
Cappuccino	£2.40
Latte	£2.40
Flat white	£2.40

MAP REF.

COFFEE 4.50 / 5   🫘 🫘 🫘 🫘 🫘

OVERALL 4.50 / 5   ★ ★ ★ ★ ⯨

Department of Coffee and Social Affairs

Whitechapel 133 Whitechapel High Street, E1 7QA

This Department of Coffee and Social Affairs is set in the ground floor of an office building. While there are other coffee places in this patch of Whitechapel, wherever the Department opens one, you know it's going to be worth taking seriously. And this one certainly is, even though its demographic means that it's open only on weekdays. Local business people and students can spend quality time here, in a spacious, lofty room whose huge windows look right out onto the high street. Despite the corporate setting, it has a nicely bohemian feel, with plenty of seating both at gleaming white tables and in low-slung sofas where you can really settle in for a serious chill session.

There's a great selection of lunch dishes if you're in need of full refuelling, and the Department's usual star showing of baked goods (you urgently need to try one of their brownies). And the coffee quality is never less than impeccable. The surrounding area plays home to numerous attractions, from the Whitechapel Gallery to the street markets and Brick Lane. The Department is one of the top spots for resting your feet after making those visits.

MAP REF.

COFFEE	OVERALL
4.50 / 5	4.25 / 5

| MON-FRI. | 7:30am - 5:00pm |
| SAT-SUN. | Closed |

First opened 2017
Roaster The Roastery Department
Machine Sanremo, 3 groups
Grinder Mazzer Robur E

Espresso	£2.50
Cappuccino	£3.05 / £3.25
Latte	£3.05 / £3.25
Flat white	£3.15

departmentofcoffee.com
 Aldgate East

Sister locations Multiple locations

Exmouth Coffee Company

83 Whitechapel High Street, E1 7QX

Exmouth has it all. It has good beans from its own roaster, expertly brewed and decorated with beautiful milk art. It has exquisite baked goods and generously portioned sandwiches at eminently reasonable prices. The amusingly eclectic décor is another big draw. But the best thing about Exmouth is the people, skilled, smiling, and genuinely warm. Come in mid-afternoon or mid-morning to savour the laid-back atmosphere of one of London's loveliest coffee spots.

+44(0)20 7377 1010
www.exmouthcoffee.co.uk
Aldgate East

MON-SUN. 7:00am - 8:00pm

First opened 2012
Roaster Exmouth Coffee Company
Machine La Marzocco Strada, 3 groups
Grinder Mazzer Robur, Mahlkönig EK 43, Mahlkönig Air

Espresso	£2.20
Cappuccino	£2.95
Latte	£2.95
Flat white	£2.95

MAP REF. 133

COFFEE 4.00 / 5   **OVERALL** 4.25 / 5 ★★★★☆

Fix 126

126 Curtain Road, EC2A 3PJ

If it ain't broke, don't fix it. This seems to be the philosophy here. This simple location ticks all the standard Shoreditch boxes with consummate skill. The food offering is small but of high quality, service is smiling and swift, even the look of the place (raw brick and wood) is done beautifully. The gleaming La Marzocco produces most of what people drink here, but don't pass up the chance to savour a batch brew. There's plenty of seating available to sit and sip with friends or open up your sketchbook and let your creativity flow.

+44(0)20 7033 9555
www.fix-coffee.co.uk
Old Street / Shoreditch High Street

MON-FRI. 7:00am - 7:00pm
SAT-SUN. 8:00am - 7:00pm

First opened 2011
Roaster Climpson & Sons
Machine La Marzocco Linea PB, 3 groups
Grinder Victoria Arduino Mythos One, Mazzer Robur E

Espresso	£1.80
Cappuccino	£2.75
Latte	£2.75
Flat white	£2.75

Sister locations Fix

MAP REF. 134

COFFEE 4.25 / 5   **OVERALL** 4.00 / 5 ★★★★☆

Friends of Ours

61 Pitfield Street, N1 6BU

You feel instantly at home in this neighbourhood hangout, even if it's your first visit. Coffee comes from Dark Arts, and the Clipper blend makes an excellent espresso on the Black Eagle Gravitech. But coffee alone doesn't sum up this venue's appeal. Regulars abound, the owners 'wanted this to be a place where we would remember names and orders.' During the week, most custom is takeaway; at weekends it swings closer to 90 per cent eating-in for the coffee and fine brunch fare.

+44(0)7545 939 751
www.friendsofourscafe.com
⊖ Old Street

MON–FRI.	8:00am – 5:00pm
SAT.	9:00am – 5:00pm
SUN.	10:00am – 5:00pm

First opened 2015
Roaster Dark Arts Coffee and guests
Machine Victoria Arduino Black Eagle Gravitech, 2 groups
Grinder Mahlkönig EK 43, Nuova Simonelli Mythos One

Espresso	£2.20
Cappuccino	£3.00
Latte	£3.00
Flat white	£2.80

MAP REF. **135**

COFFEE 4.50 / 5

OVERALL 4.25 / 5 ★★★★⯪

Holy Shot Coffee

155 Bethnal Green Road, E2 7DG

Michael Kim came into coffee via the personal route. He worked in finance but felt more passionate about the black stuff than the green stuff. After travelling and researching extensively, he opened this Bethnal Green space. It's nice to look at and a pleasure to sit in, with one big table and potted plants in abundance. Caravan's espresso blend is racy stuff, best displayed in combination with milk, and it's expertly crafted here. Have a little something baked. And do consider taking home a bar of their mega-popular homemade coffee soap.

+44(0)20 3222 0693
www.holyshotcoffee.com
⊖ Shoreditch High Street

MON-FRI.	7:00am - 6:00pm
SAT.	8:00am - 6:00pm
SUN.	9:00am - 6:00pm

First opened 2016
Roaster Caravan Coffee Roasters
Machine La Marzocco Linea PB, 2 groups
Grinder Mazzer Kony

Espresso	£2.20
Cappuccino	£2.80
Latte	£2.80
Flat white	£2.80

MAP REF. **136**

COFFEE 4.25 / 5

OVERALL 4.00 / 5 ★★★★☆

Jonestown

215 Bethnal Green Road, E2 6AB

Serial coffee entrepreneur Adrian Jones opened Jonestown in 2015, on a corner site with a bit of pavement seating and a very great deal of bright, almost Caribbean feel. Espresso from the La Marzocco is sweet enough to need no sugar, and latte art is notably accomplished. While pavement tables are a treat in fine weather, the indoor seating option of choice is the sofa, so comfortable you'll need coffee just to keep from falling asleep. Even as Bethnal Green becomes one of London's coffee hotspots, this is a local star.

+44(0)20 7739 7476
www.jonestown.co.uk
 Bethnal Green

MON–SAT.	7:00am – 7:00pm
SUN.	8:00am – 7:00pm

First opened 2015
Roaster Jonestown Coffee
Machine La Marzocco Linea AV, 3 groups
Grinder Mazzer Kold, Mahlkönig EK 43

Espresso	£1.70
Cappuccino	£2.50
Latte	£2.50
Flat white	£2.50

Sister locations Fuckoffee / Goswell Road Coffee

MAP REF.

COFFEE
4.25 / 5

OVERALL
4.50 / 5 ★★★★✦

Kahaila

135 Brick Lane, E1 6SB

Kahaila began life in 2012 as a café and local gathering place for events. Since then it has become very popular, the large room at the back crowded with groups, couples, and Brick Lane creatives tap-tapping on their devices. Coffee is a big part of the draw: very well made using beans from Climpson, and with multiple different grinders showing their attention to detail. The food offering is basic, but the big room is a very pleasant place to eat it. Even in an area that's pretty rich with coffee, Kahaila is a hot spot.

+44(0)20 7998 1388
www.kahaila.com
 Liverpool Street

MON–SAT.	9:00am – 7:00pm
SUN.	9:00am – 5:30pm

First opened 2012
Roaster Climpson & Sons
Machine La Marzocco GB5, 2 groups
Grinder Mazzer Robur, Mahlkönig EK 43

Espresso	£2.40
Cappuccino	£2.90
Latte	£2.90
Flat white	£2.90

MAP REF.

 COFFEE 4.00 / 5   **OVERALL** 4.00 / 5

Lantana Shoreditch

1 Oliver's Yard, 55 City Road, EC1Y 1HQ

TOP 35

Inner East

This branch of Lantana has helped transform East London's once arid coffee landscape into a blossoming caffeine community. A takeout bar serves those in a rush, and the large midcentury-inspired casual dining room is a fashionable spot for brunch. Lantana's formidable brunch menu and potent Alchemy coffee (a unique blend available at Lantana only) are more than a match for even the most grievous Shoreditch hangover.

+44(0)20 7253 5273
www.lantanacafe.co.uk
⊖ Old Street

Sister locations Fitzrovia / London Bridge

| MON-FRI. | 7:30am - 10:00pm |
| SAT-SUN. | 9:00am - 5:00pm |

First opened 2012
Roaster Alchemy Coffee and guests
Machine La Marzocco FB80, 3 groups
Grinder Mazzer Luigi

Espresso	£2.40
Cappuccino	£3.00
Latte	£3.00
Flat white	£2.90

MAP REF. **139**

 COFFEE 4.50 / 5

 OVERALL 4.50 / 5 ★★★★⯨

157

Lmnh Kitchen

101 Back Church Lane, E1 8LU

TOP 35

Lmnh Kitchen occupies a gorgeous ground-floor space in The Loom, a Victorian wool warehouse turned creative complex. Through clever and sensitive design, Lmnh has made this into a proper café/restaurant. Food can be anything from cakes or cheese plates to sharing platters and full meals, with a mouth-watering menu created by their talented head chef. Coffee comes from Square Mile by way of a cosseted Kees van der Westen, and it's made with consummate skill. Service is charming, and the drinks list is serious (check out the London-brewed beer selection). Weekend brunch after a walk around Whitechapel? Yes please, mum!

+44(0)20 3621 8898
www.lookmumnohands.com
⊖ Aldgate East

Sister locations Look Mum No Hands!

| MON-FRI. | 8:00am – 5:00pm |
| SAT-SUN. | 9:00am – 3:00pm |

First opened 2016
Roaster Square Mile Coffee Roasters and guests
Machine Kees van der Westen, 3 groups
Grinder Victoria Arduino Mythos One

Espresso	£2.20
Cappuccino	£2.90
Latte	£2.90
Flat white	£2.90

MAP REF.

 COFFEE 4.50 / 5

OVERALL 4.50 / 5

Lyle's

Tea Building, 56 Shoreditch High Street, E1 6JJ

With a few exceptions, restaurants are guilty of some grievous crimes against coffee. At Lyle's you can eat very handsomely (seasonal, unfussy fare) and conclude your meal with a jaw-dropping espresso. If you're in the mood for a coffee and nothing more, that's fine too. The bar is an all-day affair offering exceptional beans from the likes of Sweden's Koppi and Belleville in Paris. At Lyle's, coffee is treated with the same respect as food and wine, challenging entrenched perceptions of how restaurants think about coffee.

+44(0)20 3011 5911
www.lyleslondon.com
⊖ Shoreditch High Street

MON-FRI.	8:00am – 11:00pm
SAT.	12:00pm – 11:00pm
SUN.	Closed

First opened 2014
Roaster Belleville, Roundhill, La Cabra, James Gourmet, Koppi, Clifton
Machine Nuova Simonelli Aurelia II T3, 2 groups
Grinder Mahlkönig EK 43

Espresso	£2.00
Cappuccino	£2.50
Latte	£2.70
Flat white	£2.50

MAP REF. 141

| COFFEE 4.50 / 5 | | OVERALL 4.25 / 5 | ★★★★⯪ |

Modern Society

33 Redchurch Street, E2 7DJ

Modern Society is a lovely little café. Not surprising, since it's located in a store that sells high-end clothing, accessories and housewares. But it maximises the wow factor with particularly gorgeous floor tiles and chandeliers. Perch at the bar or grab the single table and sit right in the window to watch the hip pageantry of Redchurch Street float by. Note the filtered options supplementing the espresso-based list. And note the reasonable prices, too.

themodernsociety.com/pages/cafe
⊖ Shoreditch High Street

| MON-FRI. | 10:00am – 7:00pm |
| SAT-SUN. | 11:00am – 5:00pm |

First opened 2015
Roaster Assembly
Machine Modbar, 2 groups
Grinder Mahlkönig

Espresso	£2.00
Cappuccino	£3.00
Latte	£3.00
Flat white	£2.60

MAP REF. 142

| COFFEE 4.25 / 5 |  | OVERALL 4.25 / 5 | ★★★★⯪ |

Nkora

21 Hackney Road, E2 7NX

Nkora hums with the happy feeling you get from an attractive room, friendly staff, and a real commitment to neighbourhood. The food offer is low-key; sandwiches and baked goods. Coffee offering includes V60 in addition to the espresso-based drinks (made to a high standard by ultra-friendly baristas). The neighbourhood touches come in the form of a downstairs work space with a big table, mum-and-baby groups on Wednesdays, and a positively ecstatic policy on Man's Best Friend: 'We love dogs!'

+44(0)20 8127 1810
nkora.co.uk
⊖ Shoreditch High Street

| MON-FRI. | 7:30am - 5:00pm |
| SAT-SUN. | 9:00am - 6:00pm |

First opened 2015
Roaster Union Coffee Roasters and guests
Machine La Marzocco Linea PB, 2 groups
Grinder Nuova Simonelli Mythos One, Mahlkönig EK 43

Espresso	£2.40
Cappuccino	£3.00
Latte	£3.00
Flat white	£2.80

Sister locations
Cambridge Heath

MAP REF. 143

| COFFEE 4.25 / 5 | OVERALL 4.25 / 5 ★★★★⯪ |

Nude Espresso Hanbury Street

26 Hanbury Street, E1 6QR

You can't get much more local than this: Nude's beans are roasted across the street. The café has been here for a decade, and its popularity shows no sign of waning - it's rare to find anything less than a mob scene here. But if you can find a place to sit, you'll be well rewarded with famously ample portions of excellent food and well-made coffees. Tables at the front show you the rich pageant of Brick Lane life, while those at the back are better for seclusion. Ten years old, and still a star.

+44(0)7712 899 335
www.nudeespresso.com
⊖ Shoreditch High Street / Liverpool Street

Sister locations The Roastery (Hanbury St) / Bell Lane / Spitalfields Market

| MON-FRI. | 7:00am - 6:00pm |
| SAT-SUN. | 9:30am - 5:00pm |

First opened 2008
Roaster Nude Coffee Roasters
Machine La Marzocco Linea PB, 3 groups
Grinder Nuova Simonelli Mythos

Espresso	£2.40
Cappuccino	£3.00
Latte	£3.00
Flat white	£3.00

MAP REF. 144

| COFFEE 4.50 / 5 | OVERALL 4.50 / 5 ★★★★⯪ |

Origin Coffee Roasters Charlotte Road

65 Charlotte Road, EC2A 3PE

Photo: Juliet Murphy

Origin buys green beans through direct trade with producers and roasts them in Cornwall, where the company is based. This small London outpost does the beans proud, both in espresso and in a surprisingly popular brew bar (around 20 per cent of their trade is non-espresso-based). The ground-floor café is soothingly attractive, and there's a full training centre downstairs where they offer SCA courses covering barista skills at every level. Food is simple, service friendly and attentive. Now a key venue within the sophisticated Shoreditch coffee scene.

+44(0)20 7729 6252
www.origincoffee.co.uk
⊖ Old Street

Sister locations The British Library / Hammersmith

MON–FRI.	7:30am – 6:00pm
SAT.	10:00am – 6:00pm
SUN	11:00am – 5:00pm

First opened 2014
Roaster Origin Coffee Roasters
Machine La Marzocco Strada, 3 groups
Grinder Nuova Simonelli Mythos One, Mahlkönig EK 43

Espresso	£2.50
Cappuccino	£3.00
Latte	£3.00
Flat white	£3.00

MAP REF. 145

 COFFEE 4.50 / 5

 **OVERALL** 4.50 / 5 ★★★★✯

161

Ozone Coffee Roasters

11 Leonard Street, EC2A 4AQ

Ozone made a splash when it opened in 2012, with its two-storey space(s) creating a dramatic spectacle out of the roasting and serving of coffee beans. The ground floor is bright and airy, the basement (where the roasting happens) has a darker, cooler character with semi-industrial décor. Bag yourself a seat and you will enjoy good food and consistently exciting coffee. Pour-overs are the preferred option here, especially if you are downstairs: espresso-based drinks tend to lose a little heat on their way from the ground floor. Australia-inspired food is excellent, and staff are skilfully trained. Still one of the best in Shoreditch.

+44(0)20 7490 1039
www.ozonecoffee.co.uk
⊖ Old Street

MON-FRI. 7:30am - 10:00pm
SAT-SUN. 8:30am - 5:30pm

First opened 2012
Roaster Ozone Coffee Roasters
Machine La Marzocco Strada, 3 groups
Grinder Mahlkönig EK 43, Victoria Arduino Mythos One, Mazzer Kold

Espresso	£2.40
Cappuccino	£3.00
Latte	£3.00
Flat white	£3.00

MAP REF.

 COFFEE 5 / 5

 OVERALL 5 / 5  ★★★★★

Shoreditch Grind

213 Old Street, EC1V 9NR

Grinds have been popping up regularly around London, but the original remains unique. It's partly the unlikely location right on Old Street roundabout, and partly the early-space-age look of the building. Both of these aspects must account for some of its success, but there's plenty of other stuff to love here, including a great buzz generated by fast-moving baristas. They really know their business, and they keep the brews coming from their Linea PB even when the place is rammed. There's also high-quality food, especially baked goods. And the seats outside are an amazingly pleasant place to plant yourself, considering that they're a few steps away from a busy roundabout.

+44(0)20 7490 7490
grind.co.uk
Old Street (Exit 8)

Sister locations Multiple locations

MON-THU.	7:00am - 11:00pm
FRI.	7:00am - 1:00am
SAT.	8:00am - 1:00am
SUN.	9:00am - 7:00pm

First opened 2011
Roaster Grind & Co.
Machine La Marzocco Linea PB, 2 groups x2
Grinder Nuova Simonelli Mythos One x3, Mahlkönig Tanzania

Espresso	£2.30
Cappuccino	£3.00
Latte	£3.00
Flat white	£3.00

MAP REF. 147

COFFEE 4.50 / 5

OVERALL 4.50 / 5 ★★★★½

163

Trade

47 Commercial Street, E1 6BD

Trade is a neatly-pulled-together outfit among the textile wholesalers of Spitalfields, dealing in stout sandwiches and a no-nonsense approach to coffee making. The painted brick walls and industrial fittings may be rather hackneyed, but the interior is well-planned, spacious, and wholly redeemed by a sun-splashed terrace. Prepare to reckon with bold brunch and lunch options including formidable lobster rolls and reuben sandwiches. Boasting walloping fare and well-made coffee, Trade is a juicy morsel on an otherwise unappetising strip of Commercial Street.

+44(0)20 3490 1880
www.trade-made.co.uk
⊖ Aldgate East

MON-FRI. 7:30am - 5:00pm
SAT-SUN. 9:00am - 5:00pm

First opened 2014
Roaster Origin Coffee Roasters and guests
Machine Orchestrale Etnica, 2 groups
Grinder Nuova Simonelli Mythos One

Espresso	£1.90
Cappuccino	£2.50
Latte	£2.50
Flat white	£2.50

Sister locations Essex Road

MAP REF. 148

COFFEE 4.25 / 5	OVERALL 4.25 / 5 ★★★★☆

White Mulberries

D3 Ivory House, St Katharine Docks, E1W 1AT

The location alone would make a visit here worthwhile. White Mulberries is a few minutes from the Tower of London and sits right on the marina in St Katharine Dock. If the weather allows it, you can sit outside for an even better view of the bobbing yachts. Inside it's nicely cosy in the small, attractive space where a flat white and batch brew can be your companion for a quiet drink and a chat with friends. If you're hungry, there are egg dishes, sandwiches, soups, and scrumptious baked goods. You can almost forget you're in London at White Mulberries. And as much as we love London, that's a compliment.

www.whitemulberries.com
⊖ Tower Hill / Tower Gateway DLR

MON-FRI.	7:30am – 5:00pm
SAT.	8:00am – 6:00pm
SUN.	8:30am – 6:00pm

First opened 2012
Roaster Allpress Espresso, La Cabra Coffee Roasters and guests
Machine La Marzocco FB80, 2 groups
Grinder Victoria Arduino Mythos, Mazzer Major, Mazzer Super Jolly

Espresso	£2.00
Cappuccino	£3.00
Latte	£3.00
Flat white	£3.00

MAP REF. 149

Whitechapel Grind

10 Whitechapel High Street, E1 8DX

Coffee shops in office buildings are officially a thing, and it's a thing that makes sense: businesses run as much on caffeine as on electricity, and having high-quality brews just a lift-ride away will make workers happy. Sometimes these are pretty humdrum places, efficient rather than wonderful. But the best office-building coffee shops make you forget you're in a place of work. The crucial question is: 'would I go there even if I didn't work in the building?' If the answer is yes, you're on to a winner.

That's certainly true of Grind Whitechapel, one of the pleasantest places to sip a cappuccino anywhere in east London. Located in the expansive lobby of the

White Chapel building, it boasts seating reminiscent of a cocktail bar in addition to more conventional dining-type tables and a big, gleaming bar. You can imagine spending a whole day here, from morning meetings through light lunch and then an afternoon on the laptop - as long as you don't fall asleep in that comfy seating. Single origin filter, applied liberally, will help overcome that danger. Anyone touring Whitechapel would do well to pop in here. This place is a perfect example of how office coffee should be done.

MAP REF.

COFFEE
4.50 / 5

OVERALL
4.50 / 5 ★★★★☆

MON–WED.	8:00am – 5:00pm
THU–FRI.	8:00am – 9:00pm
SAT–SUN.	Closed

First opened 2017
Machine La Marzocco Linea PB, 3 groups
Grinder Nuova Simonelli Mythos One

Espresso	£2.30
Cappuccino	£3.00 / £3.30
Latte	£3.00 / £3.30
Flat white	£3.00 / £3.30

grind.co.uk
Aldgate East

Sister locations Multiple locations

East London has successfully shaken off its label as a rough outer region to emerge as London's booming artistic neighbourhood. A wonderful combination of cultures and a thriving creative scene have helped put the area back on the map, and provide a fertile environment for London's coffee pioneers.

East

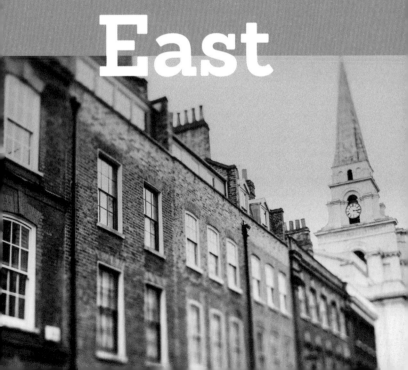

46b Espresso Hut

46b Brooksby's Walk, E9 6DA

While the space is small, the size of the welcome - and the quality of the coffee - are monumental at 46b. Square Mile's invigorating espresso blend comes through the Synesso in perfect condition, awaiting some outstanding milk art. If one of the handful of seats is free, plonk yourself down and watch the Homerton scene through the big front window - or better still, on a bench outside if the sun's out. Mouth-watering toasted sandwiches complete the picture of this perfect east London local.

+44(0)7702 063 172

⊖ Homerton

Sister locations Hand Café / Espresso Hut x Jack Wills

MON-FRI.	7:30am - 5:00pm
SAT.	8:30am - 5:00pm
SUN.	9:00am - 5:00pm

First opened 2012
Roaster Square Mile Coffee Roasters
Machine Synesso Cyncra, 2 groups
Grinder Anfim Super Caimano

Espresso	£2.20
Cappuccino	£2.70
Latte	£2.70
Flat white	£2.70

MAP REF. **152**

COFFEE 4.50 / 5	OVERALL 4.25 / 5 ★★★★⯪

56 St James

56 St James Street, E17 7PE

56 St James is a true neighbourhood coffee shop. There's something for everyone here: delicious coffee, the large communal table, a gigantic chalkboard for children, and cakes handmade by none other than the owner's mum. This café also has a penchant for pineapples: pineapple themed art cheerfully graces the walls and visitors are greeted by an enormous pineapple donning the exterior brickwork. In past centuries, this exotic fruit was a symbol of prosperity. 56 St James is a sure sign that Walthamstow's fortunes are on the up.

+44(0)7792 328 479

⇌ St James Street

MON-TUE.	Closed
WED-THU.	9:00am - 6:00pm
FRI.	9:00am - 4:30pm | 6:00pm - 11:00pm
SAT-SUN.	10:00am - 5:00pm

First opened 2014
Roaster Extract Coffee
Machine La Marzocco Linea, 2 groups
Grinder Compak K-10, Compak K-3

Espresso	£2.00
Cappuccino	£2.50
Latte	£2.50
Flat white	£2.50

MAP REF. **153**

COFFEE 4.00 / 5	OVERALL 4.00 / 5 ★★★★☆

Allpress Espresso Roastery & Café

Dalston 55 Dalston Lane, E8 2NG

Allpress is a powerful outfit, and very popular locally. This impressive roastery occupies a large and airy space on both floors of a converted joiner's factory. Expect distinct crowds: City types, mums and even students on weekday mornings, with a more mixed clientele later in the day and at weekends. Espresso-based drinks are made flawlessly, as you'd expect from Allpress, but pour-over is also executed with care. As is everything from the kitchen. Note that there is no WiFi because the owners 'want to give people a place where they can get away from work and socialise.'

+44(0)20 7749 1780
uk.allpressespresso.com
⊖ Dalston Junction

Sister locations Shoreditch

MON-FRI.	7:30am - 4:00pm
SAT-SUN.	9:00am - 4:00pm

First opened 2015
Roaster Allpress Espresso
Machine La Marzocco Strada EP, 3 groups
Grinder Nuova Simonelli Mythos One

Espresso	£2.30
Cappuccino	£2.90
Latte	£2.90
Flat white	£2.90

COFFEE 4.75 / 5	🫘 🫘 🫘 🫘 🫘	OVERALL 5 / 5	★ ★ ★ ★ ★

Brunswick East

Unit 3D Stamford Works, Gillett Street, N16 8JH

Nestled in the midst of a humming complex of offices and studios (as well as the skate-park in Gillett Square), Brunswick East is a small, ultra-friendly operation owned by two Australian sisters. They set out with three main aims. One: recreate Oz-style brunch ('our favourite meal'). Two: provide a central meeting place for the local workers who, they felt, usually operate in isolation. Three: make great coffee. They set about the task with lively spins on the Aussie breakfast and lunch staple dishes, and with Alchemy coffee expertly made. Mission accomplished.

+44(0)7570 119 708
www.brunswickeast.london
⊖ Dalston Kingsland

MON-FRI.	8:00am - 5:00pm
SAT-SUN.	9:00am - 5:30pm

First opened 2015
Roaster Alchemy Coffee
Machine La Marzocco Linea, 2 groups
Grinder Mazzer Kony E, Mahlkönig EK 43

Espresso	£2.20
Cappuccino	£2.80
Latte	£2.80
Flat white	£2.80

MAP REF. **154**

COFFEE
4.25 / 5

OVERALL
4.00 / 5 ★★★★☆

Bühler and Co

8 Chingford Road, E17 4PJ

Sisters Meg and Rosie Bühler created their café with the view that it needed to have 'good coffee, good food, good service, and a good environment.' They're four out of four. This attractive Walthamstow local does everything right, from the warm smiles, through unusually ambitious and imaginative food to beautifully brewed coffee from Climpson beans. This is a real standout in an area that's not overly supplied with good coffee. If you find yourself here later in the day, make sure to sample their evening menu. Check out the garden and snuggle up under blankets provided for when the weather's cold.

+44(0)20 8527 3652
www.buhlerandco.com
⊖ Walthamstow Central

MON-WED.	8:00am – 5:00pm
THU-FRI.	8:00am – 10:30pm
SAT.	9:00am – 10:30pm
SUN.	9:00am – 5:00pm

First opened 2016
Roaster Climpson & Sons
Machine La Marzocco Linea, 2 groups
Grinder Mazzer Major, Mahlkönig Tanzania

Espresso	£2.20
Cappuccino	£2.50
Latte	£2.50
Flat white	£2.50

MAP REF. **155**

Climpson & Sons

67 Broadway Market, E8 4PH

Nice and neat

Looks pro

20/6/18

— we need to keep an eye on the east (places)
— we need to go each of them
bike?.)

— if you find a good place you should go for it
(& (apt rocks!;)

Climpson is one of London's star roasters, and its flagship café has been a star in Broadway Market since 2005. Unless you savour the hustle and bustle (and queues) on market-day weekends, the week is the best time to come. Your brew will be served in ceramic, not paper, and you'll be able to enjoy it along with locals who love to drink and laugh. Milky drinks are made with exceptional care and skill, and the breakfast and lunch menu features ingredients bought from local suppliers.

www.climpsonandsons.com
⇌ London Fields Rail

Sister locations Old Spitalfields Market / Broadway Market Cart (Sat Only) / Climpson's Arch & Coffee Roastery / Climpson's Academy

MON-FRI.	8:30am – 6:00pm
SAT.	11:00am – 5:00pm
SUN.	10:00am – 5:00pm

First opened 2005
Roaster Climpson & Sons
Machine La Marzocco Linea PB, 2 groups
Grinder Nuova Simonelli Mythos One

Espresso	£2.20
Cappuccino	£2.80
Latte	£2.80
Flat white	£2.80

MAP REF. **156**

COFFEE 4.50 / 5

OVERALL 4.25 / 5 ★★★★☆

The Common E2

53 Old Bethnal Green Road, E2 6QA

The Common was designed to be an 'open work space' for creative people from the local area and beyond, and the main communal table is likely to be crowded with people working on laptops. But there's a nice buzz anyway, coming from groups of friends, mothers with children, and sometimes from the workers themselves, who have meetings and share ideas. And the buzz comes also from the friendly, chatty, helpful staff. Food and drink are excellent, with eggs and good toasted sandwiches prominent (at extremely reasonable prices), and superbly made brews using beans from The Roasting Shed in Clapton.

thecommone2.com

⊖ Bethnal Green / ⇌ Cambridge Heath Rail

MON-FRI.	8:00am - 5:00pm
SAT-SUN.	9:30am - 5:00pm

First opened 2015
Roaster The Roasting Shed and guests
Machine La Marzocco Linea PB, 2 groups
Grinder La Marzocco Vulcano

Espresso	£2.10
Cappuccino	£2.80
Latte	£2.80
Flat white	£2.60

MAP REF. 157

COFFEE
4.25 / 5

OVERALL
4.50 / 5
★ ★ ★ ★ ⯨

Corner Kitchen

58a Woodgrange Road, E7 0QH

Corner Kitchen is a bit of sunshine on traffic-heavy Woodgrange Road. The owners have aimed to make this a community centre as well as a café and restaurant, and you can come here for events including children's play activities in the basement and wine tastings. Or you can just eat and drink. Doppio's espresso blend is a high roast best suited to milky treatment, and it's made well. The restaurant features pizzas and many other baked goods made on the premises, and the wine list is heavy on natural wine.

+44(0)20 8555 8068
www.cornerkitchen.london
⇝ Forest Gate Rail

MON-THU.	9:00am - 10:00pm
FRI-SAT.	9:00am - 10:30pm
SUN.	9:00am - 9:00pm

First opened 2016
Roaster Doppio
Machine La Marzocco Linea 2EE, 2 groups
Grinder Mazzer Super Jolly E

Espresso	£1.50
Cappuccino	£2.50
Latte	£2.50
Flat white	£2.50

MAP REF. **158**

COFFEE
4.00 / 5

OVERALL
4.00 / 5
★ ★ ★ ★ ☆

Craving Coffee

Unit 3, Gaunson House, Markfield Road, N15 4QQ

Craving Coffee resides in a converted industrial unit shared with The Mill Co. Project studio space. Co-owner Matt Ho formerly roasted with Climpson & Sons, and his experience clearly shines through in the superb coffee service. The kitchen turns out thoughtfully-prepared dishes using seasonal ingredients from local suppliers. This large, versatile space opens weekly for Tottenham Social, where some of London's best street food traders take over the kitchen.

+44(0)20 8808 3178
www.cravingcoffee.co.uk
⊖ Seven Sisters / Tottenham Hale

MON-WED.	10:00am - 5:00pm
THU-SAT.	10:00am - 11:00pm
SUN.	10:00am - 5:00pm

First opened 2014
Roaster Climpson & Sons
Machine Synesso Hydra, 2 groups
Grinder Nuova Simonelli Mythos One

Espresso	£2.00
Cappuccino	£2.50
Latte	£2.50
Flat white	£2.50

MAP REF. **159**

Esters

55 Kynaston Road, N16 0EB

Bright, attractive, friendly - Esters gets everything right. The owners are closely involved with their operation, and you can feel it in the attention to detail. The food offering is limited but there are hot dishes as well as sandwiches and baked goods. Coffee comes from Has Bean and is featured in pour-overs as well as espresso. Esters is very much a local hangout, but you should seek it out if you're doing a bit of Stokey exploration. If the weather's good, sit on the quaint outdoor terrace out back.

+44(0)20 7254 0253
www.estersn16.com
🚉 Rectory Road Rail /
Stoke Newington Rail

MON.	Closed
TUE-FRI.	8:00am - 4:00pm
SAT.	9:00am - 4:00pm
SUN.	10:00am - 4:00pm

First opened 2013
Roaster Has Bean
Machine La Marzocco Linea, 2 groups
Grinder Nuova Simonelli Mythos One

Espresso	£2.20
Cappuccino	£2.80
Latte	£3.00
Flat white	£2.80

MAP REF. 160

COFFEE 4.25 / 5   🫘🫘🫘🫘🫘   **OVERALL** 4.25 / 5   ★★★★✩

The Grand Howl

214a Well Street, E9 6QT

Two things set Grand Howl apart from most neighbourhood coffee spots. One is the Diedrich roaster at the back which produces all their beans. The other is the all-vegetarian (and mostly vegan) food menu, varied and enticing even for those who eat meat. A lot of business is for takeaway but Howl is an extremely pleasant place to work, talk, or watch the world go by. They keep two espresso selections, one designed for drinking with milk. And that's how the house roasting style shows best. East London is lucky to have this place.

+44(0)20 3659 9631
🚇 Homerton / Hackney Central

| MON-FRI. | 8:30am - 4:30pm |
| SAT-SUN. | 9:00am - 4:00pm |

First opened 2016
Roaster Howl
Machine La Marzocco Linea PB, 2 groups
Grinder Nuova Simonelli Mythos One,
Mahlkönig EK 43

Espresso	£2.00
Cappuccino	£2.80
Latte	£2.80
Flat white	£2.60

MAP REF. 161

COFFEE 4.25 / 5   🫘🫘🫘🫘🫘   **OVERALL** 4.25 / 5   ★★★★✩

Hand Café

20 Victory Parade, E20 1FS

The vast East Village development in Stratford is lucky to have this coolly laid-back café in its midst, an indie alternative to the chains in nearby Westfield Stratford. A second project from the owner of 46b Espresso Hut in Hackney, Hand has the same Greek-accented menu with an abundance of herbs giving a lift to standard dishes. Square Mile's espresso blend is expertly handled in the Synesso, and huge windows bring in plenty of light. There are Greek sweets and other goodies to take home alongside bags of beans, and service couldn't be friendlier.

⊖ Stratford

Sister locations 46b Espresso Hut

MON-FRI.	8:00am - 6:00pm
SAT-SUN.	9:00am - 6:00pm

First opened 2016
Roaster Square Mile Coffee Roasters
Machine Synesso Cyncra, 2 groups
Grinder Nuova Simonelli Mythos One

Espresso	£2.00
Cappuccino	£2.60
Latte	£2.60
Flat white	£2.60

MAP REF. 162

COFFEE 4.25 / 5 🫘🫘🫘🫘🫘

OVERALL 4.25 / 5 ★★★★⯪

The Hive Wellbeing

286-290 Cambridge Heath Road, E2 9DA

The word chilled doesn't begin to describe the vibe at this lovely venue - a coffee bar, juice bar, wine bar and restaurant all rolled into one. The Hive Wellbeing comes from the team behind the former G&T. The accent is on healthy, from the all-vegetarian menu to the freshly squeezed fruit juices. But the coffee seems to be what most people come for, and with good reason: The Square Mile blend is crafted perfectly.

+44(0)20 8981 9245
www.thehivewellbeing.com
⊖ Bethnal Green /
⇌ Cambridge Heath Rail

MON-FRI.	8:00am - 10:00pm
SAT.	9:00am - 10:00pm
SUN.	10:00am - 6:30pm

First opened 2015
Roaster Square Mile Coffee Roasters, Workshop Coffee
Machine La Marzocco FB80, 2 groups
Grinder Mazzer Kony, Mahlkönig EK 43

Espresso	£2.40
Cappuccino	£2.80
Latte	£2.80
Flat white	£2.80

MAP REF. 163

COFFEE
4.00 / 5

OVERALL
4.25 / 5

Lanark Coffee

262 Hackney Road, E2 7SJ

Lanark is a little slip of a coffee bar named after Alasdair Gray's dystopian novel. You can rely on owner, Greg Boyce, to fix you a superb brew with an assortment of beans from top microroasters, as well as a range of teas. Coffee geeks will gravitate towards the Victoria Arduino Athena, a mythological lever-operated espresso machine with beautiful hammered metalwork and exquisite detailing. Lanark is a coffee bar with particular appeal to London's coffee purists.

www.lanarkcoffee.co.uk
⊖ Hoxton

| MON-FRI. | 8:00am - 4:00pm |
| SAT-SUN. | 10:00am - 4:00pm |

First opened 2014
Roaster Dark Arts Coffee
Machine Victoria Arduino Athena Leva, 2 groups
Grinder Mahlkönig EK 43

Espresso	£2.00
Cappuccino	£2.50
Latte	£2.50
Flat white	£2.50

MAP REF. 164

Mouse Tail Coffee Stories

307 Whitechapel Road, E1 1BY

Mouse Tail occupies a tiny, irregular space sandwiched between Whitechapel Road and the railway lines. There's little seating inside, but what it lacks in size it makes up for in the warmth of the welcome and the quality of the coffee. It's a great place to sit and watch the action in the street market. Food is nearly all homemade at their kitchen in Clapton (sandwiches are pretty enormous), and as far as coffee is concerned, their aim is to 'do all the geeky stuff right without being intimidating.'

www.mousetailcoffee.com

⊖ Whitechapel

Sister locations Borough High Street / Canary Wharf / Canada Water / Deptford Station

MON–FRI.	7:00am – 6:00pm
SAT–SUN.	9:00am – 5:00pm

First opened 2015
Roaster Mission Coffee Works
Machine La Marzocco Linea PB, 2 groups
Grinder Mahlkönig Tanzania, Mazzer Kony

Espresso	£2.20
Cappuccino	£2.80
Latte	£2.80
Flat white	£2.80

MAP REF. **165**

COFFEE
4.00 / 5

OVERALL
4.25 / 5 ★★★★⯪

Pavilion

Victoria Park, Crown Gate West, E9 7DE

You couldn't ask for a lovelier location than this: Victoria Park, with a view of the pond and its two little islands from inside the glass-domed building or outside on the deck. Pavilion would be good even without the view, because its food and drink offerings are so special. The menu's inspired by Sri Lankan cuisine, and local beers are the perfect accompaniment. Even if you're just having a cake, however, you have to finish with a brew from Origin beans, in filter or espresso form. The obvious warning is urgently needed: if you're here at the weekend, especially during lunch, expect a massive crowd.

⊖ Bethnal Green / Mile End

MON-FRI. 8:00am – 5:00pm
SAT-SUN. 8:00am – 5:30pm

First opened 2007
Roaster Origin Coffee Roasters
Machine Synesso Cyncra MVP, 3 groups
Grinder Victoria Arduino Mythos One

Espresso	£2.50
Cappuccino	£2.70
Latte	£2.70
Flat white	£2.70

Sister locations Elliots / Pavilion Bakery

MAP REF. 166

 COFFEE 4.25 / 5  OVERALL 4.25 / 5 ★★★★⯪

The Peanut Vendor

6 Gunmakers Lane, E3 5GG

This patch of Hackney might not seem a likely spot for a first-rate café, but that's just what The Peanut Vendor is. Staff are young, keen and friendly, and they brew double shots of The Barn beans alongside an excellent range of teas. Toasted sandwiches and baked goods dominate the small food offering. Locals come in with babies, laptops and especially dogs, which are more than welcome.

+44(0)20 8981 8613
www.thepeanutvendor.co.uk
⊖ Bow Road

MON-SUN. 9:00am – 5:00pm

First opened 2015
Roaster The Barn and guests
Machine La Marzocco Linea, 2 groups
Grinder Mazzer Major, Mahlkönig EK 43, Nuova Simonelli Mythos One

Espresso	£2.30
Cappuccino	£2.70
Latte	£2.90
Flat white	£2.70

MAP REF. 167

 COFFEE 4.25 / 5 OVERALL 4.00 / 5 ★★★★☆

Second Shot Coffee

475 Bethnal Green Road, E2 9QH

This dinky coffee shop in Bethnal Green is a social enterprise dedicated to working with people affected by homelessness and teaching them barista skills, hoping that they will then go on to jobs elsewhere. The coffee is noteworthy as Second Shot uses a constantly changing roster of beans. Espresso is beautifully made in their futuristic digital Nuova Simonelli. Even more enticing is the 'brewing menu', five single-origins brewed in any of three ways. Second Shot is small in size, but big in heart - and in quality.

+44(0)20 7739 1628
secondshotcoffee.co.uk
 Bethnal Green

MON-SUN. 8:00am - 6:00pm

First opened 2016
Roaster Square Mile Coffee Roasters, Cast Iron Coffee Roasters and guests
Machine Nuova Simonelli Aurelia, 2 groups
Grinder Nuova Simonelli Mythos One, Mahlkönig EK 43

Espresso	£2.10
Cappuccino	£2.70
Latte	£2.70
Flat white	£2.60

MAP REF.

COFFEE 4.25 / 5

OVERALL 4.25 / 5

Taylor St Baristas Canary Wharf

8 South Colonnade, Canary Wharf, E14 4PZ

Photo: Cephas Azariah

This lean, mean café is designed to produce a high volume of quality coffee for the district's bankers and business people. The venue is predominantly set up to serve takeaway drinks, but there are also a small number of tables. In addition to espresso-based drinks, customers can opt for a single origin coffee brewed by AeroPress. A full breakfast menu is on offer complemented by cakes and Australian classics such as lamingtons and cheese and Vegemite muffins.

+44(0)20 7519 6536
www.taylor-st.com
⊖ Canary Wharf

Sister locations Multiple locations

MON-FRI.	7:00am - 5:30pm
SAT-SUN.	Closed

First opened 2011
Roaster Taylor St Baristas
Machine Victoria Arduino White Eagle, 3 groups x2
Grinder Victoria Arduino Mythos One x3, Mazzer Robur

Espresso	£2.20
Cappuccino	£3.00
Latte	£3.00
Flat white	£3.00

MAP REF. **169**

COFFEE 4.50 / 5	OVERALL 4.50 / 5	★★★★⯪

Taylor St Baristas South Quay

1 Harbour Exchange Square, E14 9GE

London's financial district runs on regular doses of caffeine, administered by the skilled hands of Taylor St's dedicated baristas. This large café offers both a rapid takeaway service and ample seating; ideal for conducting casual business meetings. The timber-clad counter is stacked with healthy salads and Antipodean treats. At South Quay, Taylor St pulls off exceptional coffee and food within the constraints of a very busy site.

+44(0)20 3069 8833
www.taylor-st.com
⊖ South Quay

Sister locations Liverpool Street / Shoreditch / Canary Wharf / Monument / Mayfair / Bank / St Paul's

MON-FRI.	8:00am - 5:00pm
SAT-SUN.	Closed

First opened 2013
Roaster Taylor St Baristas
Machine Nuova Simonelli Aurelia II T3, 3 groups
Grinder Nuova Simonelli Mythos, Mazzer Robur, Anfim, Mahlkönig Tanzania

Espresso	£2.20
Cappuccino	£3.50
Latte	£3.50
Flat white	£3.90

MAP REF.

COFFEE 4.50 / 5

OVERALL 4.25 / 5
★★★★☆

Tina, We Salute You

47 King Henry's Walk, N1 4NH

Dalston locals are fiercely protective of Tina, We Salute You. The enigmatic Tina presides over a lush selection of tarts, cakes, sticky buns, and glorious coffee. Tina's corner location provides the perfect place to soak up the afternoon sun while engrossed in a magazine. The interior is regularly given over to creatives to use as an exhibition space, and one of the outside walls hosts street art by local artists. A true local gem.

+44(0)20 3119 0047
www.tinawesaluteyou.com
⊖ Dalston Kingsland

Sister locations Stratford

MON–FRI.	8:00am – 6:00pm
SAT–SUN.	10:00am – 6:00pm

First opened 2009
Roaster Alchemy Coffee
Machine La Marzocco Linea, 2 groups
Grinder Anfim

Espresso	£2.20
Cappuccino	£2.80
Latte	£2.80
Flat white	£2.80

MAP REF.

COFFEE
4.25 / 5

OVERALL
4.25 / 5 ★★★★⯨

Wilton Way Café

63 Wilton Way, E8 1BG

Wilton Way Café sells excellent coffee using Climpson beans. But if you left your description of the place there, you'd be missing 90 per cent of what makes this venue so special. Wilton Way takes community involvement very seriously, hosting monthly art gallery openings for a gallery down the road. It also gives over some of its floor space to London Fields Radio, which you may find broadcasting live when you drop in for your cortado. There's something wonderfully relaxed about the whole setup. Do you need more convincing? OK, the sandwiches are great too and the location is quiet. The only way is Wilton Way.

Hackney Central /
Hackney Downs Rail

| MON–FRI. | 8:00am – 4:30pm |
| SAT–SUN. | 9:00am – 5:00pm |

First opened 2009
Roaster Climpson & Sons
Machine La Marzocco Linea, 2 groups
Grinder Mazzer Luigi, Mazzer Luigi E

Espresso	£2.20
Cappuccino	£2.60
Latte	£2.50 / £2.70
Flat white	£2.50

MAP REF. **172**

COFFEE 4.25 / 5	OVERALL 4.25 / 5

Wood St Coffee

Blackhorse Workshop, 1-2 Sutherland Road Path, E17 6BX

Walthamstow has its grimier moments, but mostly it's known for its strong community, green spaces, and, like other gentrifying areas, a growing thirst for coffee. Wood St Coffee has an authentic feel, housed in the proudly blue-collar Blackhorse Workshops, busy with metalworkers, carpenters, bakers, and brewers. Come here for honest, well-made coffee enjoyed with slabs of sourdough toast baked freshly on site. The building isn't easy to locate (hidden down an alley off Blackhorse Lane), but the explorer's persistence will be amply rewarded.

+44(0)7944 888 011
www.woodstcoffee.co.uk
Ⓔ Blackhorse Road

MON-FRI.	8:30am - 5:30pm
SAT.	9:30am - 5:30pm
SUN.	10:00am - 4:00pm

First opened 2014
Roaster Dark Arts Coffee
Machine La Marzocco Linea Classic, 2 groups
Grinder Mazzer Kony, Nuova Simonelli Mythos One

Espresso	£2.20
Cappuccino	£2.60
Latte	£2.60
Flat white	£2.60

MAP REF. **173**

COFFEE 4.25 / 5		OVERALL 4.00 / 5	★ ★ ★ ★ ☆

Zealand Road Coffee

391 Roman Road, E3 5QS

There's little in the area that can compete with Zealand Road Coffee, but you get the sense that this place would thrive wherever it set up shop. Homemade food is simple but good, and there's some outdoor seat when the weather allows. And big windows give the sense of being outside even when you're in the rustically charming interior. Beans from Origin get respectful treatment and drinks are served with a great big smile. At mealtimes, Zealand's small size may make it hard to bag a seat but go there anyway. This place is just great.

+44(0)7940 235 493
Ⓔ Mile End / Bethnal Green

MON-SAT.	8:00am - 5:00pm
SUN.	9:00am - 5:00pm

First opened 2011
Roaster Origin Coffee Roasters
Machine La Marzocco Classic, 2 groups
Grinder Mazzer Major, Compak K6

Espresso	£2.20
Cappuccino	£2.60 / £2.80
Latte	£2.60 / £2.80
Flat white	£2.60

MAP REF. **174**

COFFEE 4.25 / 5		OVERALL 4.00 / 5	★ ★ ★ ★ ☆

JOIN THE PLANT-BASED REVOLUTION

Not only are our products delicious in taste and texture, but we also have OUTSTANDING sustainability credentials. So you can rest assured that by choosing Alpro, your drink will be good for you and good for the planet too.

WWW.ALPRO.COM   #ALPROXCOFFEE

ENJOY ENDLESS PLANT-BASED POSSIBILITIES

ALMOND MOCHA

ICED SOYA LATTE

COCONUT LATTE

TURMERIC COCONUT LATTE

COCONUT HOT CHOCOLATE

COLD BREW ALMOND CHAI

SOY CHAI LATTE

ALMOND CAPPUCCINO

Whatever your choice,
enjoy it with plant power.

CRAFTED WITH

enjoy plant power
alpro®

#PLANTPOWER

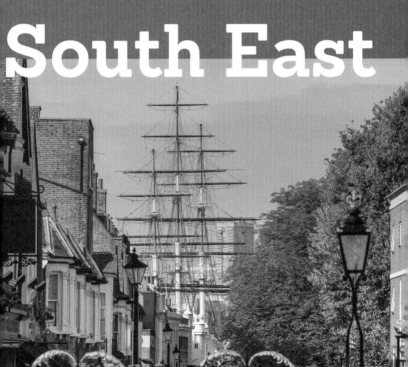

One of the capital's best kept secrets, South East London is home to a small number of quietly brilliant coffee venues, and is rapidly establishing itself on the coffee map. With the completion of the Overground line from East London to Clapham Junction via Peckham, the area is now more accessible, and rewards the urban explorer with a vibrant foodie and market scene.

South East

Anderson & Co

139 Bellenden Road, SE15 4DH

This enduringly popular Peckham spot is known mainly as an eatery, and you can expect it to be packed out at weekends. Even if you're not in the market for a full meal, you're welcome to pop in for coffee. It's well made from Square Mile beans, and if you're sitting outside you can enjoy it while watching the street life go by. Enjoy your brew with one of their homemade cakes or brownies, perfect pairing any day of the week.

+44(0)20 7469 7078
www.andersonandcompany.co.uk
⊖ Peckham Rye

| MON.-SAT. | 8:00am – 5:00pm |
| SUN. | 8:30am – 4:30pm |

First opened 2011
Roaster Square Mile Coffee Roasters
Machine La Marzocco Linea, 2 groups
Grinder Victoria Arduino Mythos

Espresso	£2.00
Cappuccino	£2.80
Latte	£2.80
Flat white	£2.80

MAP REF. 175

COFFEE 4.25 / 5   **OVERALL** 4.25 / 5 ★★★★⯪

Brick House Bakery

1 Zenoria Street, SE22 8HP

Started as a wholesale bakery in 2012, Brick House opened this retail shop and café in 2015 - and it's quickly become a local hangout. It's in a lovely space that formerly housed an electrical warehouse. The food is top-notch, made with real attention to detail. Square Mile beans are brewed in the La Marzocco Linea by a polished, friendly team. Brick House appeals to a diverse customer base with weekdays very popular with parents and babies. Generous spacing of the long tables means that buggies don't get in the way.

+44(0)20 8693 2031
www.brickhousebread.com
⇌ East Dulwich Rail

Sister locations Peckham

MON.	Closed
TUE.-FRI.	8:00am – 4:00pm
SAT.	8:00am – 5:00pm
SUN.	8:00am – 4:00pm

First opened 2015
Roaster Square Mile Coffee Roasters
Machine La Marzocco Linea, 2 groups
Grinder Mazzer Robur, Mazzer Super Jolly, Nuova Simonelli Mythos One

Espresso	£2.10
Cappuccino	£2.95
Latte	£2.95
Flat white	£2.95

MAP REF. 176

COFFEE 4.00 / 5   **OVERALL** 4.25 / 5 ★★★★⯪

Browns of Brockley

5 Coulgate Street, SE4 2RW

Coffee legend and owner Ross Brown's café now has it's own range of apparel for sale - t-shirts and caps decorated with slightly surreal illustrations. This is perhaps testament to the cult following that's built around this South East London institution. Situated directly opposite Brockley station since 2010, the long, thin space has recently been refurbished and extended to allow more seating, which is usually occupied by Brockley's bohemian clientele. They're here to enjoy Browns' consistently excellent Square Mile coffee (pulled through a gleaming Victoria Arduino Black Eagle machine), the warm, convivial atmosphere, and of course the delicious cinnamon donut muffins.

+44(0)20 8692 0722
www.brownsofbrockley.com
⊖ Brockley

MON-FRI.	7:30am - 4:00pm
SAT-SUN.	9:00am - 4:00pm

First opened 2010
Roaster Square Mile Coffee Roasters
Machine Victoria Arduino Black Eagle
Gravimetric, 2 groups
Grinder Nuova Simonelli Mythos One

Espresso	£2.00
Cappuccino	£3.00
Latte	£3.20
Flat white	£3.00

MAP REF. **177**

COFFEE 4.50 / 5  **OVERALL** 4.50 / 5 ★★★★✬

Canada Water Café

40 Surrey Quays Road, SE16 7DX

The coffee alone would make Canada Water Café worth visiting. Union's espresso blend is brewed precisely and latte art is outstanding. But the coffee's just part of the appeal of this successful venue, a combination of café, bar, and restaurant. It looks great and has a cheery vibe at busy mealtimes. The menu is wide-ranging, with an emphasis on Italian food at lunch and dinner. You get a smile and a greeting the instant you walk in the door. Those who live or work locally are fortunate. Everyone else should find a reason to pay a visit.

+44(0)20 3668 7518
www.canadawatercafe.com
⊖ Canada Water

MON–FRI.	7:00am – 11:00pm
SAT.	8:30am – 11:00pm
SUN.	8:30am – 10:00pm

First opened 2014
Roaster Union Coffee Roasters
Machine La Marzocco Linea PB, 2 group
Grinder Mahlkönig EK 43

Espresso	£1.70
Cappuccino	£2.70
Latte	£2.80
Flat white	£2.60

MAP REF. 178

COFFEE 4.50 / 5

OVERALL 4.50 / 5 ★★★★½

Caravan Bankside

30 Great Guildford Street, SE1 0HS

Having conquered the north with restaurant/cafés in Exmouth Market and King's Cross, Caravan has crossed the river to Bankside. This site is big and bustling, and like the one in King's Cross it's at the centre of a thriving local scene. Their menu has an emphasis on small plates (plenty of choice for vegetarians), pizza, and home-cured meats. Espresso-based drinks are always very well made at Caravan, but their buying and roasting skills are best appreciated in the changing roster of single-origin filter brews.

+44(0)20 7101 1190
www.caravanrestaurants.co.uk
⊖ Borough

Sister locations Exmouth Market / King's Cross / City

MON-FRI.	8:00am - 10:30pm
SAT.	10:00am - 10:30pm
SUN.	10:00am - 4.00pm

First opened 2016
Roaster Caravan Coffee Roasters
Machine Faema E71
Grinder Mazzer Kold, Mahlkönig EK 43

Espresso	£2.20
Cappuccino	£2.80
Latte	£2.80
Flat white	£2.80

MAP REF.

 COFFEE 4.50 / 5   **OVERALL** 4.75 / 5

The Coffee House by The Gentlemen Baristas

63 Union Street, SE1 1SG

Lords, ladies, barons, countesses and members of the general public can expect a cordial welcome at the splendid premises of 63 Union Street. The building itself boasts a fascinating history: it originally housed one of London's oldest coffee roasteries dating back to the 18th century. Proprietors Henry Ayers and Edward Parkes, two tweed-clad coffee chaps, have also set up a coffee training school in the space above the shop. The coffee here is really rather spiffing, but owners of particularly dashing moustaches should exercise caution when indulging in cappuccinos.

+44(0)7817 350 067
www.thegentlemenbaristas.com
⊖ Borough / London Bridge

Sister locations Store Street / The School House

MON-THU.	7:00am - 6:00pm
FRI.	7:00am - 11:00pm
SAT.	8:30am - 5:00pm
SUN.	8:30am - 4:00pm

First opened 2014
Roaster The Gentleman Baristas, Wogan Coffee Roasters, Strangers Coffee Company, Neighbourhood Coffee
Machine Faema E71, 3 groups
Grinder Nuova Simonelli Mythos x2, Mazzer Kold

Espresso	£2.00
Cappuccino	£2.70 / £2.90
Latte	£2.70 / £2.90
Flat white	£2.70

MAP REF. **180**

COFFEE 4.50 / 5		OVERALL 4.25 / 5	

The Coffee Works Project
Blackfriars Road 235 Blackfriars Road, SE1 8BF

When you walk up to the counter in this outpost of The Coffee Works Project, you'll undoubtedly begin by chatting with the disarmingly friendly staff. But then it's down to business. The Coffee Works Project espresso from their fully manual Slayer is flawless, with textbook crema and just the right extraction for a beautifully balanced cup. Food arrives daily from a central kitchen, and everything's made in-house except bread and pastries. Locals, whether in jeans or suits, have already spotted the quality. The well-spaced, generous seating, makes this a great spot to socialise with friends.

+44(0)20 7928 8456
www.coffeeworksproject.com
⊖ Southwark

MON-FRI. 7:30am - 5:00pm
SAT-SUN. Closed

First opened 2015
Roaster The Coffee Works Project
Machine Slayer V3, 3 groups
Grinder Nuova Simonelli Mythos x2, Mahlkönig EK 43

Espresso	£2.20
Cappuccino	£2.80
Latte	£2.80
Flat white	£2.80

Sister locations Angel / Leadenhall / Battersea / Hackney

MAP REF. 181

COFFEE 4.50 / 5	OVERALL 4.75 / 5

Coleman Coffee

20 Lower Marsh, SE1 7RJ

Jack Coleman has worked in the coffee business, one way or another, since he was thirteen. Perhaps that explains the complete self-confidence in every aspect of his first retail outlet. This half-pint-size café uses only full-fat Jersey milk, doesn't have loyalty cards, and serves a specialised food offering centred around Staffordshire oatcakes (sweet and savoury). It's all about the coffee here: excellent beans, expertly brewed, from a venerable Synesso or filter. Try their 'old-fashioned espresso'. And in good weather, drink it in a lovely back garden which boasts both a pomegranate tree and a mulberry tree.

+44(0)20 3267 1139
www.colemancoffee.com
⊖ Waterloo / Lambeth North

MON–FRI.	8:00am – 3:00pm
SAT–SUN.	9:30am – 3:00pm

First opened 2016
Roaster Coleman Coffee Roasters
Machine Synesso Cyncra, 3 groups
Grinder Mazzer Kony E, Ditting KR1203

Espresso	£2.20
Cappuccino	£2.80
Latte	£2.90
Flat white	£2.80

MAP REF. 182

COFFEE 4.50 / 5		OVERALL 4.25 / 5	★★★★⯪

Daily Goods

36 Camberwell Church Street, SE5 8QZ

Daily Goods is a much-needed shot in the arm for Camberwell's café scene. Run by Carter Donnell - who practised his craft at New York's renowned Ninth Street Espresso - Daily Goods has a relaxed atmosphere attracting a cross-section of Camberwell residents. In a doff of the (baseball) cap to Yankee coffee culture, the menu includes filter coffee served in American diner-style mugs. But forget any preconceptions you might have about bulk brew; the baristas at Daily Goods are anything but casual about their coffee.

www.dailygoodslondon.co.uk
◉ Denmark Hill

| MON-FRI. | 7:30am - 5:00pm |
| SAT-SUN. | 8:30am - 5:00pm |

First opened 2014
Roaster Daily Goods, Caravan, Quarter Horse, Square Mile, Round Hill
Machine La Marzocco Linea, 2 groups
Grinder Nuova Simonelli Mythos One

Espresso	£2.20
Cappuccino	£2.60
Latte	£2.60
Flat white	£2.60

MAP REF. **183**

| COFFEE 4.50 / 5 | 🫘 🫘 🫘 🫘 🫘 | OVERALL 4.25 / 5 | ★★★★✰ |

FCB Coffee

Denmark Hill Station, Windsor Walk, SE5 8BB

Talk about location! FCB sits literally on top of a busy commuter rail station and a three-minute walk from a busy teaching hospital. For several hours in the morning they operate a dedicated La Marzocco selling takeaway coffees from the window. Even when things quieten down, it can still be a lively, humming place. They sell good sandwiches, and people come to eat them here - as well as drink carefully brewed coffees from Horsham and rotating guests - at the small handful of tables.

+44(0)20 7703 9754
www.fcbcoffee.com
≥ Denmark Hill Rail

Sister locations Olympia

MON-FRI.	6:00am - 8:00pm
SAT.	7:00am - 7:00pm
SUN.	8:30am - 4:00pm

First opened 2014
Roaster Horsham Coffee Roaster and guests
Machine La Marzocco Linea AV, 2 groups x3
Grinder Nuova Simonelli Mythos One x3, La Marzocco Volcano x4, Ceado E37S

Espresso	£1.90
Cappuccino	£2.90
Latte	£2.90
Flat white	£2.60

MAP REF. **184**

| COFFEE 4.00 / 5 | 🫘🫘🫘🫘🫘 | OVERALL 3.75 / 5 | ★★★⯪☆ |

Fee & Brown

50 High Street, Beckenham, BR3 1AY

Walk in to Fee & Brown at lunchtime and you'll see a lively mix of families, solitary workers, friends catching up and young parents with snoozing toddlers. This is primarily a place for eating fine breakfasts, sandwiches or baked things, but the coffee is very well made. Laptop-slaves can perch during weekdays, but at busy weekends there's a friendly but firm machine-free policy. F&B opened a second venue late in 2017 with a larger space, a gorgeous garden, and a larger food offering.

+44(0)20 8658 1996
www.feeandbrown.com
≥ Beckenham Junction Rail

Sister locations Park Langley

| MON-SAT. | 8:00am - 4:00pm |
| SUN. | 9:00am - 4:00pm |

First opened 2012
Roaster Climpson & Sons
Machine La Marzocco Linea, 2 groups
Grinder Mazzer Robur x2

Espresso	£2.20
Cappuccino	£2.60
Latte	£2.60
Flat white	£2.60

MAP REF. **185**

| COFFEE 4.25 / 5 | 🫘🫘🫘🫘🫘 | OVERALL 4.00 / 5 | ★★★★☆ |

Four Corners Cafe

12 Lower Marsh, SE1 7RJ

Four Corners looks like a café you'd find in any city that's popular with the backpacking community. Travel books and memorabilia are all over the place, and there's an intensely casual feeling. What's not casual is their attitude to quality: milk-loving Ozone beans come through the La Marzocco Linea in fine condition, with notably beautiful milk art. Food is simple but crafted with an eye to detail. Local office workers love the place and so do tourists, some a little unsteady after a ride on the nearby London Eye. Even if you're suffering from neither Eye-sickness nor wanderlust, a first trip to Four Corners will make you love the place.

+44(0)20 8617 9591
www.four-corners-cafe.com
⊖ Waterloo / Lambeth North

MON.-FRI.	7:30am - 6:30pm
SAT.	9:00am - 5:00pm
SUN.	Closed

First opened 2013
Roaster Ozone Coffee Roasters
Machine La Marzocco Linea, 2 groups
Grinder Mazzer Major

Espresso	£2.00
Cappuccino	£2.60
Latte	£2.60
Flat white	£2.60

MAP REF. **186**

| COFFEE 4.00 / 5 | | OVERALL 4.25 / 5 | ★★★★⭒ |

Fowlds Cafe

3 Addington Square, SE5 7JZ

Tucked away on bohemian Addington Square, this charming little café is a collaboration with Fowlds upholstery firm, occupying the site since 1926. This family business continues to operate from the rear of the property, while the shopfront is given over to coffee and cake. The workshop itself is occasionally repurposed for atmospheric candle-lit supper clubs. Fowlds' beautiful old-fashioned shop sign hangs from the facade, casting an enchanting spell over this forgotten corner of Camberwell. Fowlds is a quietly brilliant coffee spot well worth a detour to visit.

+44(0)20 3417 4500
⊖ Oval / Kennington

Sister locations Louie Louie

MON.-FRI.	7:30am - 5:00pm
SAT.	8:30am - 5:00pm
SUN.	9:30am - 4:00pm

First opened 2014
Roaster Square Mile Coffee Roasters
Machine La Marzocco Linea, 2 groups
Grinder Anfim Milano v.240-50

Espresso	£2.10
Cappuccino	£2.70
Latte	£2.70
Flat white	£2.70

MAP REF. **187**

| COFFEE 4.00 / 5 | | OVERALL 4.25 / 5 | ★★★★⭒ |

205

General Store

174 Bellenden Road, SE15 4BW

Plenty of delicatessens sell coffee, but General Store isn't just any old deli. Minute in size, it sells a small range of products that have one thing in common: outstanding provenance and high quality. Foods from Italy are a particular strong point, and so are vegetables. There's a little seating space both inside and out, and it's worth resting your feet either before or after shopping to have a well-priced espresso or macchiato from the two-group Linea. You'll walk away with a happy caffeine buzz and a few hundred grams of some of the best salami this side of Siena.

+44(0)20 7642 2129
www.generalsto.re
⊖ Peckham Rye

MON-TUE.	Closed
WED-FRI.	9:00am - 7:00pm
SAT.	8:00am - 6:00pm
SUN.	9:00am - 5:00pm

First opened 2013
Roaster Workshop Coffee
Machine La Marzocco Linea, 2 groups
Grinder Mazzer Super Jolly

Espresso	£2.00
Cappuccino	£2.60
Latte	£2.60
Flat white	£2.60

MAP REF. 188

COFFEE 4.25 / 5

OVERALL 4.25 / 5

The Hub Coffee House

Oasis Centre, 1a Kennington Road, SE1 7QP

Hub is part of the Oasis Waterloo group, which provides services for the local community including food banks and debt advice. It is an admirable organisation in every way. But if you're expecting Hub to be a dreary place (especially since it shares a building with a public library), you're dead wrong. This is a lively local, good-looking and eminently hipster-friendly. The house espresso blend is best drunk with milk, or there's single-origin filter. If you have a sweet tooth, make sure to feed it a cookie or a wicked slice of cake.

+44(0)20 3267 4214
www.hubcoffeehouse.org
⊖ Lambeth North / Waterloo

MON-FRI.	8:00am - 6:00pm
SAT.	9:30am - 3:00pm
SUN.	9:30am - 11:00am

First opened 2016
Roaster Kingdom Coffee
Machine Iberital Expressions, 3 groups
Grinder Mazzer Super Jolly

Espresso	£2.00
Cappuccino	£2.65
Latte	£2.65
Flat white	£2.55

MAP REF. 189

COFFEE 4.00 / 5
OVERALL 4.25 / 5 ★★★★⯪

London Grind

2 London Bridge, SE1 9RA

Most people come here for the delicious food, though the Grind house espresso is of a high standard. London Grind focuses on delivering good food and a lively, perfectly boisterous vibe. And it's doing the job right, it seems. The place attracts crowds from nearby offices and from Borough Market (a coffee bean's throw away). Come for coffee and lunch during the day, by all means, but in the evening you may prefer a Hot Flat White Russian: espresso, vodka, Kahlua and milk.

+44(0)20 7378 1928
www.londongrind.com
⊖ London Bridge

Sister locations Multiple locations

MON-THU.	7:00am - 12:00am
FRI	7:00am - 1:00am
SAT.	8:00am - 1:00am
SUN.	9:00am - 7:00pm

First opened 2015
Roaster The Grind House Espresso
Machine La Marzocco Linea PB, 2 groups x2
Grinder Nuova Simonelli Mythos One x3, Mahlkönig Tanzania

Espresso	£2.20
Cappuccino	£2.90
Latte	£2.90
Flat white	£2.80

MAP REF. 190

COFFEE 4.25 / 5
OVERALL 4.25 / 5 ★★★★⯪

Lumberjack

70 Camberwell Church Street, SE5 8QZ

Lumberjack puts a lot of emphasis on what it calls the three C's: coffee, craftsmanship and community. Part of a charity that works to help local young people into employment by training them in carpentry or coffee, it tries to buy everything from the local south London community. You wouldn't know about the charity angle from the Lumberjack operation, however: this is a professionally managed place, with excellent food and terrific coffee. It's also a perfect local hangout, whether you're accompanied by friends, your devices, or a good book. Every high street needs a place like Lumberjack. Lucky Camberwell - it already has one.

+44(0)20 7207 9567
wearelumberjack.co.uk
⊖ Denmark Hill

MON-FRI.	7:30am - 6:00pm
SAT.	9:00am - 6:00pm
SUN.	10:00am - 4:00pm

First opened 2016
Roaster Assembly
Machine La Marzocco Linea AV, 2 groups
Grinder Mazzer Robur

Espresso	£2.20
Cappuccino	£2.70
Latte	£2.90
Flat white	£2.70

MAP REF.

 COFFEE 4.25 / 5   **OVERALL** 4.25 / 5  ★★★★✬

Monmouth Coffee Company Borough

2 Park Street, SE1 9AB

The name Monmouth is legendary in the London coffee scene, so be prepared to queue here at peak times. This location is much bigger than the original in Covent Garden, but seating is still fairly limited. Going well outside peak times - and the two peak days - is your best bet for enjoying some of London's best coffee. They make espresso-based drinks expertly, but filter is the real glory here. You'll get no choice on the milk front, just full fat Jersey - that's the way they think it shows off the beans best. Though a grand old lady of the London bean scene, Monmouth shows no sign of ageing.

+44(0)20 7232 3010
www.monmouthcoffee.co.uk
⊖ London Bridge

MON-SAT. 7:30am - 6:00pm
SUN. Closed

First opened 2001
Roaster Monmouth Coffee Company
Machine La Marzocco Linea, 2 groups x2
Grinder Mazzer Robur x2

Espresso	£1.70
Cappuccino	£2.70
Latte	£2.70
Flat white	£2.70

Sister locations Covent Garden / Bermondsey

MAP REF.

COFFEE 4.50 / 5 🫘🫘🫘🫘🫘 **OVERALL** 4.50 / 5 ★★★★⯪

No. 50 Friendly Street

50 Friendly Street, SE8 4DR

The owners of No. 50 say that outsiders often express their surprise at discovering the place. And by 'outsiders' they mean people who live just a few streets away. That's how unexpected this lovely little place is, in a beautiful residential area not far from St Johns railway station: you're most likely to discover it by accident, or by word of mouth. And there's been plenty of word of mouth since they opened last year. No. 50 is the only place in the area for excellent coffee, Ozone beans expertly pulled through their La Marzocco. It's right across the road from a nice little park, and you can park yourself there after grabbing a drink and a cake. But don't pass up the chance to sit in the sunny front room or the smaller back room with a comfy sofa for meetings or serious chilling.

+44(0)20 8305 8438

 St Johns Rail / Deptford Bridge Rail

MON-FRI.	7:00am - 5:00pm
SAT-SUN.	9:00am - 5:00pm

First opened 2017
Roaster Ozone Coffee Roasters
Machine La Marzocco PB AV, 2 groups
Grinder Nuova Simonelli Mythos One

Espresso	£2.00
Cappuccino	£2.70
Latte	£2.70
Flat white	£2.70

MAP REF. 193

COFFEE 4.25 / 5

OVERALL 4.00 / 5 ★★★★☆

Old Spike Roastery

54 Peckham Rye, SE15 4JR

Old Spike would be an admirable outfit even if it didn't make good coffee. It was founded in 2015 as a social enterprise aimed at helping people cope with homelessness by training them in the coffee trade. This tiny café showcases their beans, all of them presented as single-origin and therefore a good candidate for ordering from a filter. And don't pass up the opportunity to pick up your own bag of freshly roasted beans while you're there.

www.oldspikeroastery.com

⊖ Peckham Rye

MON-FRI.	7:30am - 3:00pm
SAT-SUN.	9:00am - 5:00pm

First opened 2015
Roaster Old Spike Roastery
Machine La Cimbali M28
Grinder Anfim Super Caimano, Ditting KR1403

Espresso	£2.00
Cappuccino	£2.50
Latte	£2.50
Flat white	£2.50

MAP REF. 194

 **COFFEE** 4.00 / 5

 **OVERALL** 3.75 / 5 ★★★★☆

Rabot 1745

2-4 Bedale Street, SE1 9AL

Rabot 1745 is a chocolate-lovers paradise. Almost every item on the carefully curated menu has an element of chocolate, from the cocoa infused gin cocktails to the white chocolate mash (a surprising delight). The venue consists of a vibrant café downstairs and an elegant cocoa degustation upstairs. Make sure to try their signature burger, complete with a 70% ganache centre - a real stand out dish. But it's not only cocoa that takes the stage here - let's not forget the 'other' bean. Whether you're popping in for a quick espresso, or finishing your meal with a fragrant flat white, the baristas are experts at getting the most from both beans. Sit back, indulge yourself, and watch the hustle and bustle of Borough Market go by below you.

www.hotelchocolat.com/uk/restaurants/rabot-1745

⊖ London Bridge

MON.	8:00am - 6:00pm
TUE-FRI.	7:30am - 10:00pm
SAT.	9:00am - 10:00pm
SUN.	9:00am - 6:00pm

First opened 2013
Roaster Hotel Chocolat
Machine La Marzocco GB5, 3 groups
Grinder Nuova Simonelli Mythos One

Espresso	£1.95
Cappuccino	£2.75
Latte	£2.75
Flat white	£2.75

MAP REF. 195

COFFEE 4.25 / 5

OVERALL 4.50 / 5

Red Lion Coffee Co.

Corner of Batavia Road and Clifton Rise, SE14 6AX

Red Lion gets everything right in a unusual space just a few minutes away from both Fordham Park and Goldsmiths College. Coffee is all from Climpsons beans and the espresso blend shows at its best with beautifully decorated milk on top. There are sweet and savoury baked goods to eat, hot dishes of the day, and small selections of beer and wine. An oasis of good coffee in New Cross, Red Lion has proven to be a roaring success.

www.redlioncoffee.co.uk
New Cross Gate

MON-WED.	8:00am - 5:00pm
THU-FRI.	8:00am - 8:00pm
SAT-SUN.	9:00am - 5:00pm

First opened 2016
Roaster Climpson & Sons
Machine La Marzocco Linea PB, 2 groups
Grinder Nuova Simonelli Mythos One, Mazzer Super Jolly

Espresso	£2.00
Cappuccino	£2.80
Latte	£2.80
Flat white	£2.80

MAP REF. 196

COFFEE 4.25 / 5

OVERALL 4.00 / 5 ★★★★

Small White Elephant

28 Choumert Road, SE15 4SE

For those days when you're furious with the world, we prescribe a trip to Small White Elephant. This café is a calming sanctuary run by Dale Carney and Jehn Richardson, two of the nicest people ever to open a coffee shop. Let us count the ways they will make you smile: local art on the walls, a veritable jungle of plants, tasty Alchemy coffee, and even monthly jazz and poetry nights. We must also mention the French toast. This is the real deal, triumphant coconutty slabs saturated in syrup. Whatever your day has thrown at you, Small White Elephant has a remedy.

www.smallwhiteelephant.com
Peckham Rye

MON-FRI.	9:00am - 5:30pm
SAT.	9:30am - 5:00pm
SUN.	10:00am - 5:00pm

First opened 2014
Roaster Alchemy Coffee, Curve Roasters
Machine La Marzocco GB5, 2 groups
Grinder Anfim Milano v.240-50

Espresso	£2.10
Cappuccino	£2.80
Latte	£3.00
Flat white	£2.60

MAP REF. 197

COFFEE 4.25 / 5

OVERALL 4.25 / 5 ★★★★

Spike + Earl

31 Peckham Road, SE5 8UB

Following on from the success of Old Spike comes Spike + Earl, an 'all day café, bar, and coffee roastery'. Set within clean whitewashed walls and cinderblocks, the minimal aesthetic is reflected in the simple but curated menus of coffee, brunch, drinks, and evening dishes. If you are here at mealtimes, be sure to sample one of their tasty and beautifully presented main meals, or treat yourself to a pastry or cake if you want something lighter. Their cocktail menu is also one to try, with exciting and reasonably prices cocktails being a great choice for an evening with friends.

Pull up a chair and watch Old Spike's coffee get roasted in the back room or relax over a filter coffee with one of south London's local newspapers or magazines, available from a pile in front of the Faema machine. The outside seating area is perfect for relaxing with friends on a sunny day, sipping a fresh lemonade and tucking into a mouth-watering burger. It's almost too easy to while away the hours from morning 'til evening in this café that not only has it all, but does it all well.

MAP REF. **198**

| COFFEE 4.50 / 5 | | OVERALL 4.25 / 5 | |

MON-THU.	8:00am - 4:00pm
FRI-SAT.	8:00am - 11:00pm
SUN.	8:00am - 4:00pm

Sister locations Old Spike Roastery

First opened 2017
Roaster Old Spike Roastery
Machine Faema E71, 2 groups
Grinder Mazzer ZM

Espresso	£2.00
Cappuccino	£2.70
Latte	£2.70
Flat white	£2.70

www.spikeandearl.com
≷ Denmark Hill Rail

St. David Coffee House

5 David's Road, SE23 3EP

St David is a treasure. A short distance from the local rail station, this is a charmingly decked-out place in a beautiful old terrace. The kitchen offers great treats from the in-house bakery as well as breakfast and brunch dishes of impeccable quality. And there are regular popups where some really exciting food can be paired with craft beer or wine. Coffee comes from Square Mile and it's brewed with skill and love. The only drawback is that you're going to be competing for space with lots and lots of Forest Hill locals. They know a good thing when they see it.

+44(0)20 8291 6646

⊖ Forest Hill

MON.	Closed
TUE–THU.	8:00am – 5:00pm
FRI.	8:00am – 11:00pm
SAT.	9:00am – 5:00pm
SUN.	10:00am – 4:00pm

First opened 2010
Roaster Square Mile Coffee Roasters and guests
Machine Victoria Arduino White Eagle, 3 groups
Grinder Victoria Arduino Mythos One

Espresso	£2.10
Cappuccino	£2.60
Latte	£2.60
Flat white	£2.50

MAP REF. **199**

COFFEE
4.00 / 5

OVERALL
4.00 / 5
★★★★☆

Tate Boiler House Kitchen and Bar

Tate Modern, Bankside, SE1 9TG

The view of St Paul's is enough to make a visit to Tate Kitchen and Bar worthwhile. But it's not the only reason to come here. Using the Tate's own beans, the baristas brew up fabulous drinks in their pair of gleaming Modbars and in filter. The house espresso blend is sweet and rounded enough to drink without sugar or milk, though the milky versions are extremely well made. Enjoy them after a meal (the cooking is simple but well done) or in one of the comfortable seats by the window. Which is closer, of course, to That View.

+44(0)20 7401 5108
www.tate.org.uk/visit/tate-modern/
kitchen-and-bar
⊖ Blackfriars

| SUN–THU. | 10:00am – 5:30pm |
| FRI–SAT. | 10:00am – 9:30pm |

First opened 2016
Roaster Tate Coffee
Machine Modbar, 4 groups
Grinder Nuova Simonelli Mythos One

Espresso	£2.55
Cappuccino	£3.35
Latte	£3.35
Flat white	£3.45

MAP REF. 200

COFFEE
4.25 / 5

OVERALL
4.50 / 5 ★★★★½

Volcano Coffee House

Parkhall Trading Estate, 40 Martell Road, SE21 8EN

TOP 35

Volcano Coffee Works has an unlikely location on a small industrial estate in otherwise strictly residential West Dulwich. The café is attached to Volcano's roaster, but it's far from being an afterthought – and it's become a valuable resource in an area that isn't exactly bursting with places to eat and drink. The food is standard fare, with sandwiches, baked goods and a few cooked dishes. It's served in a huge room with lots of space for spreading out and settling in. And needless to say, the coffee is great: single estate filters alongside the house espresso blends mean a beautiful brew no matter your mood.

+44(0)20 8670 8927
www.volcanocoffeeworks.com
⇌ West Norwood Rail / West Dulwich Rail

MON–FRI.	8:00am – 4:00pm
SAT.	9:00am – 4:00pm
SUN.	Closed

First opened 2012
Roaster Volcano Coffee Works
Machine La Marzocco Linea, 2 groups
Grinder Nuova Simonelli Mythos One

Espresso	£2.30
Cappuccino	£2.60
Latte	£2.60
Flat white	£2.60

MAP REF. 201

COFFEE 4.75 / 5

OVERALL 4.50 / 5   ★★★★½

The Watch House

199 Bermondsey Street, SE1 3UW

During the nineteenth century, the fascinating Watch House building housed guards protecting the churchyard of St Mary Magdalen against body-snatchers. This unique octagonal space has been transformed into a cosy retreat complete with rustic wooden lampshades, underfloor heating, and even a wood-burning hearth. Happily, The Watch House doesn't disappoint Bermondsey Street's discerning food lovers. In addition to hand-roasted Ozone coffee, the counter is stacked high with homemade sandwiches and indulgent goodies.

+44(0)20 7407 6431
www.watchhousecoffee.com
⊖ London Bridge

MON–SUN. 7:00am - 6:00pm

First opened 2014
Roaster Ozone Coffee Roasters
Machine La Marzocco Linea PB, 2 groups
Grinder Nuova Simonelli Mythos

Espresso	£2.40
Cappuccino	£3.00
Latte	£3.00
Flat white	£2.80

Sister locations Tower Bridge / Fetter Lane

MAP REF. 202

COFFEE 4.00 / 5

OVERALL 4.25 / 5 ★★★★★

PROFESSIONAL
— GUIDE TO —
Steaming
FOR EVERYONE

 1

Keep It Cool!
Pour chilled, keep steam temperature lower than milk *(à la cappuccino).*

 2

While stretching you should hear *a whisper.*

3

After 3-5 seconds, tip pitcher to side to begin *whirlpool.*

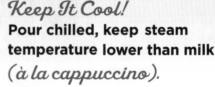

Chat with @CalifiaFarms

www.califiafarms.co.uk
For information or sales inquiries,
contact: hello@califiafarms.com

Steams·
REMARKABLY

BARISTA | CHOICE

Available at

WHOLE
FOODS
MARKET

Chill For Better Steaming
ORIGINAL
BARISTA · CHOICE

CALIFIA
FARMS®

BARISTA
BLEND

ALMOND
DAIRY FREE
CARRAGEENAN FREE
SOY FREE

STEAMS REMARKABLY

946 ml

CARRAGEENAN FREE

KOSHER

VEGAN

BPA FREE

GLUTEN FREE

NON GMO Project VERIFIED
nongmoproject.org

South West London contains a dizzying array of cultural influences, from the Afro-Caribbean heritage of Brixton to the Antipodean-influenced lifestyle of Clapham and the genteel suburban rhythms of Putney. The area's colourful and creative coffee culture reflects these unique influences and local quirks.

South West

Artisan East Sheen

139 Sheen Lane, SW14 8LR

Artisan's East Sheen location occupies a great spot, with light flooding in through huge windows and recycled wood décor that will put a smile on your face. Behind the big counter, the baristas know just what to do with Allpress beans - and with textured milk, too. But the greatest thing is the warm and welcome feel. The owners say this area has a distinctive village feel, and 'a lot of customers bring their cups and plates up to the counter when they're finished.' Just like home.

+44(0)7712 657 476
www.artisancoffee.co.uk
⊖ Mortlake

Sister locations Ealing / Stamford Brook / Putney

MON-FRI.	7:30am – 5:00pm
SAT.	8:00am – 5:00pm
SUN.	8:30am – 5:00pm

First opened 2015
Roaster Allpress Espresso,
Curious Roo Coffee Roasters
Machine La Marzocco FB80, 3 groups
Grinder Victoria Arduino Mythos One,
Mahlkönig Tanzania

Espresso	£2.20
Cappuccino	£2.70 / £2.90
Latte	£2.70 / £2.90
Flat white	£2.90

MAP REF. 203

COFFEE 4.50 / 5	OVERALL 4.50 / 5

Artisan Putney

203 Upper Richmond Road, SW15 6SG

Artisan Putney has a natural, effortless rapport with the local community. Whenever you come here, you see young and old, hip and not-so-hip, singles, doubles, groups. And always lots of young parents with children, who are made more than welcome. The cheery corner spot with its big windows is one draw, but the high quality of the food and drink offer is the main attraction. Baked goods are sensational, and beans from Allpress and Curious Roo go into making wonderful cups every time.

+44(0)20 8617 3477
www.artisancoffee.co.uk
⊖ East Putney / ⇌ Putney Rail

Sister locations Ealing / Stamford Brook / East Sheen

MON-FRI.	7:00am – 6:00pm
SAT.	8:00am – 6:00pm
SUN.	8:30am – 6:00pm

First opened 2011
Roaster Allpress Espresso, Curious Roo Coffee Roasters
Machine La Marzocco FB80, 3 groups
Grinder Victoria Arduino Mythos One, Mahlkönig Tanzania

Espresso	£2.20
Cappuccino	£2.70 / £2.90
Latte	£2.70 / £2.90
Flat white	£2.90

MAP REF. **204**

| COFFEE 4.50 / 5 | | OVERALL 4.50 / 5 | ★★★★✬ |

Batch & Co Coffee

54 Streatham Hill, SW2 4RD

Jen Batchelor, the owner of Batch, wants it to be a community centre - her background is in social enterprise and community work. But there's a lot more to Batch than good intentions: this is a great local. The food is great, with sandwiches, toasties, and pastries all strong points, and they've got Caravan to roast a bespoke espresso blend for them. If you're dawdling a while in the 'lending library' at the back, a V60 from the changing selection of single-origin beans may be your drink of choice.

+44(0)20 8616 6767
www.batchandco.com
⇌ Streatham Hill Rail

MON-FRI.	7:00am – 4:30pm
SAT.	9:00am – 5:00pm
SUN.	10:00am – 4:00pm

First opened 2016
Roaster Caravan Coffee Roasters
Machine La Marzocco Linea Classic, 2 groups
Grinder Mazzer Robur E, Mazzer Jolly

Espresso	£2.30
Cappuccino	£2.70
Latte	£2.70
Flat white	£2.70

MAP REF. **205**

| COFFEE 4.25 / 5 | | OVERALL 4.00 / 5 | ★★★★☆ |

Birdhouse

123 St John's Hill, SW11 1SZ

MON–FRI.	7:00am – 4:00pm
SAT–SUN.	9:00am – 5:00pm

Birdhouse has changed little since it opened in 2011. And that's great, because it was perfect right from the start. They've always taken exceptional care with every detail of their small, focussed offering both in drinks and in food. And in the décor – cool grey walls livened up by colourful pictures. They make a Climpsons espresso perfectly, brewing to preserve maximum sweetness. And if it's too early for one of their excellent sandwiches, indulge in one of their antipodean-style baked goods. Fly over to Birdhouse – a worthy competitor in the Wandsworth coffee scene.

+44(0)20 7228 6663
www.birdhou.se
⊖ Clapham Junction

First opened 2011
Roaster Climpson & Sons
Machine La Marzocco Linea, 3 groups
Grinder Anfim, Mazzer Robur E

Espresso	£2.20
Cappuccino	£2.60 / £2.90
Latte	£2.60 / £2.90
Flat white	£2.60

MAP REF.

COFFEE 4.50 / 5	OVERALL 4.25 / 5

The Black Lab Coffee House

18 Clapham Common Southside, SW4 7AB

The Black Lab Coffee House is a warm and cosy place to enjoy your coffee. The venue has comfortable seating and is a great place to catch up with friends but can fill up rapidly at weekends. Black Lab has a great coffee offering with a roster including Alchemy, Round Hill and Square Mile. They also offer a range of home brewing gear and beans ground to order. Single estate coffees, brewed by AeroPress, are also offered at less busy periods.

+44(0)20 7738 8441
www.blacklabcoffee.com
⊖ Clapham Common

MON-FRI.	7:00am – 5:00pm
SAT.	8:00am – 4:30pm
SUN.	9:00am – 4:30pm

First opened 2010
Roaster 8 rotating UK roasters
Machine La Marzocco Linea PB, 2 groups
Grinder Mazzer Kony x2, Nuova Simonelli Mythos One x2, Mahlkönig EK 43

Espresso	£2.00
Cappuccino	£2.90
Latte	£3.00
Flat white	£2.80

MAP REF.

COFFEE 4.25 / 5

OVERALL 4.25 / 5 ★★★★⯪

Brew

45 Northcote Road, SW11 1NJ

Brew is one of the best Australian-style café groups, and their Battersea branch is justly popular with locals. Now ten years old, it always seems to have a crowd outside at weekends eager for one of the best brunches in the area. While Brew takes a lot of pride in its careful sourcing of raw food ingredients, it takes equal care with coffee; all espresso-based drinks using Allpress beans, and the milk art is particularly lovely. Arrive early if you want to be sure of getting a seat.

+44(0)20 7585 2198
www.brew-cafe.com
Clapham Junction

Sister locations Wimbledon / Wandsworth / Chiswick

SUN-MON.	7:00am - 5:00pm
TUE-WED.	7:00am - 8:00pm
THU-SAT.	7:00am -10:00pm

First opened 2008
Roaster Allpress Espresso
Machine La Marzocco Linea Classic, 2 groups
Grinder Mazzer Major

Espresso	£2.60
Cappuccino	£2.90
Latte	£2.90
Flat white	£2.90

MAP REF. 208

COFFEE 4.00 / 5

OVERALL 4.25 / 5 ★★★★½

Brickwood Balham

11 Hildreth Street, SW12 9RQ

This place looks outstanding. Corrugated steel, distressed woods and recycled coffee bags dominate the décor - you can almost imagine you're riding the rails in a 1930s American black-and-white movie. The appearance is rugged, but the coffee and service are smooth and polished. The Brickwood interpretation of Caravan's blend produces great results, crema standing proud in a little glass beaker. All the food for the three branches is cooked here, so it's always in tiptop shape - like everything else at this lovely hangout.

+44(0)20 8772 6818
www.brickwoodlondon.com
 Balham

MON-FRI.	7:00am - 6:00pm
SAT-SUN.	9:00am - 6:00pm

First opened 2015
Roaster Caravan Coffee Roasters
Machine La Marzocco FB70, 2 groups
Grinder Mazzer Robur

Espresso	£2.50
Cappuccino	£2.80
Latte	£2.80
Flat white	£2.80

Sister locations Clapham / Tooting / Streatham

MAP REF. 209

COFFEE 4.25 / 5

OVERALL 4.25 / 5

Brickwood Clapham

16 Clapham Common South Side, SW4 7AB

The Clapham Brickwood is perfectly located right near the Common, but would do well anywhere. The food is standard breakfast/brunch fare but done to a very high quality and with a lot of flair. The look of the place also follows well-trodden paths, with bare brick and rough wood much in evidence, but that too is beautifully executed. And the coffee's great, with beans from Caravan and flawless technical skill in the execution. Huge popularity with all of south London's coffee-loving population means that the place is crowded and heaving at weekends. When you take a seat, you'll see why.

+44(0)20 7819 9614
www.brickwoodlondon.com
Clapham Common

| MON-FRI. | 7:00am – 6:00pm |
| SAT-SUN. | 9:00am – 6:00pm |

First opened 2013
Roaster Caravan Coffee Roasters
Machine La Marzocco FB80, 2 groups
Grinder Mazzer Luigi

Espresso	£2.50
Cappuccino	£2.70
Latte	£2.70
Flat white	£2.70

Sister locations Balham / Tooting / Streatham

MAP REF. 210

COFFEE 4.25 / 5

OVERALL 4.50 / 5 ★★★★½

Brickwood Tooting

21 Tooting High Street, SW17 0SN

The newest of the Brickwood venues, this corner spot in Tooting Market has become a hugely popular destination for weekend breakfast/brunch/lunch. Be prepared for queues, in other words. Weekdays are quieter, but there may still be a good lunchtime crowd: friends of all ages, sometimes with babies in tow, eating toasties, eggs or salads. Brickwood's variation on the Caravan espresso blend produces a cup with fine red-berry sweetness, a perfect companion while you watch market life pass before your eyes.

+44(0)20 7819 9614
www.brickwoodlondon.com
Tooting Broadway

| MON-FRI. | 7:00am – 6:00pm |
| SAT-SUN. | 9:00am – 6:00pm |

First opened 2015
Roaster Caravan Coffee Roasters
Machine La Marzocco FB70, 2 groups
Grinder Mazzer Luigi

Espresso	£2.30 / £2.50
Cappuccino	£2.60 / £2.80
Latte	£2.60 / £2.80
Flat white	£2.60 / £2.80

Sister locations Clapham / Balham / Streatham

MAP REF. 211

COFFEE 4.25 / 5

OVERALL 4.25 / 5 ★★★★½

Brixton Blend

8 Tunstall Road, SW9 8BN

Brixton Blend sits bang opposite the David Bowie mural, and it's a welcome indie in an area dominated by chains. Expect three things here: a nice-looking space, friendly service, and excellent coffee - some of the best latte art we've seen floated on a BB latte. You'll be offered your choice of Nude or Volcano for an espresso-based drink, which is a nice touch. Make sure to pair your brew with one of BB's delicious treats; choose from a range of tantalising pastries, cakes and sandwiches. Whether you sit in or take it with you, you'll be on to a winner with any BB brew.

+44(0)20 7733 0775
www.brixtonblend.co.uk
⊖ Brixton

Sister locations Brockwell Blend

MON-FRI.	7:00am - 5:00pm
SAT.	9:00am - 5:00pm
SUN.	9:30am - 5:00pm

First opened 2016
Roaster Nude Coffee Roasters, Volcano Coffee Works
Machine La Marzocco GB5, 3 groups
Grinder Nuova Simonelli Mythos One, Mazzer Mini, Mahlkönig EK 43

Espresso	£2.10
Cappuccino	£2.80
Latte	£2.80
Flat white	£2.80

MAP REF.

 COFFEE 4.25 / 5   **OVERALL** 4.00 / 5

231

Brockwell Blend

19 Tulse Hill, SW2 2TH

This sister café to Brixton Blend has a great location just a few minutes away from Brockwell Park. Locals going for a walk in the greenery can (and do) stop in to fetch something hot to drink while they exercise the pooch or the kiddies. But it's worth stopping here, too. The space is attractive, the WiFi's good, and there's outdoor seating at the back. Not to mention some good sandwiches (bagels are a strong point) and extremely well-made coffees, all espresso-based, from Nude and Volcano.

www.brockwellblend.co.uk
⊖ Brixton

Sister locations Brixton Blend

MON-FRI.	7:00am – 4:00pm
SAT.	8:00am – 4:00pm
SUN.	9:30am – 4:00pm

First opened 2016
Roaster Nude Coffee Roasters, Volcano Coffee Works
Machine La Marzocco GB, 2 groups
Grinder Nuova Simonelli Mythos One

Espresso	£2.10
Cappuccino	£2.80
Latte	£2.80
Flat white	£2.80

MAP REF. 213

COFFEE 4.25 / 5		OVERALL 4.25 / 5	★★★★⯪

Brother Marcus

9 Chestnut Grove, SW12 8JA

Brother Marcus is a lively local with very friendly baristas. Beans come from Caravan and keep the La Marzocco Linea working hard throughout the day. Food focuses on brunch dishes with some excruciatingly punning names, which you can enjoy with a cocktail if you're in the mood. The evenings often feature popup supper clubs (they're very popular; book well in advance). And check out their hidden garden out the back; a lovely retreat. Brother Marcus sits less than 50 metres away from Balham station, so it's also a good place to pick up your pick-me-up before the morning commute.

+44(0)20 3674 2141
brothermarcus.co.uk
⊖ Balham

MON-FRI.	8:00am – 4:30pm
SAT.	9:00am – 4:00pm
SUN.	9:30am – 4:00pm

First opened 2016
Roaster Caravan Coffee Roasters
Machine La Marzocco Linea, 2 groups
Grinder Fiorenzato F64 EVO

Espresso	£2.00
Cappuccino	£2.50
Latte	£2.50
Flat white	£2.50

MAP REF. 214

COFFEE 4.25 / 5		OVERALL 4.00 / 5	★★★★☆

Bump&Grind

64 Clapham High Street, SW4 7UW

Walking down Clapham High Street, you may be surprised to see a large Lego head peering out at you from the windows of 64th and Social. Even more surprising is to find out that the venue - a bar and local hotspot by night - is home to an excellent café by day. Sip your beverage of choice in Bump&Grind's bright yellow cups (to match the Lego, of course) or grab a cuppa to takeaway. You can also sample Mat's espresso on the bar menu as the eponymous Bump&Grind espresso martini.

bumpandgrind.london
⊖ Clapham North

Sister locations Venn St Market

MON–TUE.	7:30am – 2:00pm
WED.	Closed
THU–FRI.	7:30am – 2:00pm
SAT–SUN.	Closed

First opened 2014
Roaster Climpson & Sons
Machine Promac Green Compact ME, 2 groups
Grinder Mazzer Super Jolly E

Espresso	£2.20
Cappuccino	£2.70
Latte	£2.70
Flat white	£2.70

MAP REF. **215**

COFFEE 4.00 / 5		OVERALL 4.00 / 5 ★★★★☆

Café Fleur

198 St Ann's Hill, SW18 2RT

Many of London's cafés buy in at least part of the food they serve, especially baked stuff, but at Café Fleur it's 100 per cent home-made. They'll even bake you birthday and wedding cakes if you want one. But you can also just settle down with breakfast or lunch, perhaps with a glass of organic wine or craft beer. The coffee comes from Brixton's own Volcano roastery, and it's served up by a friendly team with some particularly lovely latte art in evidence.

+44(0)20 8874 1930
www.cafefleurwandsworth.com
≋ Wandsworth Town Rail

MON-FRI.	8:00am - 5:00pm
SAT-SUN.	9:00am - 4:00pm

First opened 2013
Roaster Volcano Coffee Works
Machine La Marzocco FB80,. 2 groups
Grinder Victoria Arduino Mythos One

Espresso	£2.20
Cappuccino	£2.80
Latte	£2.80
Flat white	£2.40

MAP REF. **216**

COFFEE 4.00 / 5 **OVERALL** 4.25 / 5 ★★★★½

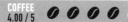

234

Caya

344 Coldharbour Lane, SW9 8QH

Set away from the centre of Brixton's lively scene, Caya is an attractive place with two separate areas: a café at the front and a custom-made 'work space' at the back with a long table, electrical outlets, and WiFi that promises blazing-fast speeds. You rent space in the back by the hour or the day, with bottomless coffee or tea, so you get your workspace for a very reasonable rent. If you're just relaxing, however, the comfortable front area is a lovely place to enjoy Ozone's espresso blend (best with milk) or a single-origin filter.

www.cayaclub.com

⊖ Brixton

MON-FRI.	7:30am - 5:30pm
SAT-SUN.	8:30am - 5:00pm

First opened 2016
Roaster Ozone Coffee Roasters
Machine La Marzocco Linea AV, 2 groups
Grinder Mazzer Major

Espresso	£2.00
Cappuccino	£2.60
Latte	£2.60
Flat white	£2.60

MAP REF.

COFFEE
4.25 / 5

OVERALL
4.25 / 5 ★★★★⯪

The Eclectic Collection

575 Garratt Lane, SW18 4ST

Ramtin Fatemi had been collecting antiques of all kinds for years, and planning details of how he'd use them in a coffee shop for many months, before opening The Eclectic Collection in May 2017. The planning paid off. This astoundingly lovely place marries old and new in a way that's simultaneously soothing and amusing. If Mr Fatemi is on the premises, he will happily give you the lowdown on everything in the place, and there are some fascinating objects of great antiquity in the mix. The funny thing is, even the oldest items look as if they had been made specifically for the space they now occupy.

The same attention to detail shines through in the coffee, made mainly using beans from The Barn in Berlin and brewed to maintain exceptional sweetness even in a simple espresso. This was one of the star cups of the year and the milk art is fabulous. Food is taken very seriously, from breakfast through to ambitious cooking at dinner, and short wine and cocktail lists make this a one-stop pleasure-seeking shop. This is one of those places where coffee, food and alcohol all get equal billing.

It took nerve to open such an unusual place in Earlsfield. In this case, the nerve had it right. There's something here for everyone, whether hipsters or young mums with babies in pushchairs. One of the best new openings of 2017, and a model for aspiring coffee-entrepreneurs.

MAP REF.

COFFEE 4.25 / 5	OVERALL 4.50 / 5

MON-THU.	8:00am - 5:00pm	
FRI-SAT.	8:00am - 10.30pm	
SUN.	9:00am - 5:00pm	

First opened 2017
Roaster The Barn and guests
Machine Victoria Arduino Black Eagle,
3 groups
Grinder Nuova Simonelli Mythos One,
Mahlkönig EK 43

Espresso	£2.20
Cappuccino	£2.50 / £2.70
Latte	£2.50 / £2.70
Flat white	£2.50 / £2.70

+44(0)20 8265 2007
theeclecticcollection.co.uk
⊖ Earlsfield

F.Mondays

112a Brixton Hill, SW2 1AH

F.Mondays is a small place, but it has a good choice of seating options including a counter in the window, a few individual tables, and a larger table where 'a good cross-section of the community' gathers round to work, talk, and eat. They come for excellent Alchemy espresso-based brews, and for great-looking food that includes wickedly indulgent cakes. But the best thing here (apart from the coffee) is the exceptionally attractive garden at the back, a hidden haven that will make you forget that the Brixton Hill traffic is just a stone's throw away.

www.fmondayscoffee.com

⊖ Brixton

MON-FRI. 7:00am - 4:00pm
SAT-SUN. 8:00am - 5:00pm

First opened 2014
Roaster Alchemy Coffee
Machine La Marzocco Linea, 2 groups
Grinder Anfim SCODY II,
Mahlkönig Guatemala

Espresso	£2.00
Cappuccino	£2.60
Latte	£2.60
Flat white	£2.50

MAP REF.

 COFFEE 4.00 / 5 **OVERALL** 4.25 / 5 ★★★★✫

Federation Coffee

Unit 77-78 Brixton Village Market, Coldharbour Lane, SW9 8PS

Federation has led a flourishing of foodie culture in the rapidly developing Brixton Village Market and is surrounded by a host of other cafés and restaurants following its lead. The seating arrayed around the outside of the café affords a prime position to people-watch and soak up the lively atmosphere of the covered market. Federation offers a small but high-quality food menu and has a brew bar serving filter coffee with beans from a changing roster of guest roasters.

www.federationcoffee.com
⊖ Brixton

MON-FRI.	8:00am - 5:00pm
SAT.	9:00am - 6:00pm
SUN.	9:00am - 4:00pm

First opened 2010
Roaster Curve Roasters and guests
Machine La Marzocco Linea PB, 3 groups
Grinder Nuova Simonelli Mythos One, Mahlkönig EK 43

Espresso	£2.10
Cappuccino	£2.70
Latte	£2.70
Flat white	£2.70

MAP REF. 220

 COFFEE 4.50 / 5

 OVERALL 4.50 / 5 ★★★★½

Flotsam & Jetsam

4 Bellevue Parade, SW17 7EQ

Proving once again that beginners can do great things in the world of coffee. Kiwi-born Hana McEwan - who had never worked in the business before - has created a first-rate local hangout. The nautical theme in the décor is handled subtly, so it looks 'like a beach house' but doesn't ride the theme too hard. There's a highly accomplished kitchen (weekend brunch is mega-popular) and an equally skilful team working with the Allpress beans. McEwan says, 'We wanted to welcome everyone.' And the locals appreciate it. Great place to sit and relax after a walk on the Common.

+44(0)20 8672 7639
www.flotsamandjetsamcafe.co.uk
⊖ Wandsworth Common

MON-SUN. 8:00am - 5:00pm

First opened 2015
Roaster Allpress Coffee Roasters
Machine La Marzocco Linea PB, 3 groups
Grinder Mazzer Super Jolly, Mazzer Robur

Espresso	£2.00
Cappuccino	£2.70
Latte	£2.70
Flat white	£2.40

MAP REF. 221

COFFEE 4.25 / 5

OVERALL 4.25 / 5 ★★★★⯪

Ground Coffee Society

79 Lower Richmond Road, SW15 1ET

This star of the Putney coffee scene puts Ground Coffee Society's own beans to excellent use in both a three-group La Marzocco Linea, and in batch brews. The menu is short but pushes all the right buttons for brunch and lunch, and baked goods are taken very seriously - check out the cake offering, whatever it happens to be when you visit. They also sell loose-leaf tea or smoothies if that's more to your liking - which of course it shouldn't be. In fine weather, be sure to grab a seat outside.

+44(0)845 862 9994
www.groundcoffeesociety.com
⊖ Putney Bridge / ⇌ Putney Rail

Sister locations Upper Richmond Road

| MON-FRI. | 7:00am - 6:00pm |
| SAT-SUN. | 8:00am - 6:00pm |

First opened 2010
Roaster Ground Coffee Society Roasters
Machine La Marzocco Linea PB, 3 groups
Grinder Victoria Arduino Mythos One x3

Espresso	£2.00
Cappuccino	£2.50 / £2.70
Latte	£2.50 / £2.70
Flat white	£2.50 / £2.70

MAP REF. 222

COFFEE 4.50 / 5  **OVERALL** 4.25 / 5 ★★★★⯨

The Lido Cafe

Brockwell Lido, Dulwich Road, SE24 0PA

We all know that swimming is one of the healthiest things you can do, but any discussion of The Lido must come with a health warning. This place is at the Brockwell Park Lido and it can get insanely busy with both swimmers and non-swimmers. Fortunately, you can book - and it's a good idea at weekends, at least several days in advance if possible. Once you're in, you're set to enjoy a lovely space, the view of the pool, excellent food, and Allpress beans brewed with skill. When it's heaving, service can struggle a little. But it's always accompanied by a smile.

+44(0)20 7737 8183
www.thelidocafe.co.uk
⇌ Herne Hill Rail

| MON-SUN. | 9:00am - 5:00pm |

First opened 2009
Roaster Allpress Espresso
Machine La Marzocco FB80, 3 groups
Grinder Mazzer Robur

Espresso	£1.90
Cappuccino	£2.75
Latte	£2.75
Flat white	£2.60

MAP REF. 223

COFFEE 4.25 / 5   **OVERALL** 4.25 / 5 ★★★★⯨

Milk

20 Bedford Hill, SW12 9RG

Milk is immediately striking for its corner location with great big windows for looking in or out. It's also easily identified by the people queuing outside for a table, who can range in number from a handful to a horde. This is one of Balham's most popular brunch and lunch spots, winning hearts and stomachs with its Australian-inspired menu featuring some of the best egg dishes south of the Thames. Weekdays, outside normal mealtimes, are the best opportunity for sampling the pleasures here. But even when things are crazy, the baristas work patiently and with an artisan's care using their Kees van der Westen machine to pull shot after perfect shot. This place couldn't be better, and Balhamites know it.

+44(0)20 8772 9085
www.milk.london
⊖ Balham

| MON-SAT. | 8:00am - 5:00pm |
| SUN. | 9:00am - 5:00pm |

First opened 2012
Roaster The Barn, Koppi
Machine Kees van der Westen Spirit, 3 groups
Grinder Mahlkönig EK 43, Mahlkönig Peak

Espresso	£2.00
Cappuccino	£2.60
Latte	£2.60
Flat white	£2.60

Sister locations Milk Teeth

MAP REF. 224

COFFEE 4.50 / 5   OVERALL 4.25 / 5 ★★★★☆

Saucer & Cup

159 Arthur Road, SW19 8AD

Saucer & Cup is small in size - tiny really, with seating for just a dozen customers. But it aims for huge quality in everything it does. Beans come from Workshop and you can have them from the La Marzocco or in batch brew form. The counter is loaded throughout the day with great-looking food - everything from sandwiches and salads to indulgent cakes and small bakes. Saucer & Cup lies just outside Wimbledon Park station but it's more than just a pitstop before the morning commute.

+44(0)20 3774 0390
www.saucerandcup.com
Wimbledon Park

MON-FRI.	7:30am - 5:00pm
SAT.	8:30am - 5:00pm
SUN.	9:00am - 4:30pm

First opened 2015
Roaster Workshop Coffee and guests
Machine La Marzocco Strada EP
Grinder Mahlkönig EK 43, Mahlkönig Peak x2

Espresso	£2.20
Cappuccino	£2.80
Latte	£2.80
Flat white	£2.80

MAP REF. 225

COFFEE
4.25 / 5

OVERALL
4.00 / 5 ★★★★☆

Social Pantry Café

170a Lavender Hill, SW11 5TG

This Lavender Hill café is part of a catering company, which helps to explain the emphasis on beautiful presentation. But it's not all about good looks - even though everything here, from the food through the plates to the décor, is designed to be easy on the eye. It's about quality, from the light bites, filling brunches, lovely cakes and biscuits, to the skilfully brewed coffee from Redemption Roasters.

+44(0)20 7924 4066
socialpantry.co.uk
⊖ Clapham Junction

MON–WED.	7:30am – 4:00pm
THU–FRI.	7:30am – 5:00pm
SAT.	8:30am – 5:00pm
SUN.	9:00am – 5:00pm

First opened 2013
Roaster Redemption Roasters
Machine La Marzocco Linea Classic,
2 groups
Grinder Fiorenzato F64 EVO

Espresso	£2.30
Cappuccino	£2.60
Latte	£2.60
Flat white	£2.60

MAP REF.

 COFFEE 4.00 / 5   **OVERALL** 4.00 / 5

Stir Coffee

111 Brixton Hill, SW2 1AA

Photo: Cephas Azariah

Stir is set on a corner site with big windows allowing plenty of natural light to flood in, and the back room is the perfect setting to escape from the outside world. It's impossible not to notice the mouth-watering array of sandwiches, and the baked goods are equally tempting.
The coffee, which is made with care using a variety of roasters, is well made, and latte art is so lovely you won't want to drink it. Friendly and eager service completes the picture at this Brixton local.

+44(0)20 8333 1203
www.stircoffee.co.uk
⊖ Brixton

| MON-FRI. | 7:00am - 5:00pm |
| SAT-SUN. | 8:00am - 5:00pm |

First opened 2016
Roaster Mission Coffee Works, Campbell & Syme, Round Hill Roastery and guests
Machine La Marzocco FB70, 2 groups
Grinder Mazzer ZM, Mahlkönig EK 43

Espresso	£2.20
Cappuccino	£2.70
Latte	£2.70
Flat white	£2.60

MAP REF. **227**

COFFEE
4.25 / 5

OVERALL
4.25 / 5

Story Coffee

115 St John's Hill, SW11 1SZ

TOP
35

Story Coffee rather belongs to a different world. A world where a person's golden time isn't bullied by smartphones, menial tasks, or wailing offspring. A world where delicious things are handed to them across the counter. A world where a beautifully-poured coffee has the power to unscramble the scrambled. Floods of light, blonde wood, fresh flowers on the tables, charming owners and an impeccable list of suppliers: it's all there. Like a great novel, Story transports you to an altogether better place.

+44(0)20 7998 3303
www.storycoffee.co.uk
⊖ Clapham Junction

Sister locations Clapham Junction

MON-FRI.	7:00am - 4:00pm
SAT.	8:00am - 5:00pm
SUN.	9:00am - 5:00pm

First opened 2014
Roaster Square Mile Coffee Roasters and guests
Machine Kees van der Westen Spirit, 2 groups
Grinder Nuova Simonelli Mythos, Mahlkönig EK 43

Espresso	£2.20
Cappuccino	£2.80
Latte	£2.80
Flat white	£2.80

MAP REF. 228

 COFFEE 4.50 / 5 　 OVERALL 4.50 / 5 ★★★★⯪

Tamp Coffee

1 Devonshire Road, W4 2EU

Nestled between the chichi boutiques of Devonshire Road, Tamp resembles a rustic lodge with its wood-clad floor, ceiling, and bar. This isn't just a destination to put your feet up, though. Tamp offers coffee from Bristol-based Extract Coffee Roasters, and even the non-homogenised milk has been carefully sourced from West Sussex's Goodwood Estate, making deliciously sweet and creamy cappuccinos.

www.tampcoffee.co.uk
 Turnham Green

MON–WED.	8:00am – 5:30pm
THU–SAT.	8:00am – 6:00pm
SUN.	9:00am – 6:00pm

First opened 2014
Roaster Extract Coffee Roasters
Machine La Marzocco Linea PB
Grinder Mahlkönig EK 43, Nuova Simonelli Mythos One, Sanremo SR70 EVO

Espresso	£2.00
Cappuccino	£2.80
Latte	£2.80
Flat white	£2.80

MAP REF. 229

COFFEE 4.25 / 5

OVERALL 4.25 / 5 ★★★★✩

Tried & True

279 Upper Richmond Road, SW15 6SP

'Please take a seat. Relax.' Yay! As table service becomes increasingly rare among London's coffee shops, it's one thing that makes a visit to Tried & True such a true pleasure. Add onto that some incredibly friendly service, a generous food offering (they make a much-celebrated pulled pork), and the size of the outdoor seating space - we love the little terrace at the back - and you see a model of a lovely local hangout. And then there's the coffee, Square Mile beans from an FB80 as well as pour over. Take a seat, sit back and let the coffee come to you.

+44(0)20 8789 0410
www.triedandtruecafe.co.uk
≷ Putney Rail

MON-FRI. 8:00am - 4:00pm
SAT-SUN. 8:30am - 4:30pm

First opened 2012
Roaster Square Mile Coffee Roasters
Machine La Marzocco FB80, 3 groups
Grinder Mazzer Robur E, Mazzer Super Jolly

Espresso	£2.20
Cappuccino	£3.00
Latte	£3.20
Flat white	£3.00

MAP REF. **230**

COFFEE 4.25 / 5

OVERALL 4.25 / 5 ★★★★⯪

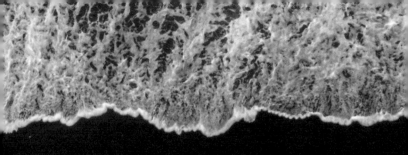

NITRO IS THE NEW BLACK

@newnorthcoffee

TREE OF LIFE
Making health easy

+44 1782 567 120
treeoflife.co.uk

+44 20 8884 1639
jdsfoodgroup.co.uk

NEW NORTH

+44 20 3637 8931
newnorth.coffee

GREAT COFFEE, GOODWILL.

#UKCOFFEEWEEK

Image: Gavin Gough, Splash International

JOIN US FOR UK COFFEE WEEK AND SUPPORT PROJECT WATERFALL, BRINGING CLEAN DRINKING WATER TO COFFEE GROWING COMMUNITIES.

Home to some of London's wealthiest residents, world-renowned museums and lavish department stores, West London has a well established café culture. The number of quality-focussed coffee bars has grown in recent months, but still has a long way to go to match other London neighbourhoods.

West

A Wanted Man

330 King's Road, SW3 5UR

This is a pleasant curiosity, the first UK branch of a Singapore-based café operator (and numerous other non-coffee-related retail businesses). It has a Wild West theme, with wanted posters and such-like. If that strikes you as a strange idea for deepest Chelsea, don't let it deter you. This is a well-run, welcoming place. The high espresso roast is best suited to milky treatments, and the short menu has some imaginative dishes. Upstairs there is a beauty salon specialising in eyebrows and waxing.

+44(0)20 7351 5166
www.awantedman.co.uk
Sloane Square / South Kensington

MON–FRI.	8:00am – 7:00pm
SAT.	9:00am – 7:00pm
SUN.	9:00am – 6:00pm

First opened 2016
Roaster Caravan Coffee Roasters
Machine Synesso Cyncra, 2 groups
Grinder Victoria Arduino Mythos One, Mahlkönig EK 43

Espresso	£2.20
Cappuccino	£3.00
Latte	£3.00
Flat white	£3.00

MAP REF. 231

COFFEE 4.25 / 5

OVERALL 3.75 / 5 ★★★☆

Antipode

28 Fulham Palace Road, W6 9PH

Australians may have afflicted us with Vegemite and Mel Gibson, but when it comes to coffee and brunch, we must concede they have something to be proud of. Antipode embodies the Australian café culture Londoners have grown to adore: velvety 'flatties', delicious smashed avocado on sourdough, and disarmingly casual service. In the evening Antipode whips out a selection of Australian craft beers and wines, with negronis thrown in for good measure. Despite hunkering in the shadow of the Hammersmith flyover, hang out here and you could just as easily be in sunny Melbourne.

+44(0)20 8741 7525
⊖ Hammersmith

MON–WED.	7:00am – 6:00pm
THU.	7:00am – 9:00pm
FRI.	7:00am – 10:00pm
SAT.	8:00am – 10:00pm
SUN.	9:00am – 4:00pm

First opened 2014
Roaster Square Mile Coffee Roasters
Machine La Marzocco Linea PB, 3 groups, Synesso Cyncra, 3 groups
Grinder Nuova Simonelli Mythos One, Mahlkönig EK 43

Espresso	£2.00
Cappuccino	£2.90 / £3.30
Latte	£2.90 / £3.30
Flat white	£2.90 / £3.30

MAP REF. 232

COFFEE 4.25 / 5

OVERALL 4.25 / 5 ★★★★✩

Artisan Ealing

32 New Broadway, W5 2XA

TOP 35

Most coffee entrepreneurs would be content with two successful coffee shops. Not Artisan founders, Edwin and Magda Harrison. Not only have they continued to open new sites, they have also launched a coffee school. Connected to the main café space, the school runs home brewing masterclasses and professional SCAE-accredited qualifications. The Artisan team's enthusiasm is infectious; baristas and trainers alike are eager to surprise customers with superb Allpress and Curious Roo coffees, and constantly challenge themselves in pursuit of coffee excellence.

+44(0)7712 657 475
www.artisancoffee.co.uk
⊖ Ealing Broadway

Sister locations Putney / Stamford Brook / East Sheen

MON-FRI.	7:30am - 5:00pm
SAT.	8:30am - 5:30pm
SUN.	9:00am - 5:30pm

First opened 2014
Roaster Allpress Espresso, Curious Roo Coffee Roasters
Machine La Marzocco FB80, 3 groups
Grinder Victoria Arduino Mythos One, Mahlkönig Tanzania

Espresso	£2.20
Cappuccino	£2.70 / £2.90
Latte	£2.70 / £2.90
Flat white	£2.90

MAP REF. 233

COFFEE 4.75 / 5 🫘🫘🫘🫘🫘

OVERALL 4.50 / 5 ★★★★⯪

Artisan Stamford Brook

372 King Street, W6 0RX

This local legend is loved by people of all ages. The room is big and open, with amply spaced tables and huge windows on two corners providing plenty of natural light. Most people come here for something to eat, and we can see why. But the raison d'etre is coffee brewed from Allpress and Curious Roo beans. This is some of London's best coffee, served with smiling pride.

+44(0)7712 657 474
www.artisancoffee.co.uk
⊖ Stamford Brook

Sister locations Ealing / Putney / East Sheen

MON-FRI.	7:00am – 6:00pm
SAT.	8:00am – 6:00pm
SUN.	8:30am – 6:00pm

First opened 2013
Roaster Allpress Espresso, Curious Roo Coffee Roasters
Machine La Marzocco FB80, 3 groups
Grinder Victoria Arduino Mythos One, Mahlkönig Tanzania

Espresso	£2.20
Cappuccino	£2.70 / £2.90
Latte	£2.70 / £2.90
Flat white	£2.90

MAP REF. **234**

COFFEE 4.50 / 5	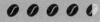	OVERALL 4.50 / 5	★★★★½

Beany Green

Unit 6C, Sheldon Square, W2 6EZ

The area north of Paddington station may not abound in charm, but Beany Green creates its own. From the slightly wacky décor down to the smiling service and indulgent baked goods, this place is just a joy. The food centres on wraps and salads with an Australian-style emphasis on healthy eating – and in quality it is several notches above the London coffee-shop average. Espresso drinks using beans from The Roasting Party have a sweetly rounded character. Here and at its other locations, Beany Green leaves the competition looking green with envy.

+44(0)20 7289 3344
www.daisygreenfood.com
⊖ Paddington

MON-FRI.	7:00am – 6:00pm
SAT-SUN.	9:00am – 6:00pm

First opened 2014
Roaster The Roasting Party
Machine La Marzocco Strada EP, 3 groups
Grinder Mazzer Luigi

Espresso	£2.90
Cappuccino	£2.90
Latte	£2.90
Flat white	£2.90

Sister locations Multiple locations

MAP REF. **235**

COFFEE 4.25 / 5		OVERALL 4.25 / 5	★★★★½

Black Sheep

189 Victoria Street, SW1E 5NE

West

Black Sheep's mission to spread the gospel of specialty robusta has now arrived in Victoria. Sitting next to a busy tube station exit means that this particular outlet is focused on high volume and takeaway. But that doesn't mean that it lacks character. Stepping inside is a breath of fresh air from the staid, suited nature of west London, with graffiti art splashed across the rough wood walls. Bottled cold brew and other refreshing drinks are also available to grab and go; though should you wish to stay and take a break from the hustle and bustle, there are a few tables and high seats available for perching and watching the world rush by.

+44(0)20 3883 3406
www.leavetheherdbehind.com
⊖ Victoria

MON–FRI.	7:00am – 7:00pm
SAT.	8:00am – 6:00pm
SUN.	9:00am – 5:00pm

First opened 2017
Roaster Black Sheep Coffee
Machine Faema E71, 3 groups
Grinder Victoria Arduino Mythos One

Espresso	£2.20
Cappuccino	£3.20
Latte	£3.50
Flat white	£3.00

Sister locations Multiple locations

MAP REF. 236

COFFEE 4.25 / 5

OVERALL 4.25 / 5 ★★★★☆

258

Bluebelles

320 Portobello Road, W10 5RU

Bluebelles has been in W10 since 2012 and has built up a dedicated local following for its warm welcome, soul-satisfying brunch dishes, and outstanding coffee. But it never rests on its laurels and is always looking for ways to raise its game. Coffee is beautifully brewed from Caravan beans, and the display of baked goods is dangerously enticing, with an ever-expanding gluten-free range. Even in an area with no shortage of cafés, Bluebelles is a standout.

+44(0)20 8968 4572
Ladbroke Grove

Sister locations Mill Hill

MON–FRI.	8:30am – 4:30pm
SAT–SUN.	9:00am – 4:30pm

First opened 2012
Roaster Caravan Coffee Roasters
Machine La Marzocco Linea, 2 groups
Grinder Mazzer Robur

Espresso	£1.80
Cappuccino	£2.50
Latte	£2.50
Flat white	£2.80

MAP REF. **237**

COFFEE 4.00 / 5 🫘🫘🫘🫘🫘   OVERALL 4.00 / 5 ★★★★★

Cable Co.

4 Bridge House, Chamberlayne Road, NW10 3NR

The spartan interior of this unassuming coffee bar follows a factory theme: concrete, raw timber, and black tiling contrast with copper lamp shades, which provide welcome flashes of colour. An oil drum repurposed as a sugar station completes the industrial atmosphere. Aromatic Climpson & Sons coffee is complemented by a tempting range of raw vegan and gluten free cakes. And if you're looking for a milk alternative, make sure to sample their house-made almond milk.

cableco.london
⊖ Kensal Rise

MON–FRI.	7:00am – 4:30pm
SAT–SUN.	8:30am – 4:30pm

First opened 2014
Roaster Climpson & Sons
Machine La Marzocco Linea PB, 3 groups
Grinder Victoria Arduino Mythos One, Mazzer Major E, Mahlkönig Tanzania

Espresso	£2.10
Cappuccino	£2.70
Latte	£2.70
Flat white	£2.60

Sister locations Wired Co.

MAP REF. 238

COFFEE 4.25 / 5

OVERALL 4.25 / 5 ★★★★⯨

Chairs and Coffee

512 Fulham Road, SW6 5NJ

Chairs and Coffee is the labour of two friends, Simone Guerini Rocco and Roberto D'alessandro. The duo's passion emanates from every facet of the café: their Italian pride pours from the La Marzocco Linea. Coffee is skilfully extracted from the 80 Stone beans, and the chairs casually suspended from the ceiling (because they like 'being ridiculous') embody their unbridled eccentricity. Truly authentic cafés like Chairs and Coffee are a rarity; this is one to be cherished.

+44(0)20 7018 1913
www.chairsandcoffee.co.uk
⊖ Fulham Broadway

MON–FRI. 8:00am – 5:00pm
SAT–SUN. 9:00am – 5:00pm

First opened 2013
Roaster 80 Stone Coffee Roasters
Machine La Marzocco Linea, 2 groups
Grinder Mazzer Major E, Mahlkönig EK 43

Espresso	£2.00
Cappuccino	£2.50
Latte	£2.50
Flat white	£2.50

Sister locations Elephant and Castle

MAP REF. ②③⑨

COFFEE
4.25 / 5

OVERALL
4.25 / 5 ★ ★ ★ ★ ⯨

Chief Coffee

Turnham Green Terrace Mews, W4 1QU

Located in a mews around the corner from Turnham Green station, Chief Coffee occupies a building that began life as a Victorian bottling factory. Their regular beans come from Workshop and Allpress, but there might also be a guest pour-over from the excellent Barn roaster in Berlin. You can have a light lunch, a cake or one of their brownies. And if you're feeling nimble-fingered, they have a pinball lounge with nine machines. Seriously consider one of those pour overs. But if you order an espresso-based drink, ask for a swan on top.

+44(0)20 8994 0636
www.chief-coffee.com
⊖ Turnham Green

MON–FRI.	8:00am – 5:30pm
SAT.	9:00am – 6:00pm
SUN.	10:00am – 5:30pm

First opened 2015
Roaster Allpress Espresso, Workshop Coffee, The Barn
Machine La Marzocco FB80, 2 groups
Grinder Mahlkönig EK 43, Mazzer Kony

Espresso	£2.20
Cappuccino	£2.80
Latte	£2.80
Flat white	£2.80

MAP REF.

COFFEE 4.25 / 5		OVERALL 4.00 / 5	

Coffee Geek and Friends

Unit 22 Cardinal Place, 6 Cathedral Walk, SW1E 5JH

The new developments around Victoria Station are not exactly big on warmth, but Coffee Geek lives up to the second part of its name: this is a really friendly place. It's a great spot for enjoying lunch, baked goods, or just a beautifully brewed coffee. Two espresso machines (total of five groups) are needed to cope with peak times, and three chefs make most of their baked goods on the premises, a rarity in a place this size. While you're there, be sure to check out the incredibly clever water filtration system.

+44(0)20 3417 3600
www.coffeegeekandfriends.co.uk
◉ Victoria

MON-FRI.	7:00am - 5:00pm
SAT.	9:00am - 5:00pm
SUN.	9:00am - 3:00pm

First opened 2015
Roaster Allpress Espresso
Machine La Marzocco Linea PB, 3 groups, La Marzocco Linea PB, 2 groups
Grinder Nuova Simonelli Mythos One, Mazzer Kold, Mahlkönig EK 43

Espresso	£2.10
Cappuccino	£2.90
Latte	£2.90
Flat white	£2.90

MAP REF. **241**

COFFEE 4.25 / 5

OVERALL 4.25 / 5 ★★★★⯨

District

50 Parsons Green Lane, SW6 4HU

District is one of the exceptional openings of 2017, a place whose tiny size belies its massive commitment to quality. The commitment is particularly noticeable in the baked goods, which are far better than they need to be for a place that caters in large part to takeaways. Get a slice of the banana bread, home-made specially for them. (Customers ask if they can order a whole loaf, and are turned down with regret.) But the quality is also there in the coffee, made from Roasting Party beans. There isn't much space for sitting, but you'll find more seating at their second location in Nine Elms. District is a formula for mega-success; don't be surprised to see them grow and grow.

Parsons Green

Sister locations Nine Elms

MON-FRI.	6:30am – 5:00pm
SAT.	8:00am – 5:00pm
SUN.	9:00am – 4:00pm

First opened 2017
Roaster The Roasting Party
Machine La Marzocco Linea AV, 2 groups
Grinder Nuova Simonelli Mythos One

Espresso	£2.20
Cappuccino	£2.80
Latte	£2.80
Flat white	£2.80

MAP REF.

COFFEE 4.25 / 5	OVERALL 4.25 / 5
	★★★★☆

Electric Coffee Co.

40 Haven Green, W5 2NX

Ealing seems to regard Electric as a precious local resource, and that's an entirely appropriate view: you could plonk this narrow, attractive room down anywhere in London and it would be one of the best coffee hangouts in the area. Coffee from their own roastery produces brews of excellent quality, and it's served with smiling efficiency. The other big draw at Electric - quite apart from its location near Ealing Broadway station for those seeking coffee on the go - is the exciting lunch menu, not just sandwiches but cooked dishes as well. Ealing locals, you are lucky. And you know it.

+44(0)20 8991 1010
www.electriccoffee.co.uk
🚇 Ealing Broadway

Sister locations Helterskelter Beatles Coffee Shop

MON-FRI.	7:00am - 6:00pm
SAT.	8:00am - 6:00pm
SUN.	9:00am - 6:00pm

First opened 2008
Roaster Electric Coffee Co. Roasters
Machine Kees van der Westen Mirage Veloce, 3 groups
Grinder Mazzer Robur E x2, Anfim Super Caimano

Espresso	£2.10
Cappuccino	£2.70 / £2.90
Latte	£2.70 / £2.90
Flat white	£2.70

MAP REF. 243

 COFFEE 4.50 / 5 🫘🫘🫘🫘🫘 **OVERALL** 4.50 / 5 ★★★★⯨

The Elgin

255 Elgin Avenue, W9 1NJ

West

The La Marzocco gets a good workout when The Elgin is busy. And it's busy a lot, even during the week, when local kids (and their parents) congregate for food and drinks. The ground-floor café/bar/restaurant was originally an old-fashioned pub and takes advantage of that large space, now with a combination of traditional and industrial décor. Food is serious, changing three times a day and combining modern British with a good dose of Italian and Spanish flair.

+44(0)20 7625 5511
www.theelgin.com
Maida Vale

MON–THU.	8:00am – 11:00pm
FRI.	8:00am – 12:00am
SAT.	9:00am – 12:00am
SUN.	9:30am – 10:30pm

First opened 2013
Roaster Coleman Coffee Roasters
Machine La Marzocco Linea, 2 groups
Grinder Mazzer Luigi, Mazzer Luigi Robur E

Espresso	£2.40 / £2.80
Cappuccino	£2.80
Latte	£2.80
Flat white	£2.80

MAP REF. 244

COFFEE 4.25 / 5

OVERALL 4.25 / 5 ★★★★

266

Farm Girl

59a Portobello Road, W11 3DB

When Farm Girl first appeared in 2015 on iconic Portobello Road, it quickly became apparent that this was the right place opening at the right time. This Australian outpost has become a major destination, and it's not just because of visitors hitting the antique markets (though Saturday lunch will guarantee a long queue). Its emphasis on healthy living is so hard-core Notting Hill that they cook their omelettes in coconut oil, and don't even offer full-fat milk in their coffees.

+44(0)20 7229 4678
www.thefarmgirl.co.uk
⊖ Notting Hill Gate

Sister locations Chelsea / Soho

MON-FRI.	8:30am - 5:00pm
SAT.	9:00am - 5:00pm
SUN.	9:00am - 4:00pm

First opened 2015
Roaster The Roasting Party
Machine La Marzocco Linea Classic, 3 groups
Grinder Mazzer Kold E

Espresso	£2.20
Cappuccino	£2.90
Latte	£2.90
Flat white	£2.90

MAP REF. **245**

COFFEE 4.25 / 5

OVERALL 4.50 / 5 ★★★★½

Fernandez & Wells South Kensington

8a Exhibition Road, SW7 2HF

If you crave a light meal in South Kensington and don't want to spend a fortune, Fernandez & Wells could be your new best friend. The location is just a few minutes from the Science Museum, Natural History Museum and the V&A. And the place itself is a pleasure to look at, especially the nautical-style lights. Outdoor seating is the ideal choice. In poor weather, indoor seating is fairly abundant and very comfortable. Round-off your meal with a well brewed flat white from Has Bean.

+44(0)20 7589 7473
www.fernandezandwells.com
⊖ South Kensington

Sister locations Denmark Street / Duke Street / Lexington Street / Somerset House

MON.-SAT.	8:00am - 11:00pm
SUN.	8:00am - 8:00pm

First opened 2012
Roaster Has Bean
Machine La Marzocco Linea PB, 3 groups
Grinder Nuova Simonelli Mythos One

Espresso	£2.60
Cappuccino	£2.95
Latte	£2.95
Flat white	£2.95

MAP REF. **246**

COFFEE 4.25 / 5		OVERALL 4.25 / 5	★ ★ ★ ★ ☆

Granger & Co Notting Hill

175 Westbourne Grove, W11 2SB

Bill Granger's Australia-style approach to eating and drinking makes a perfect fit with this posh patch of Notting Hill, which has taken to it enthusiastically. The downside is that if you show up without a booking at mealtimes, you'd better resign yourself to waiting. This is not Granger & Co's biggest site, and even on a cold day there may well be a queue. But it's a pleasure to come outside peak mealtimes for a cookie or piece of fudge, washed down with well-made milky drinks or (our favourite) their cold drip coffee.

+44(0)20 7229 9111
grangerandco.com
⊖ Notting Hill Gate

MON.-SAT.	7:00am - 11:00pm
SUN.	8:00am - 10:30pm

First opened 2011
Roaster Allpress Espresso
Machine La Marzocco Linea AV, 3 groups
Grinder Mazzer Robur, Mazzer Super Jolly

Espresso	£3.00
Cappuccino	£3.00
Latte	£3.00
Flat white	£3.00

Sister locations Chelsea / Clerkenwell / King's Cross

MAP REF. **247**

COFFEE 4.25 / 5		OVERALL 4.25 / 5	★ ★ ★ ★ ☆

Hally's

60 New Kings Road, SW6 4LS

The vibe at Hally's is airy California cool. The reclaimed clapboard and whitewashed brick walls are punctuated by citrus yellow bar stools and neon signs. You may just be popping in for a Monmouth coffee, but be prepared to stay for longer once you catch sight of the food on offer, which includes an outstanding array of salads and a bold-flavoured brunch menu. Across the street, sister shop Little H offers a condensed Hally's menu including breakfast, lunch and fabulous fresh juices and smoothies.

+44(0)20 3302 7408
www.hallyslondon.com
⊖ Parsons Green

Sister locations Little H

MON-SUN. 8:00am - 6:00pm

First opened 2013
Roaster Monmouth Coffee Company
Machine La Marzocco Linea, 2 groups
Grinder Mazzer Kold

Espresso	£2.00
Cappuccino	£2.70 / £3.00
Latte	£2.70 / £3.00
Flat white	£2.70 / £3.00

MAP REF. **248**

COFFEE **4.25 / 5** OVERALL **4.50 / 5** ★★★★½

Iris & June

1 Howick Place, SW1P 1WG

The arrival of Iris & June (named after the owner's grandparents) marked a turning point in the fortunes of the neighbourhood. The interior's concrete floors, exposed ventilation ducts, and industrial tiling gives the café an air of Shoreditch cool. Upon entering, customers are greeted by a sumptuous display of salads and sandwiches behind polished glass. Iris & June feels like a keystone in the new Victoria, injecting a dose of vigour and setting a high standard for a stylish, intelligent coffee bar in an area previously bereft of speciality coffee.

+44(0)20 7828 3130
www.irisandjune.com
⊖ Victoria / St James's Park

MON-FRI.	7:30am – 5:30pm
SAT-SUN.	9:00am – 4:00pm

First opened 2014
Roaster Ozone Coffee Roasters
Machine La Marzocco Strada, 3 groups
Grinder Mazzer Luigi Robur E, Mahlkönig EK 43

Espresso	£2.50
Cappuccino	£2.90
Latte	£2.90
Flat white	£2.90

MAP REF.

COFFEE
4.50 / 5

OVERALL
4.50 / 5

Notes Victoria

Nova Building, 10 Sir Simon Milton Square, SW1E 5DJ

Notes excels at turning small spaces into memorable coffee havens, and their Victoria branch - one of numerous eating and drinking places on the ground floor of the new Nova Building - is yet another example of that skill. The company has a reliable formula: good, simple food and beautifully made coffee from their own beans. Local office workers, tourists and commuters heading for the nearby mainline station - Notes knows how to sing their tune. And the small size means they don't have to attract hordes to do well, unlike some of the competition. A sure winner.

+44(0)20 7976 6335
notes-uk.co.uk
⊖ Victoria

MON-TUE.	7:00am - 7:00pm
WED-FRI.	7:00am - 9:00pm
SAT.	10:00am - 6:30pm
SUN.	10:00am - 5:00pm

First opened 2017
Roaster Notes Coffee Roasters
Machine La Marzocco Linea PB, 2 groups
Grinder Nuova Simonelli Mythos One

Espresso	£2.20
Cappuccino	£3.00
Latte	£3.00
Flat white	£3.00

Sister locations Multiple locations

MAP REF.

 COFFEE 4.25 / 5  OVERALL 4.25 / 5 ★★★★⯪

271

Over Under

181a Earls Court Road, SW5 9RB

Over Under is a tiny little diamond of a place in Earl's Court, an area that doesn't have many jewels in its crown. And the emphasis should be on the word tiny - there's seating here for no more than a dozen or so people. You will probably be able to hear every word spoken by the people at the front of the room, even if you're sitting at the back. That won't bother the busy commuters who crowd in for their morning hit, but if you want to sit down and relax you should plan to come outside rush hour.

What makes Over Under so completely lovable is the happy vibe, the ultra-chilled atmosphere, and the feeling that you're a welcome guest.

The coffee comes from Assembly by way of a two-group Linea, and it is expertly made. Perhaps the nicest thing of all here is that they have music nights, which will startle you when you see the closet-sized space. If you're living or staying in the area, drop in for a coffee and find out when the music's next on. Sounds like a hoot. Note: despite the address, the entrance is in Hogarth Road.

MAP REF. **251**

COFFEE		OVERALL	
4.25 / 5	🫘🫘🫘🫘◗	4.25 / 5	★★★★☆

MON-FRI.	6:30am - 4:30pm
SAT.	8:00am - 4:30pm
SUN.	9:00am - 4:30pm

Sister locations Soho

First opened 2017
Roaster Assembly
Machine La Marzocco Linea AV, 2 groups
Grinder Victoria Arduino Mythos One

Espresso	£2.20
Cappuccino	£2.90
Latte	£2.90
Flat white	£2.90

www.overundercoffee.com
⊖ Earl's Court

Rude Health Café

212 New King's Road, SW6 4NZ

Rude Health is anything but rude: the welcome here is about as warm and smiley as you could ask for. Branching out with its first café, the Rude Health company (makers of healthy food and drink products) has created a space where virtue and hedonism walk hand in hand. It's a pretty small space, and tables may be hard to find at lunchtime. But turnover is fast, so it's definitely worth waiting. The food offering is small but you'll find good salads, sandwiches and baked goods. And the coffee is great; Caravan beans handled with care and artfully decorated.

+44(0)20 7731 3740
rudehealth.com/cafe
⊖ Putney Bridge

MON-FRI.	7:30am – 5:00pm
SAT.	8:30am – 4:00pm
SUN.	Closed

First opened 2017
Roaster Caravan Coffee Roasters
Machine La Marzocco PB, 2 groups
Grinder Mazzer Robur

Espresso	£2.00
Cappuccino	£2.60
Latte	£2.60
Flat white	£2.60

MAP REF.

COFFEE 4.25 / 5

OVERALL 4.25 / 5

Saint Espresso Baker Street

214 Baker Street, NW1 5RT

It's the great cliché about retail businesses: the three things that matter are location, location, and location. On these terms, Saint Baker Street is a three-time winner. Sherlock Holmes's house is across the street; Madame Tussaud is a three-minute walk away; and Regent's Park is even closer. And that's before you even mention the busy station next door. So there's a huge market of local business people and tourists for Saint's very good coffee, their own blends and single origins in espresso and filter. The space here is small but it's attractive, and gives a good view of the busy street outside. The morning rush gets busiest (7:30-9:00), afternoons can be very chilled. Take advantage of it: there's nothing else nearly this good anywhere in the area.

www.saintespresso.com

⊖ Baker Street

MON-FRI.	7:30am - 6:00pm
SAT-SUN.	9:00am - 6:00pm

First opened 2016
Roaster Saint Espresso
Machine La Marzocco PB, 2 groups
Grinder Nuova Simonelli Mythos One, Mahlkönig EK 43

Espresso	£2.30
Cappuccino	£2.80 / £3.20
Latte	£2.80 / £3.20
Flat white	£2.70

Sister locations Angel / Kentish Town / Leyas

MAP REF. 253

  COFFEE 4.50 / 5 OVERALL 4.25 / 5 ★★★★☆

St Clements Cafe

201 New Kings Road, SW6 4SR

The menu at St Clements is so good it presents some tough decisions. Agonising choices must be made between seductive salads and tantalising tarts. Olivia Cundy, a professional chef with ten years' experience, composes marvellous plates of seasonal fare, paired with hand-roasted coffee from Cast Iron Coffee Roasters. The café offers comfortable seating and a delightful terrace opening out to the street. Little details like bone-handled knives and tasteful teal decor lend the café an air of elegance.

+44(0)20 7998 8919
www.stclementscafe.co.uk
⊖ Parsons Green

MON-FRI.	8:00am - 5:00pm
SAT.	8:30am - 5:30pm
SUN.	9:00am - 5:30pm

First opened 2014
Roaster Cast Iron Coffee Roasters
Machine La Marzocco FB80, 2 groups
Grinder Mazzer Kony, Mazzer Super Jolly

Espresso	£2.30
Cappuccino	£3.00
Latte	£3.00
Flat white	£2.80

MAP REF. 254

COFFEE 4.00 / 5   OVERALL 4.25 / 5

Timmy Green

Nova Building, 11 Sir Simon Milton Square, SW1E 5DJ

Timmy Green is a radical departure from the other Beany Green venues; a gleaming modern box, set in a new building near Victoria, with huge windows and two floors. It's also much more a 'proper restaurant': if you want a cocktail or a steak, you'll find it here. But coffee remains at the centre of what they do, whether from the canary-yellow La Marzocco or filter-fed by an SP9 brewer. You can grab and go, but the fabulous space (inside or out) makes it worth perching here for a while.

+44(0)20 3019 7404
www.daisygreenfood.com
⊖ Victoria

Sister locations Multiple locations

| MON-SAT. | 7:30am - 11:00pm |
| SUN. | 9:00am - 10:00pm |

First opened 2017
Roaster The Roasting Party
Machine La Marzocco FB80, 3 groups
Grinder DIP DK-30, Mazzer Kold E

Espresso	£2.20 / £2.60
Cappuccino	£2.90 / £3.20
Latte	£2.90 / £3.20
Flat white	£2.90 / £3.20

MAP REF. 255

COFFEE 4.25 / 5   OVERALL 4.50 / 5

CUPPA, MOCHA, MATCHA.

WE'VE GOT YOU COVERED

NATURALLY FROTHABLE | ORGANIC | NO ARTIFICIAL ANYTHINGS

The London Coffee Festival

28 – 31 MARCH 2019
THE OLD TRUMAN BREWERY

www.londoncoffeefestival.com

Behind every cup of coffee is a unique story. On its journey from coffee tree to cup, coffee passes through the hands of a number of skilled individuals. Over the following pages, expert contributors share their specialist knowledge. As you will see, the coffee we enjoy is the result of a rich and complex process, and there is always something new to learn.

Coffee
Knowledge

Coffee at Origin

by **Mike Riley**, Falcon Speciality Green Coffee Importers

If you go into London's vibrant coffee community today and ask any good barista what makes a perfect cup of coffee, they will always tell you that it starts with the bean. Beyond the roasting technique, the perfect grind, and exact temperatures and precision pressure of a modern espresso machine, we must look to the dedicated coffee farmer who toils away in the tropical lands of Africa, Asia and Latin America. They are the first heroes of our trade.

Approximately 25 million people in over 50 countries are involved in producing coffee. The beans, or seeds to be exact, are extracted from cherries that most commonly ripen red but sometimes orange or yellow. The cherries are usually hand-picked then processed by various means. Sometimes they are dried in the fruit under tropical sunshine until they resemble raisins - a process known as 'natural'. The 'honey process' involves pulping the fresh cherries to extract the beans which are then sundried, still coated in their sticky mucilage. Alternatively, in the 'washed process', the freshly pulped beans are left to stand in tanks of water for several hours where enzyme activity breaks down the mucilage, before they are sundried on concrete patios or raised beds. Each method has a profound impact on the ultimate flavour of the coffee.

The term 'speciality coffee' is used to differentiate the world's best from the rest. This means it has to be Arabica, the species of coffee that is often bestowed with incredible flavours - unlike its hardy cousin Robusta which is usually reserved for commercial products and many instant blends. But being Arabica alone is by no means enough for a coffee to achieve the speciality tag, since the best beans are usually those grown at higher altitude on rich and fertile soils. As well as country and region of origin, the variety is important too; Bourbon, Typica, Caturra, Catuai, Pacamara and Geisha to name but a few. Just as Shiraz and Chardonnay grapes have their own complex flavours, the same is true of coffee's varieties. Some of the world's most amazing coffees are the result of the farmer's innovative approach to experimentation with growing and production techniques, meaning that today's speciality roaster is able to source coffees of incredible complexity and variation.

A good coffee establishment will showcase coffees when they are at their best - freshly harvested and seasonal, just like good fruit and vegetables. Seasonal espresso blends change throughout the year to reflect this.

As speciality coffee importers we source stand-out coffees by regularly travelling to origin countries. Direct trade with farmers is always our aim. Above all, we pay sustainable prices and encourage them to treat their land, and those who work it, with respect. Such an approach is increasingly demanded by London's speciality coffee community in order to safeguard the industry's future.

Small Batch Roasting

by **Kurt Stewart**, Roaster and Co-owner, Volcano Coffee Works

I was brought up in a household dedicated to pickling, baking, sauce making and preserving. After experimenting with home brewing and wine making, my first foray into the aromatic world of small batch roasting was inevitable.

My own first experiments in small batch roasting started at home with some green beans and a wok. Of course roasting at home is much like home cooking, but when the term is applied to a commercial enterprise, it encompasses the passion and adventure of a home cook with the control and precision of a gourmet chef.

The art behind developing and building a roasting profile for a particular coffee is approached in the same way a chef develops cuisine, or a vintner crafts a wine. Culinary rules and science apply in equal measure. The roaster builds layers of flavour, working with the ingredients, sometimes pushing or manipulating the properties of an individual bean, to achieve the desired balance of sweetness, acidity, body, and the right mouth-feel and aftertaste. Coffee and wine share a vocabulary of descriptors, but as coffee has more flavour molecules than wine, coffee descriptors reach further into the culinary world. You will hear words describing aspects of flavour and taste senses, such as fruit acidity, sweet roundness, viscous syrup body, juicy plum, creamy, buttery, velvet chocolate textures. Delicious!

When a green bean is roasted, three fundamental processes occur that impact the flavours of the bean: enzyme by-products develop (giving the floral, citrus and fruity aromas), sugars brown (giving the sweet, caramel and nutty aromas), and plant fibres in the bean are roasted, known as dry-distillation (giving the spicy and smokey flavours). Only the enzyme by-products (which come from the coffee plant itself) are due to the bean chosen for roasting, whilst the remaining two processes are the result of how the bean is roasted. This is why no two small batch roasters will create an identical flavour profile from the same bean. Like chefs, each roaster will identify with, single out and highlight a flavour or combination of flavours which pleases, satisfies or amazes their palate.

Small Batch Roasting is a term reserved for those using roasting equipment controlled by the human hand rather than computers. A skilled roaster who understands his equipment, maintains ducting, understands heat/air ratios and extraction principles, coupled with following some basic fundamentals, can draw out origin characteristics and individual nuances, and create a roast where the optimum flavour potential is realised.

The roasting equipment itself is fundamentally a steel drum, which is usually heated by a gas flame. The drum constantly revolves, and at around 10 minutes of roasting at 203-205°C the developing beans reach 'first crack' (a bit like popcorn cracking). If roasting stops here, it will be a mild or lighter roast. When roasting continues, samples are taken with every revolution of the drum and the roaster observes the developing bean's colour, mass and aroma. The roaster may apply more or less heat or air and will remove the beans once they have reached the desired roast profile. This is usually within a 20 minute roasting time and often before second crack is reached as beyond this point the beans can lose their subtle origin characteristics and begin to take on a generic burnt flavour. The beans then enter the cooling tray until cool to touch. This process is in stark contrast to the large scale computer controlled commercial roasting process that takes between 90 seconds and 10 minutes at temperatures in excess of 360 °C. The beans are then doused with water to cool them. Although this is the most economic way to roast beans, it takes away any input by the roaster and does not give the bean enough time to develop fully.

When a roastery operation gets to such a scale that the roaster becomes distanced from their beans due to mechanised roasting processes and machinery, the instinct and hands-on effect that define a small batch roaster's product will always become somewhat diminished. And therein lies the excitement and diversity that small batch roasting offers over and above large-scale operations. It comes down to the physical ability of a talented roaster to exercise his or her senses, passion, enthusiasm, and the art of roasting.

Coffee Tasting

by **Lynsey Harley**, Founder, Modern Standard Coffee

Coffee tasting is the process of identifying the characteristics of a particular coffee. In the coffee industry, professional 'cupping' sessions are conducted to evaluate coffees on a range of attributes. Cupping helps coffee buyers select which coffees to buy, and identify desirable attributes for formulating blends.

Coffee is most commonly scored using The Specialty Coffee Association of America (SCAA) system. Coffees achieving a score of 85 or higher (from a maximum of 100) are regarded as 'specialty' grade. These coffees have no defects and have a very distinct pleasant flavour profile. Coffees are scored on the following attributes: aroma, flavour, aftertaste, acidity, body, sweetness, cleanliness, uniformity and balance.

The cupping process follows a set procedure: 8.25g of coarsely ground coffee is measured into a shallow cup, specifically designed for the purpose. 150ml of water heated to 92°C is added and left for 4 minutes. Next, a spoon is used to break and remove the 'crust', which provides the first opportunity to sample the coffee's aroma. After a further 6 minutes, the cupper begins to taste the coffee. Different attributes are evaluated at intervals as the coffee cools.

70°C: Flavour and Aftertaste

Flavour: The coffee's principle flavour; what are your taste buds telling you?

Aftertaste: The length of positive flavour qualities after the coffee has been swallowed.

70°C – 60°C: Acidity and Body

Acidity: Bright for positive acidity, sour for negative. Positive acidity adds to the coffee's sweetness.

Body: The 'weight' of the brew. Is it heavy like a good red wine, or light and refined like a sauvignon blanc?

38°C: Sweetness and Cleanliness

Sweetness: Is the coffee sweet and pleasing?

Cleanliness: When no defects are found, the cup is clean.

Balance: Greater than the sum of its parts. Flavour, aftertaste, acidity and body work together to achieve balance.

One coffee can taste dramatically different depending on the processing method. Washing coffees increases the acidity, whilst the semi-washed process gives a honeyed sweetness to the coffee. The natural processing method can increase the sweetness, and can also encourage development of more obscure flavours including strawberry, blueberry and creamy notes.

Tasting coffee at home can be fun; exploring what a coffee can offer in terms of flavour, sweetness and other attributes is exciting. Your local speciality coffee shop can offer advice on which coffees are in season, and many will sell beans for you to experiment with at home. There's a coffee out there for everyone.

SCAA Coffee taster's wheel

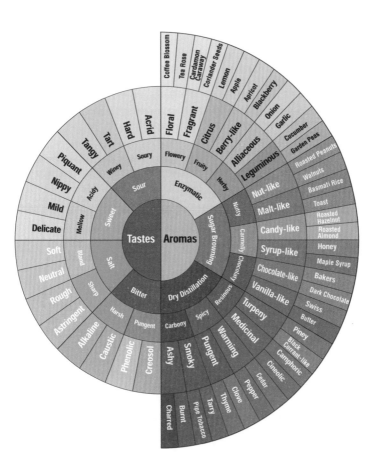

Coffee Grinding

by **Jeremy Challender**, Former Co-owner and Director of Training, Prufrock Coffee and the

Grinder technology is about to change radically. Machine design, techniques behind the bar and hand brewing methodology have improved rapidly over recent years. Manufacturers are starting to address this by seeking feedback from users as well as lab testing. Home users can benefit from these changes too. New designs entering the market have drawn directly from the experiences of barista champions. Grinder designers are seeking professional and consumer feedback on taste, flavour and ergonomics through direct collaboration and field testing. Manufacturers are aware that we need development to continue and, now more than ever, baristas have a voice in this process. To be a barista in this time of grinder development is very exciting.

With all brew methods the challenge is replicating flavour and strength. Once we've got a precise brew recipe for a coffee we stand a better chance of extracting our coffee consistently. Commercially, the easiest way to navigate from this baseline towards the optimum extraction level is with micro-adjustments in the exposed surface area of the grinds - so the grinder is key to managing flavour in the cup.

The challenge grinder designers face is how to create consistency of grind size and shape. If you get out the microscope, and a set of test sieves, you start to realise all your grinds aren't the same size, nor are they all the same shape. If they were all the same size and shape,

brewing would be much easier to control. In espresso you will have seen tiny granules in your cup that are smaller than the holes in the filter basket. We call these fines. These small particles have very high surface area and extract very quickly. As a home brewer, you could consider following the example of many championship baristas; invest in laboratory test sieves to remove a portion of particles under a certain size to reduce over-extracted flavours.

There is a portion of particles that fit side-on between the burrs and are planed rather than ground. We call these larger particles boulders. They have a much lower surface area relative to their size and in a 30 second espresso extraction will under-extract. Wobbly hand grinders are real offenders in the production of boulders. These too can be sieved out.

Sharp burrs are considered to reduce fines production. Ceramic burrs, which many hand grinders are fitted with, are very durable but are often not very sharp to start with. The material of choice at the moment is titanium-coated steel. Large burr diameter is linked to lower production of fines and boulders (more 'modal' distribution) so enormous bag grinders are being examined for application in espresso making. Cutting systems like spice grinders produce a very high proportion of fines and boulders, so are not recommended.

Keeping the coffee cool during grinding is a challenge. Burrs get hot in use because of friction, and some of the most exciting developments recently have focused on temperature stability of the burrs and burr casing with the addition of heating elements and fans. A warm grinder behaves differently to a cold or a hot one, so the particle shape and size are dependent on both grind setting and temperature.

Modern grinder design is very focussed on ease of access for regular cleaning. Arabica coffee has up to 17% fat content. We only extract a small percentage of this into a beverage but even after a day of commercial use, a grinder will have a slick of fats and tiny fine particles built up around the burr casing and the barrel and throat of the grinder. Oils oxidise, so grinders must be opened up and thoroughly swept out on a regular basis. Burrs can be washed in soapy water or coffee cleaner, or abrasive oil absorbing grinder cleaning granules can be used. Home baristas have an advantage here by

being able to clean after a few shots rather than after a full day's usage.

The final hurdle to overcome is grind retention: many grinders on the market have large barrels and throats that can store as much as 40g of grinds that must be squeezed out before fresh grinds appear. At Prufrock, we are moving away from grinders with a high retention of grinds as we are looking to optimise freshness. When grind changes are required we want the benefit of micro-adjustment to be immediate. Here, home baristas are also well placed, as hand grinders have zero retention of grinds and some very high quality espresso hand grinders are now available on the market.

Over the last decade we have felt that machine technology has been in advance of grinders. We often comment that a barista's top priority should be the choice of grinder. Find a great grinding solution and great coffee will follow.

Photo: Jacob Thue

Espresso

by **Ben Townsend,** Trainer, London School of Coffee

The last 8 years have seen a rapid pace of development for coffee in London. The emergence of new cafés and roasteries continues apace as does the evolution of espresso technique. This "new world" culture is constantly pushing the boundaries of what is possible with the equipment, coffee and scientific knowledge that we currently have.

In a curious way, some of what is new is in fact quite old, and refers back to the largely disregarded tradition of Italian espresso. Of course, many practices remain deliberately different to traditional espresso - but it's instructive to note that the cutting edge of machine and grinder technology belongs again to the Italians, albeit achieved by recruiting non-Italian "new world" baristas to consult on the design.

Probably the most important series of changes over the last few years has been an increased understanding of grinding and extraction. Put simply, we can accurately measure with a laser refractometer how much of the desirable (or undesirable) soluble compounds in coffee have been extracted from the ground coffee by the brew water and the resulting effect on flavour.

To many people, notably espresso traditionalists, much London espresso has been unpalatably sour. We realise now that a combination of light roasting and short Antipodean style shots has been severely underextracting our coffee, producing sour brews and overly simple flavour profiles.

All of London's serious cafés are now using brew recipes. A recipe describes per shot how much ground coffee goes in, how much liquid coffee comes out and over what time duration. Apart from allowing much more consistency from shot to shot, brew recipes are typically designed to produce as much sweetness and complexity as possible, without losing too much texture. We realise now that we should have been pushing more water through our coffee to extract more solubles and reduce sourness - the Italians have been doing this for decades!

I sincerely hope that we will not see the return of stale, over-roasted or Robusta coffee made on dirty machines. Traditional goals like thick crema on an espresso are very unreliable indicators of quality. The specialty scene has its colours firmly nailed to the mast of traceable, high quality, well processed and freshly roasted beans. Balanced, clean and fresh flavours that truly reveal the character of each coffee should be the goal of both barista and consumer.

Accordingly, it appears that the next wave of machine technology has finally lost the bewildering obsession with temperature and pressure control and moved onto technology to automate the brew recipe process. In practice, this means accurately dosing grinders and new "gravimetric" machines that cut the output of the shot using beverage mass instead of water volume or time. It will not be long before the weakest link in the physical production process will be the barista - a sobering thought!

The increased understanding of brew process and its resultant focus on brew recipes and extraction yield has turned scrutiny on roast profile. Those roasters producing the most soluble coffees, without baking or over-roasting, will be favoured by the best cafés.

We have also seen the emergence of a well-informed prosumer barista. Many home setups rival that of commercial cafés, and some home baristas are more technically informed than virtually all professional baristas, via internet blogs and some excellent new books.

When asked, I still advise that espresso is a drink to be enjoyed in a communal environment. For that reason I always go out for my flat whites and espresso. Coffee is about flavour, but not just that. It's an enjoyable route to shared social experience, whether you are leaning on a marble bar in Rome or a grungy wooden counter in Hackney.

Photo: Vagabond

Water - The Enigma

by **Maxwell Colonna-Dashwood**, Co-owner, Colonna and Small's, UK Barista Champion 2012 & 2014

This vital ingredient is the foundation of every cup of coffee you have ever tasted, apart from the bean itself of course.

It's not just coffee that relies so dramatically on this everyday and seemingly straightforward substance. The worlds of craft beer and whisky are suitable comparisons, with breweries and distilleries proudly signifying the provenance of their water as being a vital part of their product.

A roaster, though, sells coffee, the water bit comes post sale. The water will be different and unique based on the locality of brewing, and this is on top of all of the other variables that define coffee brewing such as grinding, temperature and brew ratios. The reality is that the impact of water is rarely directly witnessed, with the other variables often being seen as the cause for dramatic flavour changes. You may be wondering right now, how big an impact can it really have?

I'm yet to present the same coffee brewed with different waters to drinkers and not have them exclaim "I can't believe how different they are, they taste like different coffees'. These aren't "coffee people" either, but customers who contested prior to the tasting that "you may be able to taste the difference but I doubt I can tell."

It may make you question whether the coffee that you tried and weren't particularly keen on, was a representative version of what the bean actually tastes like, or at the least what it is capable of tasting of like.

So, why the big difference, what is in the water?

Nearly all water that trickles out of a tap or sits in a bottle is not just water. As well as the H_2O there are other bits and bobs in the water. Minerals mainly. These have a big impact not only on what we extract from the coffee but also how that flavour sits in the cup of coffee.

It's fair to say that currently the way the coffee industry discusses water is through the use of a measurement called Total Dissolved Solids (TDS).

TDS has become the measurement which is relied upon to distinguish and inform us about how water will affect our coffee. It gives us a total of everything in the water. The problem though, is that TDS doesn't tell us everything we need to know about the water; it doesn't tell us about what those solids are. On top of this, TDS meters don't measure some non-solids that have a huge impact on flavour.

In the water, we need the minerals calcium and magnesium to help pull out a lot of the desirable flavour in the coffee, but we also need the right amount of buffering ability in the water to balance the acids. This buffering ability can be noted as the bicarbonate content of the water. So for example an "empty" soft water with no minerals will lack flavour complexity and the lack of buffer will mean a more vinegary acidity.

A good test is to make the same coffee with both Evian and Tesco Ashbeck water. Evian has a good amount of calcium and magnesium to pull flavour out, but this is accompanied by a high bicarbonate content which flattens everything out and results in a heavy, bitter and chalky brew. The Ashbeck has little extraction power so is quite empty but has a low buffer so the acidity verges on sour. For bottled waters, Waitrose Essential yields pleasant results.

However the coffee shops in this guide will most likely have a trick up their sleeve.

The industry filtration systems that have been developed primarily to stop scale build up in the striking and valuable espresso machines, also produce water compositions that are more often than not preferable for coffee brewing. Speciality coffee shops require all manner of specifics to be obsessed over and carefully executed. That cup of coffee that hits you and stops you in your step with intense, balanced and complex flavour will owe its brilliance to careful brewing, a knowledgeable brewer and superb equipment. However, it also owes a significant part of its beautiful character and flavour to the water it is brewed with.

Brewing Coffee at Home

by **Christian Baker, David Robson, Sam Mason & The London Coffee Guide**

Y ou may be surprised to know that coffee brewed at home can rival that of your favourite coffee shop. All you need are good quality ingredients and some inexpensive equipment. Keep in mind that small variations in grind coarseness, coffee /water ratio and brew time will make a significant difference to flavour, and that trial and error is the key to unlocking perfection.

Whole Beans: Whole bean coffee is superior to pre-ground. Coffee rapidly deteriorates once ground, so buy your coffee in whole bean form and store it in an air-tight container at room temperature. It should be consumed between three and thirty days after roast and ground only moments before brewing.

Water: Water is important because it makes up over 98% of the finished drink. Only use bottled water, preferably with a dry residue between 80-150mg/l. London tap water is not suitable for brewing - it will inhibit your ability to extract flavour and reveal only a fraction of a coffee's potential.

Digital scales: Get a set of scales accurate to 1g and large enough to hold your coffee brewer. Coffee is commonly measured in 'scoops' or 'tablespoons', but coffee and water are best measured by weight for greater accuracy and to ensure repeatability. Small changes in the ratio of coffee to water can have a significant impact on flavour. A good starting point is 60-70g of coffee per litre of water. Apply this ratio to meet the size of your brewer.

Grinder

A burr grinder is essential. Burr grinders are superior to blade grinders because they allow the grind coarseness to be set and produce a more consistent size of coffee fragment (critical for an even extraction). As a general rule, the coarser the grind the longer the brew time required, and vice versa. For example, an espresso needs a very fine grind whereas a French Press works with a coarser grind.

French Press

Preheat the French Press with hot water, and discard. Add 34g of coarsely ground coffee and pour in 500g of water just below boiling point (94/95°C). Steep for 4 to 5 minutes then gently plunge to the bottom. Decant the coffee straight away to avoid over-brewing (known as over-extraction).

AeroPress

The AeroPress is wonderfully versatile. It can be used with finely ground coffee and a short steep time, or with a coarser grind and a longer steep time. The latter is our preferred method for its flavour and repeatability. Preheat the AeroPress using hot water, and discard. Rinse the paper filter before securing, and place the AeroPress over a sturdy cup or jug. Add 16g of coffee and pour in 240g of water at 95°C. Secure the plunger on top, creating a seal. Steep for 3 minutes then plunge over 20 seconds.

Pour Over

We recommend using a pouring kettle for better pouring control. Place a filter paper in the cone and rinse through with hot water. Add 15g of coffee and slowly pour 30g of 95°C water to pre-soak the coffee grounds. This creates the 'bloom'. After 30 seconds add 250g of water, pouring steadily in a circular motion over the centre. It should take 1 minute and 45 seconds to pour and between 30-45 seconds to drain through. The key is to keep the flow of water steady. If the water drains too quickly/slowly, adjust the coarseness of the grind to compensate.

Stovetop

A stovetop will not make an espresso, it will, however, make a strong coffee. Pour hot water into the base to the fill-line or just below the pressure release valve. Fill the basket with ground coffee of medium coarseness (between Pour Over and French Press). Traditional wisdom suggests a fine grind in pursuit of espresso, but stovetops extract differently to espresso machines and grinding fine is a recipe for bitter, over-extracted coffee. Screw the base to the top and place on the heat. When you hear bubbling, remove immediately and decant to ensure the brewing has stopped.

Illustrations: Zoë Barker

Traditional Pump Espresso Machine

Traditional pump espresso machines are ideal for that barista experience to create espresso-based coffee at home. Coffee should be freshly and finely ground and dosed into single or double shot filter baskets. It is then tamped to extract full flavour aroma and coffee crema. The machine controls temperature for a more consistent cup. To enjoy milk drinks such as flat whites and cappuccinos simply froth fresh milk using the steam wand (stay below 70°C) and top up your espresso.

Bean to Cup Machine

Bean to Cup provides the perfect 'coffee shop' fix and fast. It gives you all the versatility of choice and personalisation of a traditional pump machine. At the touch of a button, it burr-grinds fresh beans and froths milk (some machines even have a built in carafe), creating a fresh taste for your cup. You can personalise the strength, length, temperature, and even the froth setting. One-touch drink options make your personalised coffee time and again, without mess or fuss.

Guidelines for creating perfect latte art

by **Dhan Tamang**, UK Latte Art Champion 2013–2018

4 essential steps to create beautiful latte art.

1 Preparation

You'll need fresh, cold whole milk and a cold, clean pitcher. A pitcher with the right spout is essential. Use a straight spout for a one go, continuous pattern and a narrow spout for a drawn pattern. For the best results, place the pitcher in the fridge for 30 minutes before use. This will ensure your milk steams slowly, decreasing the chances of scalding it. Have a liquid thermometer handy so you can check the temperature of your steamed milk.

2 Milk Steaming Process

Make sure the steam wand starts at the bottom of the pitcher. Once the steam is turned on, slowly raise the wand to the top of the milk. For the best results, keep the wand 1cm away from the top of the milk as it rises. You need the milk between 60-65°C with a glossy, full bodied foam and no air bubbles. Once the milk is up to temperature take the steamer out.

3 The Perfect Espresso

For the ideal shot use 7-8 grams of ground espresso. Make sure your espresso is fresh and has a thick, strong layer of crema. Pull the perfect shot between 21-24 seconds. Don't let your espresso sit for more than 10 seconds without adding milk.

4 Pouring Technique

Before you pour make sure there are no air bubbles. If you see any, swirl the milk and pound the pitcher on the counter to get rid of them. Hold the cup slightly tilted and make sure you are comfortable with how you are holding the cup. Whatever pattern you pour, it has to focus on contrast, symmetry and detail.

For all beginners I would recommend the rosetta pattern, it is the easiest and will give you the best results.

Photo: Prufrock Coffee

Coffee Cocktails

by **Sam Trevethyen**, Grind

W̲e all love a coffee in the morning and a cocktail in the evening (or the afternoon!). However, in recent years we have seen an explosion of cafés and bars venturing into a cocktail offering environment that blends the two.

Why Coffee & Cocktails?

It's simple, they are the perfect pairing. The rise of specialty coffee perfectly marries the rise of the artisanal approach to bartending. Weird and wonderful spiriting, mixed with a whole cornucopia of different coffees, different brew methods, homemade syrups and who knows what else!

A bit of History

All good drinks need a good story, and this is no exception. Rumour has it that the legendary bartender Dick Bradsell gave birth to this title while working at the Soho Brasserie on Greek Street. An unnamed model (it was the 90's, use your imagination) asked him for a drink that would 'wake her up'. A few shakes later, she got exactly what she wanted.

The Perfect Espresso Martini

This is an easy one. Start with an amazing, freshly pulled espresso shot. Add vodka and sugar syrup. Shake vigorously over ice and double strain into a chilled coupe glass.

One of the reasons we have had so much success at Grind with this drink is a combination of the fact we pull every shot of espresso used to order (you need the crema on the shot to be fresh to give you that rich creamy head we all know and love) and we only use coffee, vodka and sugar syrup. After all, it's safe to say coffee and Grind are more than friends.

How did we get into it?

At Grind, we started opening our original site (Shoreditch Grind) rather organically - we were building an awesome vibe during the day, and then shutting the doors and chucking people out at 6pm - why not keep the party going we thought? Not to mention the financial sense behind getting more out of a space you pay rent on 24/7. For us, as with many, the jump happened with the Espresso Martini. We now have 8 sites across London, but our approach to coffee cocktails has not changed since experimenting in the evenings of Shoreditch Grind. Simple, powerful combinations, blending fresh ingredients that look awesome.

Education & Training

by **Edwin Harrison**, Co-owner, the Artisan Coffee School

The London third wave coffee scene is well established and thriving. So let's look behind the coffee machines for a moment to better understand what impact education and training has on your daily cup of coffee. Making coffee is a complex art and science; any number of small variables, from plantation to barista, can make the difference between a mouthwatering cup and one that ends up being poured down the drain. Owners and managers spend hours focusing on training in order to drive their coffee shops forward and do justice to the coffee growers, roasters and other professionals who have in some way contributed to delivering those amazing beans to our grinder hoppers.

To understand where coffee training and education has arrived today, it's useful to take a brief look at its history. The explosion of branded coffee shop chains in the 1990s lead to the birth of the barista manual. Manuals served to formalise training, systems and techniques by introducing a workflow process for baristas to follow. Together with mass training sessions, the barista manual successfully addressed problems of inconsistency and the coffee chains flourished, but little progress was made to realise coffee's full potential.

The complexity and potential of coffee was too great to be boxed up into a manual

or process; the third wave independents were eager to take coffee to the next level. Top baristas started to get excited about what could be achieved through experimentation; everything from milk texturing to coffee flavour profiles came under meticulous scrutiny. Baristas challenged conventional wisdom and investigated the science behind coffee making to understand how it could be improved. Today a new breed of dedicated training schools has emerged exploring coffee theory as well as practical brewing skills. What's more, coffee schools are no longer the preserve of industry professionals, they now offer classes tailored specifically to interested coffee lovers wishing to improve their home brewing.

An introductory barista course run over one or two days would typically include theory with a discussion on processing techniques, different roast types, and establish what flavours we are looking to achieve. The white board will then turn into something you would expect to see in an in-depth physics presentation as coffee enthusiasts discover how to create their own brew ratio. This process alone indicates just how much influence the barista has over the coffee they produce.

Then it's on to the machine, working out variables and learning how to keep these consistent is fundamental to success.

Exploring extraction times, tamping and grind adjustments are just some of the many aspects covered and the trainer will always bring it back to what impact your actions have on the flavour of the coffee. This is key to developing a deeper knowledge of the process you are responsible for. This approach to training becomes infectious as suddenly the world of coffee begins to unfold in front of students' eyes. This is why we see so many students progress from the barista foundation courses through to intermediate and professional level.

The industry as a whole has stepped up and taken notice of this revolution in education. The Speciality Coffee Association of Europe (SCAE) addressed the wide gap in formalised training, gathering top industry figures to formalise a structure with inspiration from the wine industry. The result is the Coffee Diploma System, taking a modular form incorporating the many different aspects of coffee education, and assessed with exams. Many coffee schools offer SCAE accredited courses in addition to running their own classes.

The rise of coffee schools demonstrates that the industry is taking the next big step and realising that barista training is not a single shadow shift at the start of a job, but an ongoing process that has a very significant impact on the success of a business; from staff retention to the consistency and quality of coffee they serve.

Coffee Glossary

Acidity: the pleasant tartness of a coffee. Examples of acidity descriptors include lively and flat. One of the principal attributes evaluated by professional tasters when determining the quality of a coffee.

AeroPress: a hand-powered coffee brewer marketed by Aerobie Inc., and launched in 2005. Consists of two cylinders, one sliding within the other, somewhat resembling a large syringe. Water is forced through ground coffee held in place by a paper filter, creating a concentrated filter brew.

Affogato: one or more scoops of vanilla ice cream topped with a shot of espresso, served as a dessert.

Americano, Caffè Americano: a long coffee consisting of espresso with hot water added on top. Originates from the style of coffee favoured by American GIs stationed in Europe during WWII.

Arabica, Coffea arabica: the earliest cultivated species of coffee tree and the most widely grown, Arabica accounts for approximately 70% of the world's coffee. Superior in quality to Robusta, it is more delicate and is generally grown at higher altitudes.

Aroma: the fragrance produced by brewed coffee. Examples of aroma descriptors include earthy, spicy and floral. One of the principal attributes evaluated by professional tasters when determining the quality of a coffee.

Barista: a professional person skilled in making coffee, particularly one working at an espresso bar.

Blend: a combination of coffees from different countries or regions. Mixed together, they achieve a balanced flavour profile no single coffee can offer alone.

Body: describes the heaviness, thickness or relative weight of coffee on the tongue. One of the principal attributes evaluated by professional tasters when determining the quality of a coffee.

Bottomless portafilter, naked portafilter: a portafilter without spouts, allowing espresso to flow directly from the bottom of the filter basket into the cup. Allows the extraction to be monitored visually.

Brew group: the assembly protruding from the front of an espresso machine consisting of the grouphead, portafilter and basket. The brew group must be heated to a sufficient temperature to produce a good espresso.

Brew pressure: pressure of 9 bar is required for espresso extraction.

Brew temperature: the water temperature at the point of contact with coffee. Optimum brew temperature varies by extraction method. Espresso brew temperature is typically 90-95°C. A stable brew temperature is crucial for good espresso.

Brew time, extraction time: the contact time between water and coffee. Espresso brew time is typically 25-30 seconds. Brew times are dictated by a variety of factors including the grind coarseness and degree of roast.

Burr set: an integral part of a coffee grinder. Consists of a pair of rotating steel discs between which coffee beans are ground. Burrs are either flat or conical in shape.

Café con leche: a traditional Spanish coffee consisting of espresso topped with scalded milk.

Caffeine: an odourless, slightly bitter alkaloid responsible for the stimulating effect of coffee.

Cappuccino: a classic Italian coffee comprising espresso, steamed milk and topped with a layer of foam. Traditionally served in a 6oz cup and sometimes topped with powdered chocolate or cinnamon.

Capsule: a self-contained, pre-ground, pre-pressed portion of coffee, individually sealed inside a plastic capsule. Capsule brewing systems are commonly found in domestic coffee machines. Often compatible only with certain equipment brands.

Chemex: A type of pour over coffee brewer with a distinctive hourglass-shaped vessel. Invented in 1941, the Chemex has become regarded as a design classic and is on permanent display at the Museum of Modern Art in New York City.

Cherry: the fruit of the coffee plant. Each cherry contains two coffee seeds (beans).

Cold brew: Cold brew refers to the process of steeping coffee grounds in room temperature or cold water for an extended period. Cold brew coffee is not to be confused with iced coffee.

Cortado: a traditional short Spanish coffee consisting of espresso cut with a small quantity of steamed milk. Similar to an Italian piccolo.

Crema: the dense caramel-coloured layer that forms on the surface of an espresso. Consists of emulsified oils created by the dispersion of gases in liquid at high pressure. The presence of crema is commonly equated with a good espresso.

Cupping: a method by which professional tasters perform sensory evaluation of coffee. Hot water is poured over ground coffee and left to extract. The taster first samples the aroma, then tastes the coffee by slurping it from a spoon.

Decaffeinated: coffee with approximately 97% or more of its naturally occurring caffeine removed is classified as decaffeinated.

Dispersion screen, shower screen: a component of the grouphead that ensures even distribution of brewing water over the coffee bed in the filter basket.

Dosage: the mass of ground coffee used for a given brewing method. Espresso dosage is typically 7-10g of ground coffee (14-20g for a double).

Double espresso, doppio: typically 30-50ml extracted from 14-20g of ground coffee. The majority of coffee venues in this guide serve double shots as standard.

Drip method: a brewing method that allows brew water to seep through a bed of ground coffee by gravity, not pressure.

Espresso: the short, strong shot of coffee that forms the basis for many other coffee beverages. Made by forcing hot water at high pressure through a compressed bed of finely ground coffee.

Espresso machine: in a typical configuration, a pump delivers hot water from a boiler to the brew group, where it is forced under pressure through ground coffee held in the portafilter. A separate boiler delivers steam for milk steaming.

Extraction: the process of infusing coffee with hot water to release flavour, accomplished either by allowing ground coffee to sit in hot water for a period of time or by forcing hot water through ground coffee under pressure.

Fifth Wave / 5th Wave™: A new era for the coffee industry signifying the creation of 'boutique at scale'. This means aspiring to

Coffee Glossary contd.

and achieving the highest quality of output across one's business or café, including, but not limited to, atmosphere, coffee quality, service level, staff training, business and IT systems. This era represents an advance on previous 'waves' most notably the 3rd Wave or artisan coffee era typified by craft coffee, or The 4th Wave, the science of coffee. 5th Wave businesses tend to be aspirational, professionally run businesses targeting a savvy millennial audience.

Filter method: any brewing method in which water filters through a bed of ground coffee. Most commonly used to describe drip method brewers that use a paper filter to separate grounds from brewed coffee.

Flat white: an espresso-based beverage first made popular in Australia and New Zealand. Made with a double shot of espresso with finely steamed milk and a thin layer of microfoam. Typically served as a 5-6oz drink with latte art.

Flavour: the way a coffee tastes. Flavour descriptors include nutty and earthy. One of the principal attributes evaluated by professional tasters when determining the quality of a coffee.

French press, plunger pot, cafetiere: a brewing method that separates grounds from brewed coffee by pressing them to the bottom of the brewing receptacle with a mesh filter attached to a plunger.

Green coffee, green beans: unroasted coffee. The dried seeds from the coffee cherry.

Grind: the degree of coarseness to which coffee beans are ground. A crucial factor in determining the nature of a coffee brew. Grind coarseness should be varied in accordance with the brewing method.

Methods involving longer brew times call for a coarse grind. A fine grind is required for brew methods with a short extraction time such as espresso.

Grinder: a vital piece of equipment for making coffee. Coffee beans must be ground evenly for a good extraction. Most commonly motorised, but occasionally manual. Burr grinders are the best choice for an even grind.

Group: see Brew Group

Grouphead: a component of the brew group containing the locking connector for the portafilter and the dispersion screen.

Honey process, pulped natural, semi-washed: a method of processing coffee where the cherry is removed (pulped), but the beans are sun-dried with mucilage intact. Typically results in a sweet flavour profile with a balanced acidity.

Latte, caffè latte: an Italian beverage made with espresso combined with steamed milk, traditionally topped with foamed milk and served in a glass. Typically at least 8oz in volume, usually larger.

Latte art: the pattern or design created by pouring steamed milk on top of espresso. Only finely steamed milk is suitable for creating latte art. Popular patterns include the rosetta and heart.

Lever espresso machine: lever machines use manual force to drive a piston that generates the pressure required for espresso extraction. Common in the first half of the 20th century, but now largely superseded by electric pump-driven machines.

Long black: a coffee beverage made by adding an espresso on top of hot water. Similar to an Americano, but usually shorter and the crema is preserved.

Macchiato: a coffee beverage consisting of espresso 'stained' with a dash of steamed milk (espresso macchiato) or a tall glass of steamed milk 'stained' with espresso (latte macchiato).

Matcha: Finely ground powder of specially grown and processed green tea. The matcha plants are shade-grown for three weeks before harvest.

Microfoam: the preferred texture of finely-steamed milk for espresso-based coffee drinks. Essential for pouring latte art. Achieved by incorporating a lesser quantity of air during the milk steaming process.

Micro-lot coffee: coffee originating from a small, discrete area within a farm, typically benefiting from conditions favourable to the development of a particular set of characteristics. Micro-lot coffees tend to fetch higher prices due to their unique nature.

Mocha, caffè mocha: similar to a caffè latte, but with added chocolate syrup or powder.

Natural process: a simple method of processing coffee where whole cherries (with the bean inside) are dried on raised beds under the sun. Typically results in a lower acidity coffee with a heavier body and exotic flavours.

Over extracted: describes coffee with a bitter or burnt taste, resulting from ground coffee exposed to hot water for too long.

Peaberry: a small, round coffee bean formed when only one seed, rather than the usual two, develops in a coffee cherry. Peaberry beans produce a different flavour profile, typically lighter-bodied with higher acidity.

Piccolo: a short Italian coffee beverage made with espresso topped with an equal quantity of steamed milk. Traditionally served in a glass.

Pod: a self-contained, pre-ground, pre-pressed puck of coffee, individually wrapped inside a perforated paper filter. Mostly found in domestic espresso machines. Often compatible only with certain equipment brands.

Pour over: a type of drip filter method in which a thin, steady stream of water is poured slowly over a bed of ground coffee contained within a filter cone.

Pouring kettle: a kettle with a narrow goose-neck spout specifically designed to deliver a steady, thin stream of water.

Portafilter: consists of a handle (usually plastic) attached to a metal cradle that holds the filter basket. Inserted into the group head and locked in place in preparation for making an espresso. Usually features a single or double spout on the underside to direct the flow of coffee into a cup.

Portafilter basket: a flat bottomed, bowl-shaped metal insert that sits in the portafilter and holds a bed of ground coffee. The basket has an array of tiny holes in the base allowing extracted coffee to seep through and pour into a cup.

Puck: immediately after an espresso extraction, the bed of spent coffee grounds forms compressed waste matter resembling a small hockey puck.

Pull: the act of pouring an espresso. The term originates from the first half of the 20th century when manual machines were the norm, and baristas pulled a lever to create an espresso.

Ristretto: a shorter 'restricted' shot of espresso. Made using the same dose and brew time as for a regular espresso, but with

Coffee Glossary contd.

less water. The result is a richer and more intense beverage.

Roast: the process by which green coffee is heated in order to produce coffee beans ready for consumption. Caramelisation occurs as intense heat converts starches in the bean to simple sugars, imbuing the bean with flavour and transforming its colour to a golden brown.

Robusta, Coffea canephora: the second most widely cultivated coffee species after arabica, robusta accounts for approximately 30% of the world's coffee. Robusta is hardier and grown at lower altitudes than arabica. It has a much higher caffeine content than arabica, and a less refined flavour. Commonly used in instant coffee blends.

Shot: a single unit of brewed espresso.

Single origin, single estate: coffee from one particular region or farm.

Siphon brewer, vacuum brewer: an unusual brewing method that relies on the action of a vacuum to draw hot water through coffee from one glass chamber to another. The resulting brew is remarkably clean.

Small batch: refers to roasting beans in small quantities, typically between 4-24kg, but sometimes larger.

Speciality coffee: a premium quality coffee scoring 80 points or above (from a total of 100) on the SCAA grading scale.

Steam wand: the protruding pipe found on an espresso machine that supplies hot steam used to froth and steam milk.

Stovetop, moka pot: a brewing method that makes strong coffee (but not espresso). Placed directly on a heat source, hot water is forced by steam pressure from the lower chamber to the upper chamber, passing through a bed of coffee.

Tamp: the process of distributing and pressing ground coffee into a compact bed within the portafilter basket in preparation for brewing espresso. The degree of pressure applied during tamping is a key variable in espresso extraction. Too light and the brew water will percolate rapidly (tending to under extract), too firm and the water flow will be impeded (tending to over extract).

Tamper: the small pestle-like tool used to distribute and compact ground coffee in the filter basket.

Third wave coffee: the movement that treats coffee as an artisanal foodstuff rather than a commodity product. Quality coffee reflects its terroir, in a similar manner to wine.

Under extracted: describes coffee that has not been exposed to brew water for long enough. The resulting brew is often sour and thin-bodied.

V60: a popular type of pour over coffee brewer marketed by Hario. The product takes its name from the 60° angle of the V-shaped cone. Typically used to brew one or two cups only.

Washed process: one of the most common methods of processing coffee cherries. Involves fermentation in tanks of water to remove mucilage. Typically results in a clean and bright flavour profile with higher acidity.

Whole bean: coffee that has been roasted but not ground.

A-Z List of Coffee Venues

A-Z List of Coffee Venues contd.

A-Z List of Coffee Venues contd.

* NEW
◊ TOP 35

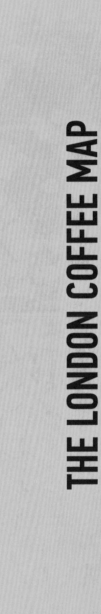

THE LONDON COFFEE MAP

The London Coffee Guide.

The London Coffee Guide.

THE DEFINITIVE GUIDE TO THE BEST
INDEPENDENT COFFEE VENUES IN LONDON

Download on the
App Store